I0039945

THE TRUTH ABOUT
ADHD

DANIEL R. BERGER II

ALETHIA
INTERNATIONAL
MINISTRIES.

The Truth About ADHD, 2nd edition

Library of Congress Control Number: 2017901582
Second Edition Trade Paperback ISBN: 978-0-9976077-4-1
First Edition Trade Paperback ISBN: 978-0-9864114-0-3

Cover Artwork by: Elieser Loewenthal
Edited by: Laurie Buck

First Copyright © in 2014 / Second Edition Copyright © in 2017
by Daniel R. Berger II

All rights reserved. No part of this publication may be reproduced
or transmitted in any form or by any means, electronic or
mechanical, including recording, photocopying, or by any
retrieval system or information storage except for brief quotations
in printed reviews, without the prior written permission of the
publisher, except as provided by USA copyright law.

Published by Alethia International Publications - Taylors, SC

www.drdanielberger.com

Printed in the United States of America.

To

My loving father and mother

"Train up [dedicate] a child in the way he should go; even when
he is old he will not depart from it."

Proverbs 22:6

TABLE OF CONTENTS

INTRODUCTION   1

CHAPTER 1 - ADHD IS A CONSTRUCT   6

CHAPTER 2 - ADHD REDEFINES NORMALCY   40

CHAPTER 3 - ADHD DESCRIBES BEHAVIOR   58

CHAPTER 4 - ADHD IS NOT A MEDICAL CONDITION   114

CHAPTER 5 - ADHD HAS A REMEDY   168

CONCLUSION   198

APPENDICES   201

BIBLIOGRAPHY   216

ACKNOWLEDGMENTS

I first want to thank my Lord Jesus Christ, whose grace is both the reason for writing this book and the reason my own mindsets, emotions, and behaviors are changing to reflect His character. Additionally, God allowed me the privilege of administrating and pastoring in numerous ministries that forced me to search and study-out practical answers and hope for our human needs. Specifically, I want to thank Pastor Marc Mortensen at First Baptist Church of Westwood Lakes, Miami for allowing me the opportunity to pastor alongside of him, counsel under his leadership, and for his continued friendship.

I also want to thank my wife, Oriana, for her love, patience, support, and prayer for this book, our family, and our ministry. Furthermore, I want to thank my parents and grandparents for their own teaching of God's wisdom that modeled true love for God and the pursuit of His wisdom above all other values. Likewise, my close friends and teachers throughout my life have been an encouragement, a sounding board, and a group of solid counselors and prayer warriors. I am blessed to have such godly and faithful friends and family. I wish to also thank my editor who diligently and patiently edited this book, and last but not least, I am grateful to the many families to which I have had the privilege of counseling or speaking. Your humble response to the gospel has been an ongoing encouragement and motivation.

DISCLAIMER

The material contained in this book is the result of years of experience, research, and professional interviews, but it is not intended in any way to be taken as medical advice. Rather, the views and material expressed in this book are philosophical and historical in nature and written in order to provide God's wisdom that will enable parents, counselors, educators, pastors, therapists, physicians, and other professionals to be better equipped to offer genuine truth, love, and hope to those in their care.

OTHER BOOKS BY DR. BERGER

Mental Illness: The Necessity for Faith and Authority

Mental Illness: The Reality of the Spiritual Nature

Mental Illness: The Reality of the Physical Nature

Mental Illness: The Influence of Nurture

Mental Illness: The Necessity for Dependence

Teaching a Child to Pay Attention: Proverbs 4:20-27

ABBREVIATIONS

AAP	American Academy of Pediatrics
APA	American Psychiatric Association
ADD	Attention Deficit Disorder
ADHD	Attention Deficit Hyperactivity Disorder
ADHD-I	ADHD-Inattentive type
ADHD-HI	ADHD-Hyperactivity-Impulsivity type
ADHD-C	ADHD-Combined type
CDC	Centers for Disease Control and Prevention
DSM-IV	*Diagnostic & Statistical Manual of Mental Disorders –IV*
DSM-5	*Diagnostic & Statistical Manual of Mental Disorders – 5*
EEG	Electroencephalogram
EF	Executive Function
ES	Executive System
ESV	*English Standard Version*
FMRI	Functional Magnetic Resonance Imaging
JAMA	*Journal of the American Medical Association*
KJV	*King James Version*
NAS	*New American Standard*
NAMI	National Alliance for the Mentally Ill
NEJM	*New England Journal of Medicine*
NIH	National Institutes of Health
NIMH	National Institute of Mental Health
NoSC	*ADHD and the Nature of Self-Control*
ODD	Oppositional-Defiant Disorder
TCoA	*Taking Control of ADHD*

FOREWORD

Since the late 1950s and early 1960s influential figures have purposely led America away from the traditional and biblical understanding of our children and toward a disease model. Much of society has fully accepted this psychiatric perspective, and many are now unaware or have denied that an alternative and proved approach to children's behavior still exists. I myself once believed that a child's maladaptive behavior constituted a valid disease that required medical attention. But after thoroughly studying the claims asserted by the psychological party line about alleged Attention Deficit Hyperactivity Disorder (ADHD) and recognizing the absence of any biological or empirical evidence to validate the idea, I accepted the clear evidence and concluded years ago that ADHD is not a disease that children contract or inherit. Rather, ADHD is a label children acquire from people who have learned to interpret kid's bad behavior from the medical model. In short, ADHD is a construct, not a reality.

By exploring every major aspect of the construct of ADHD, Dr. Berger has taken a giant step in this book to shatter some cherished but false psychiatric beliefs which have convinced far too many parents that their children are abnormal. For the last several decades, I have lectured and written on our need to return to a traditional role in parenting. With this book, Berger provides further evidence and important discussions on the historical and philosophical contexts surrounding the theory of ADHD that are sure to encourage the reader to return to biblical parenting and traditional discipline. His research and writing, both thorough and significant, provide clarity and emphasize the importance of viewing our children from the Creator's perspective in order to understand their genuine problems and discover reliable and proven solutions.

There is a revolution occurring in our country where many parents — fed up with the failed psychiatric system — are returning to a perspective and approach to children that has consistently worked for centuries. Daniel's contribution to this trend is undeniable.

— John Rosemond, Family Psychologist,
Speaker, and Author of over 20 books

INTRODUCTION

"There was a long record of speculation within medicine that
extremely hyperactive children suffered from brain dysfunction of
some kind, which was certainly a reasonable thought, but the nature
of that dysfunction was never discerned, and then, in 1980,
psychiatry simply created, with a stroke of its pen in *DSM-III*, a
dramatically expanded definition of "hyperactivity." The fidgety
seven-year-old boy who might have been dubbed a "goof-off" in
1970 was now suffering from a psychiatric disorder."[1] – Journalist,
Robert Whitaker

Since the introduction of the Attention Deficit Hyperactivity
Disorder (ADHD/ADD) label, the number of children being said
to have ADHD has risen dramatically. In 2011, the Centers for
Disease Control and Prevention (CDC) estimated that 11
percent[2] of U.S. children and as high as 18 percent in some
schools[3] have been handed the diagnosis known today as

---

[1] Robert Whitaker, *Anatomy of an Epidemic: Magic Bullets, Psychiatric Drugs,
and the Astonishing Rise of Mental Illness in America* (New York: Broadway Books,
2015), 221.

[2] "Key Findings: Trends in the Parent-Report of Health Care Provider-
Diagnosis and Medication Treatment for ADHD: United States, 2003-2011,"
http://www.cdc.gov/ncbddd /adhd/features/key-findings-adhd72013.html.
Compare 11 percent to almost 8 percent in 2003 (Maggie Fox, "Number of Young
Adults on ADHD Drugs Soars," http://www.nbcnews.com/ health/health-
news/number-young-adults-adhd-drugs-soars-n50856). The American
Psychiatric Association claims only 5 percent of American children have ADHD
(ibid).

[3] Julian Haber, *ADHD: The Great Misdiagnosis* (New York: Taylor Trade,
2003), 1.

ADHD/ADD. Some leading experts (such as psychologist and professor emeritus at Duke University, Keith Conners) believe that 15 percent of all high school-age children have now been diagnosed as having the disorder.[4] There are so many children bearing the label that prominent psychiatrists recognize ADHD to be an epidemic.[5] Psychiatrist and chair of the *Diagnostic and Statistical Manual IV (DSM-IV)* task force, Allen Frances, explains how under his leadership the American Psychiatric Association (APA) made specific changes to the *DSM-IV* that would increase the number of children diagnosed as having ADHD. Unfortunately, these psychiatrists did not accurately anticipate just how great the numbers would be:

> The carefully done *DSM-IV* attention deficit predicted at our proposed changes would cause only a 15 percent increase in rates. This was probably a fairly accurate estimate given the reality when the data were gathered in the early 1990s. We couldn't foresee the abrupt switch in this reality that occurred in 1997, when drug companies brought new and expensive medicine for ADD to market and were simultaneously set free to advertise them directly to parents and teachers. Soon the selling of ADHD as a diagnosis was ubiquitous in magazines, on your TV screen, and in pediatricians' offices — an unexpected epidemic was born, and the rates of ADHD tripled.[6]

Words and labels matter in how we perceive normal and abnormal, and, as Frances's statement attests, whoever is

---

[4] Keith Conners quoted by Alan Schwarz, "The Selling of Attention Deficit Disorder," *New York Times*, December 14, 2013, http://www.nytimes.com/2013/12/15/health/the-selling-of-attention-deficit-disorder.html?action=click&contentCollection=Health&module=RelatedCoverage&pgtype=article&region=Marginalia&utm_campaign=Constant+Contact&utm_medium=email&utm_source=January+2015&_r=0, accessed 2 January 2017.

[5] Allen Frances, *Saving Normal: An Insider's Revolt against Diagnosis, DSM-5, Big Pharma, and the Medicalization of Ordinary Life* (New York: HarperCollins, 2013), 75-76.

[6] Ibid., 26.

granted the authority to choose definitions, descriptions, and classifications of people's mindsets and behaviors is typically also granted the privilege of determining who is considered to be normal and who is designated to be abnormal. His statement also reveals just how fluid the idea of ADHD is. Though the actual number of children diagnosed with ADHD is unknown,[7] the number of families and educators who are directly affected by the psychiatric label and who desire reliable answers is growing at a break-neck-speed.[8]

Parents and teachers alike recognize the urgency to find valid and reliable answers to what causes children to behave in such a way as to be diagnosed with ADHD, how exactly to objectively define and diagnose ADHD, and how to genuinely remedy a child's maladaptive/bad behavior. While the APA has created the ADHD label, it has failed to answer the most pressing questions about children or provide empirical evidence to validate its anthropology. There certainly are numerous theories of speculated causes, spurious claims of remedies, and many subjective systems of diagnoses, but children's bad behaviors and underlying problems are not being fixed.

In fact, in the current psychiatric system, there is growing evidence that the most prominent suggested treatments cause worse mental and physical conditions in children.[9] Psychiatric

---

[7] Paul Wender, "the dean of ADHD," claims 10 percent is more accurate (Paul Wender, *ADHD: Attention-Deficit Hyperactivity Disorder in Children, Adolescents, and Adults* [New York: Oxford University Press, 2000], 4).

[8] Edward M. Hallowell and John J. Ratey, *Driven to Distraction: Recognizing and Coping with Attention Deficit Disorder from Childhood through Adulthood* (New York: Pantheon Books, 1994), xi.

[9] Robert Whitaker, *Anatomy of an Epidemic: Magic Bullets, Psychiatric Drugs, and the Astonishing Rise of Mental Illness in America* (New York: Broadway Books,

theory has not healed children from their behavior; it has left them — along with their families and society — with more perplexing questions and greater problems. It seems the more alleged scientific discoveries and technological advances made, the more children magically qualify as mentally ill. All the while, families who are struggling for answers are given only more false hope.

But where there is truth, there is genuine hope, and as this book will expose, the Word of God has been the faithful and unchanging authority throughout history, which can perfectly define all people, positively transform the spiritual mind, and indisputably change behavior without adverse effects. Those who desire to obtain this genuine hope, though, must both discover and accept the truth about the construct of ADHD from the Creator's perspective.

The goal of this book is to offer genuine hope and truth from Scripture that can transform families and answer the most pressing questions about the idea of ADHD. The first chapter examines the underlying philosophies and theories that both created and sustain the construct of ADHD. Chapter one also briefly reviews the history of the label and shows how the label's changing descriptions have offered not a better understanding of children, but a better understanding of secular theory. Chapter two sets forth the only two standards of normalcy currently available in defining and treating children's behavior and attentional problems. Chapter three examines the construct's specific behaviors, which the *DSM* claims are criteria of a child's having ADHD. Chapter four reveals that ADHD is not a medical disorder because it lacks biological diagnostic markers, known

---

2015), 235-37. See also University of Minnesota, http://open.lib.umn.edu/intropsyc /chapter/5-2-altering-consciousness-with-psychoactive-drugs/.

biological causes (etiologies), and a confirmed biological remedy. Finally, chapter five offers practical advice to help children pay attention, to have right values, and to behave in a way that please the Lord and benefits society.

CHAPTER 1

ADHD IS A CONSTRUCT

"We saw *DSM-IV* as a guidebook, not a bible—a collection of temporarily useful diagnostic constructs, not a catalog of 'real' diseases [emphasis added]."[10] – Psychiatrist and chairman of the *DSM-IV* task force, Allen Frances

"Psychotherapy may be the only treatment that creates the illness it treats."[11] – Professor of psychiatry at Johns Hopkins University Medical School, Jerome Frank

Though the psychiatric disorder known as Attention Deficit-Hyperactivity Disorder (ADHD) is controversial and claimed by many to be a biological disease, in truth, ADHD is a construct. A construct is a perspective, paradigm, or ideology, which attempts to explain something that is not real in the physical sense, but it is clearly a reality that must be understood and interpreted:

> Constructs are abstract concepts of something that is not real in the physical sense that a spoon or motorcycle or cat can be seen and touched. Constructs are shared ideas, supported by general agreement. . . . Mental illness is a construct. . . . The category itself is an invention, a creation. It may be a good and useful invention, or it may be a confusing one. *DSM* is a compendium of constructs. And

---

[10] Frances, *Saving Normal*, 73.

[11] Mark Hubble, Barry Duncan, and Scott Miller, *The Heart and Soul of Change: What Works in Therapy* (Washington, D.C.: American Psychological Association, 1999), 2.

like a large and popular mutual fund, *DSM's* holdings are constantly changing.[12]

The ADHD construct represents a definition or description of a child's real and observable maladaptive behavior from the perspective of the American Psychiatric Association (APA). Of course, other vantage points and definitions concerning the same mindsets and behaviors also exist. Drs. Ed Hallowell and John Ratey—considered by many to be some of the leading experts on ADHD—explain further: "We do not have one concise definition for ADD. Instead, we have to rely on descriptions of symptoms to define ADD."[13] The "symptoms"—which are really behaviors—represent the reality in the child's life and are undeniably problematic. But the construct of ADHD is simply one attempt to describe, categorize, and approach a child's ongoing bad/impairing actions.

Evaluating and even categorizing children's behavior from one's worldview is part of human nature. In fact, the Bible points this out in passages such as Proverbs 20:11: "Even a child is known by his doings, whether his work be *pure*, and whether it be *right*" (KJV). This proverb also emphasizes that discerning a child's behavior correctly requires moral discretion; how we interpret character traits and tendencies will always be based on our moral position (what we perceive to be pure and right). But even without accepting God's moral standard or acknowledging a child's morality, all parents, counselors, and educators must still apply moral judgment to observable human tendencies. As

---

[12] Herb Kutchins and Stuart A. Kirk, *Making us Crazy: DSM: The Psychiatric Bible and the Creation of Mental Disorders* (New York: Free Press, 1997), 22-25.

[13] Edward M. Hallowell and John J. Ratey, *Driven to Distraction: Recognizing and Coping with Attention Deficit Disorder* (New York: Pantheon Books, 1994), 151.

we will discuss in this chapter, this need is precisely why the construct of ADHD exists.

It is fairly safe to say that most all types of ADHD theory recognize that the child's observable and impairing behavior is a serious problem. But as previously noted, there exist other ways to describe and approach the same behavior and mindsets which the *DSM* suggests to qualify children as being abnormal. Psychiatrist, Allen Frances (who at the turn of the century was said to be "perhaps the most powerful psychiatrist in America"[14]) explains,

> The labeling of mental disorder has evolved over time because the lens of cultural attention extracts figure from ground in many different ways. We see elephants in clouds if we look for them. But could equally well find whales or rabbits if these better fit our preconceptions—the cloud doesn't have to change for people to see different shapes in it. Psychiatric diagnosis is seeing something that exists, but with a pattern shaped by what we expect to see.[15]

The construct of ADHD is not a verified fact; rather, it is a theory which seeks to explain "something [the behavior] that exists" and resolve these behavioral problems through a specific presupposition or worldview.

---

[14] Gary Greenberg, *The Book of Woe: The DSM and the Unmaking of Psychiatry* (New York: Blue Rider Press, 2013), 22.

[15] Frances, *Saving Normal*, 36.

FITTING REALITY INTO OUR PERSPECTIVE

Even among prominent psychiatrists, there are various interpretations and theories surrounding children's maladaptive behavior. Take for example neurologist Dr. Richard Saul, who believes that the label of ADHD is merely an attempt to describe "comorbid conditions" (other combined mental struggles), which he claims, "are in fact the only cause of distractibility and impulsivity symptoms."[16] Or take as other examples, clinicians who believe that ADHD describes a child's struggles in school,[17] problems with excessive playing of video games and watching television,[18] or the result of wrong dietary choices.[19] The reality

---

[16] Richard Saul, *ADHD Does Not Exist: The Truth about Attention Deficit and Hyperactivity Disorder* (New York: HarperCollins, 2014), 14.

[17] Leigh Pretnar Cousins, "Might Schools Be Teaching ADHD?" http://psychcentral.com/ lib/2010/might-schools-be-teaching-adhd/.

[18] Robin Weiss, "Babies and TV," http://pregnancy. about.com/od/ yourbaby/a/babiesandtv.htm.

[19] Vincent J. Monastra, *Parenting Children with ADHD: 10 Lessons that Medicine Cannot Teach* (Washington, DC: American Psychological Association, 2005), 75-91.

that all children by nature need the attention and supervision of authority has led psychiatrist Peter Breggin and his wife to use the label "DADD"[20] (Dad Attention Deficit Disorder) to describe their years of clinical observation of the true nature of ADHD being — in their minds — a dad's failure to give his children proper attention.[21] Observing these varied opinions further exposes ADHD to be a subjective psychiatric construct. To deny the secular construct of ADHD is in no way claiming that children do not have behavioral problems that need to be addressed; it simply means that the American Psychiatric Association's perspective — used to define and categorize children's maladaptive/bad behavior — has been rejected.

As people's fundamental perspectives/beliefs change, so too do their descriptive labels and categorization of people. Dr. Frances remarks on this tendency and why the number of children being diagnosed as having ADHD continues to grow:

> There is no reason to think that kids have changed, it is just that the labels have. We now diagnose as mental disorder attentional and behavioral problems that *used to be seen as part of life and normal individual variation* [emphasis added].[22]

Secular psychiatrist Bessel van der Kolk also remarks,

> Now a new paradigm was emerging: Anger, lust, pride, greed, avarice, and sloth — as well as all the other problems we humans

---

[20] Peter and Ginger Breggin, "The Hazards of Treating 'Attention-Deficit/Hyperactivity Disorder'"with Methylphenidate (Ritalin)," *Journal of College Students Psychotherapy* 10, no. 2 (1995): 55-72.

[21] Ibid.

[22] Frances, *Saving Normal*, 141.

have always struggled to manage — were recast as "disorders" that could be fixed by the administration of appropriate chemicals.[23]

The construct of ADHD has widely been accepted and continues to spread, not because children are getting worse or because a new disease of ADHD has suddenly been discovered. It is,

FITTING CHILDREN INTO OUR WORLDVIEWS

however, because society in general has gradually changed the lens through which children are viewed — exchanging the biblical vantage point for the psychiatric perspective found in the *DSM*. The secular construct of ADHD is an unproven ideology, which attempts to explain and resolve a child's maladaptive or unwanted tendencies within the framework of evolutionary thinking; it is not objective or factual.

As I have had the opportunity to speak and counsel numerous families, it has become apparent that many parents/guardians of children diagnosed as having ADHD do not truly understand what the label actually states about their

---

[23] Bessel van der Kolk, *The Body Keeps the Score: Brain, Mind, and Body in the Healing of Trauma* (New York: Penguin Group, 2014), 27.

children. The definitions of most widespread valid diseases are public knowledge and well-defined. But alleged mental illnesses (like ADHD) are widely accepted as dogma without the general public's understanding of how children (or the proposed disease) are actually being described. Many well-respected psychiatrists, like Dr. Karl Menninger, realize that constructs of mental illness cannot be defined:

> To define illness and health is an almost impossible task. We can define mental illness as being a certain state of existence which is uncomfortable to someone. The suffering may be in the afflicted person or those around him or both, but a disturbance has occurred in the total economics of a personality.[24]

Even without clear definitions or understanding of what is actually suggested in the construct of ADHD, people have come to believe that the idea is valid on the sole basis that they are able to observe a child's impairing behavior and poor academic performance. A great number of parents and educators have not taken the time to study the qualifications/criteria for being diagnosed as ADHD.[25] Still, it is often educators who suggest to parents that a child appears to have ADHD, and some educators even insist that children cannot return to the classroom until they have been professionally evaluated.

Parents and educators have a concept of ADHD — which typically includes inattentiveness, impulsivity, and hyperactivity — but they are unaware of how these terms are actually used in constructing the idea of ADHD. In order to understand not only the construct of ADHD, but also what a child's genuine problems are, it is imperative that one first

---

[24] Karl Menninger, *The Vital Balance: The Life Process in Mental Health and Illness* (New York: Viking Press, 1968), 77.

[25] It is recommended to purchase the *DSM-5* in order to fully understand what the construct proposes about children.

become familiar with the ideas of ADHD presented in the *Diagnostic and Statistical Manual of Mental Disorders- 5,*[26] hereafter referred to as the *DSM.*[27]

Psychiatrists and psychologists in general consider the APA's *DSM* to be the authority on ADHD and claim it contains "some of the most rigorous and most empirically derived criteria ever available in the history of clinical diagnosis."[28] Because most clinicians consider the *DSM* to be authoritative and empirically sound, it is the primary tool used to describe the construct of ADHD and to establish the diagnostic process.[29] The concept of ADHD and the diagnostic process — which are both based entirely on the observations and interpretations of a child's "maladaptive behaviors"[30] — were essentially conceived and are sustained in this book of psychiatric classifications. The *DSM* should be understood, not as an objective book of medical

---

[26] American Psychiatric Association, *Diagnostic and Statistical Manual of Mental Disorders: DSM-5* (Washington, D.C.: American Psychiatric Association, 2013). Hereafter referred to as *DSM-5* in the footnotes.

[27] This book does reproduce the APA's entire concept of ADHD. To study the complete construct of ADHD according to the APA, it is recommended that the *DSM-5* be purchased. For argument sake, the law allows portions of the book to be reproduced under the fair use law (17 U.S.C. § 107 : US Code - Section 107: Limitations on exclusive rights: Fair use. See more at http://codes.lp .find law .com/uscode/17/1/107# sthash.dG94ebei.dpuf).

[28] Russell A. Barkley, *ADHD and the Nature of Self-Control* (New York: Guilford, 2005), 14. Hereafter referred to as *NoSC.*

[29] Melody Petersen, *Our Daily Meds* (New York: Sarah Crichton Books, 2008), 98. Many secularists are beginning to realize that the *DSM* is not a standard or even an authority but merely a set of manmade guidelines (Saul, *ADHD Does Not Exist,* 178).

[30] Wender, *ADHD,* 159.

nosology, but as a subjective humanistic interpretation and categorization of impairing/distressful human mindsets, emotions, and behavior.

Psychiatrists have divided the *DSM*'s classification of ADHD into two main categories (which consist of nine observable behaviors in each group): *inattention* and the combination of *hyperactivity-impulsivity*. At least six of the nine behaviors in one group or the other must be observable in a child's life over a period of at least six months, and it must be clear that the child's behavior is negatively affecting his/her life (significant impairment).[31] Symptoms (behaviors) must also be present in a child prior to age twelve; they must be present in at least two different life environments (typically at school and at home), and the behaviors must not be caused by other disorders or syndromes.[32] The child's behaviors also distinguish which subtype of ADHD he/she allegedly has: "predominantly inattention" (ADHD-I), "predominantly hyperactive/impulsive" (ADHD-HI), and "combined presentation" (ADHD-C)."[33] Two more subtypes of ADHD also exist for children who don't behave well but who do not meet the *DSM* diagnostic criteria. Psychiatrists refer to these types of ADHD as "Other Specified" and "Unspecified" ADHD,[34] and their existence sheds light on just how subjective the construct of ADHD is.

---

[31] APA, *DSM-5*, 60.

[32] Ibid., 60-61.

[33] Ibid. See also Barkley, *NoSC*, 14.

[34] APA, *DSM-5*, 65-66. This subtype will be discussed further in this chapter.

Any construct of children's behavior must be formed on the basis of a presuppositional worldview/system of morality. One simply cannot approach the idea of ADHD without first establishing a perspective of humanity (anthropology) and a more fundamental view of human origins. The psychiatric theory of ADHD exists from the need to explain, understand, and approach behavioral problems that would otherwise fall outside of evolutionary theory or expose theorists' spurious claims. How a parent, counselor, or educator chooses to explain a child's behavior, how the child is approached, how bad behavior is sought to be remedied, and the demarcations between normal and abnormal behavior and normal and abnormal children will inevitably reflect each person's worldview and established authority.

Humanism

Shortly after Darwin introduced his theory of origins, his half cousin Francis Galton proposed a corresponding theory of the mind and intellect based on the philosophy of humanism. Humanism is the worldview or system that perceives people rather than God as the highest good and determiner of morals, the deliverer of human problems, and the source of the greatest wisdom in the universe.

Galton asserted that people's intellect, mental capacity, outworking behavior, and even their personalities were all determined by their genes. Galton's humanistic theory marked the birth of eugenics, and it also introduced and promoted the ideas of materialism (the idea that people are only biological masses) and determinism (the idea that people cannot choose who they are or what they do but are instead products of their biology and environments). Still to this day, materialism and

15

determinism are necessary ideas to maintain the theory of evolution, the philosophy of humanism, and the construct of mental illness.[35]

Decades after Galton first proposed his eugenics theory, German psychiatrist Emil Kraepelin proposed a similar theory of the mind based upon Galton's original ideas. Kraepelin's theory, however, sought to define abnormal minds—what was then called "madness." A humanist himself, Kraepelin maintained Galton's ideas of materialism and genetic determinism while adding his own theory of brain-dysfunction or neuro-determinism. He also proposed psychopharmacology as the remedy to alter/restore the mind. It was on his principles— derived from his belief in the evolutionary theory and humanistic ideology—that the construct of mental illness was built and is maintained today.[36] Today's construct of ADHD is fully neo-Kraepelinian—reflecting his humanistic faith.

All secular theories about ADHD presuppose the theory of evolution and a humanistic worldview. The prominent secular theorist Russell Barkley's admitted belief in evolution typifies the secular underpinning of ADHD and explains secularists'

---

[35] For further study on Francis Galton or the genetic theory of mental illness, see Daniel R. Berger II, *Mental Illness: The Influence of Nurture* (Taylors, SC: Alethia International Publications, 2016), 55-63.

[36] Emil Kraepelin was a German psychiatrist who is widely recognized to be the author of the current construct of mental illness, the father of psychopharmacology, the father of the psychiatric-genetics theory, and the originator of the *DSM*-like categorization of mental disorders. For further study on Emil Kraepelin, see Daniel R. Berger II, *Mental Illness: The Necessity for Faith and Authority* (Taylors, SC: Alethia International Publications, 2016), 63-72, and Daniel R. Berger II, *Mental Illness: The Reality of the Spiritual Nature* (Taylors, SC: Alethia International Publications, 2016), 101-28.

approaches to behavioral problems.[37] As the predominant worldview began to change at the turn of the twentieth century from aligned biblical views to more distinct secular perspectives, so followed psychological theories and practices of caring for the souls of men:

> [Man] was now seen as being part of the natural order, different from non-human animals only in degree of structural complexity. This made it possible and plausible, for the first time, to treat man as an object of scientific investigation, and to conceive of the vast and varied range of human behavior, and the motivational causes from which it springs, as being amenable in principle to scientific explanation. Much of the creative work done in a whole variety of diverse scientific fields over the next century was to be inspired by, and derive sustenance from, this new world-view.[38]

This evolutionary view also explains why the ADHD construct is so widely accepted in American culture that denies the rightful worship of God and rejects the biblical worldview. Despite the reality that secular psychology and psychiatry explain, diagnose, and treat human behavior from the presupposition that people are evolved animals[39] and reduce all human functions — including spiritual and moral behavior — to materialistic thinking, many believers choose to accept their proposed theories of anthropology and subsequent theories of maladaptive behavior.

---

[37] For more on Barkley's evolutionary beliefs and subsequent theories, see Russell A. Barkley, *Executive Functions: What They Are, How They Work, and Why They Evolved* (New York: Guilford, 2012).

[38] "Sigmund Freud (1856-1939)," http://www.iep.utm.edu/freud/#H2; accessed 21 April 2014.

[39] Hallowell and Ratey, *Driven to Distraction*, 270.

Utilitarianism

Rather than admitting that the construct of ADHD is a philosophical, anthropological, and theological matter, leading psychiatrists insist that utilitarianism is the only standard able to sustain their theory of mental illness/abnormality. Utilitarianism is the belief that "the greatest good, for the greatest number" should guide human thinking, systems, and policies.[40] Instead of absolute truth establishing morality/normalcy, a practical utilitarian trusts that humanity's collective (but ever-changing) thinking provides the best form of goodness to guide the community's thinking and establish an ambiguous standard. But utilitarianism most often amounts to what the greatest established authority determines is best for its own good. Dr. Frances remarks on how utilitarianism is dangerous and has historically brought about pain and suffering:

> There are also undeniable uncertainties in being a practical utilitarian, and even worse there are dangerous value land mines. "The greatest good for the greatest number" sounds great on paper, but how do you measure the quantities and how do you decide what's the good? It is no accident that utilitarianism is currently least popular in Germany, where Hitler gave it such an enduringly bad name.[41]

Despite Frances' recognition of the moral nature of utilitarianism—that it lacks ways to objectively measure goodness apart from morality—and that its application brought about the Nazi Holocaust, the American Psychiatric Association has chosen to view and approach humanity through this same philosophical lens:

> Utilitarianism provided the first, and remains the only practical philosophic guidance on how and where to set a boundary between "normal" and "mental disorder." The guiding assumptions are that "normal" has no universal meaning and can never be defined with

---

[40] Frances, *Saving Normal*, 5.

[41] Ibid.

precision by the spinning wheels of philosophical deduction—it is very much in the eye of the beholder and is changeable over time, place, and cultures. From this it follows that the boundary separating "normal" from "mental disorder" should be based not on abstract reasoning, but rather on the balance between the positive and the negative consequences that accrue from different choices. . . . Granted that, in the wrong hands, utilitarianism can be blind to good values and twisted by bad ones, it still remains the best or only philosophical guide when we embark on the difficult task of setting boundaries between the mentally "normal" and the mentally "abnormal." *This is the approach we used in DSM-IV* [emphasis added].[42]

But even if utilitarianism is asserted as the only valid definition of normalcy, psychiatrists are still dogmatically claiming their definition of abnormalities/deviances. They are not actually denying absolutes; they are insisting that society accept their moral system in defining abnormalities as absolute truth. Their moral system, however, is built upon a logical fallacy which asserts that so-called absolutes are necessary until another absolute can replace it. When the first absolute (or as is commonly stated, scientific fact) is replaced, it is exposed to have been false from the beginning. In psychiatric thinking, a theory and its application are considered good if they best benefit a majority or at least are perceived by an authority as good.

Psychiatrists once claimed that homosexuality, for example, was genetically proven to be a mental illness. But they then revoked the claim because of political pressure. This is the practical nature of utilitarianism.[43] Two former reviewers for the *DSM-III*, Drs. Herb Kutchins and Stuart Kirk explain:

The homosexuality controversy illustrates [a major] theme, namely, that science is often not central to the decision to include or exclude a diagnosis from [the] *DSM*. The dispute over the inclusion of homosexuality in the *DSM* was not about research findings. *It was a 20-year debate about beliefs and values.* Although the professionals who formulated diagnoses couched their arguments in the language of science, the actual influence of empirical data was negligible. *More*

---

[42] Ibid.

[43] For further study on how and why homosexuality was removed from the *DSM*, see Berger, *Necessity for Faith and Authority*, 78-79; 94-98.

> *often than not, the issues were settled by political compromises that promoted personal interests* [emphasis added].[44]

Without valid empirical evidence, the fluid psychiatric constructs are marketed as dogma and proclaimed to be absolute medical conditions.

Utilitarianism requires that psychiatric constructs be always changing. Instead of describing a genuine-absolute standard of normalcy — truth, the ADHD construct relies on ever-changing/evolving theories. The *DSM* explains this reality in its introduction: "The science of mental disorders continues to evolve."[45] Many prominent ADHD theorists admit that they have not arrived at truth in describing children, but hope to someday fully understand what causes children to lack self-control and to misbehave. Psychologist Russell Barkley — self-proclaimed as the "internationally recognized authority on ADHD,"[46] — views psychology and psychiatry's lack of absolute truth or changing theory of ADHD as both expected and as part of the scientific process.

> Since we ask not for perfection [in ADHD theory], but utility, we seek to build a ship that can be floated to be tested and revised, enabling us to build an even better ship that can be floated, tested, revised, and so on. Theories, like all accumulated information, are Darwinian in nature, evolving as their conceptual feet are held to empirical fires of experimentation, falsifiability, and revision.[47]

Similarly, *DSM-III* task force member Z.J. Liposwski remarks on "the proper scope of psychiatry":

---

[44] Kutchins and Kirk, *Making Us Crazy,* 56.

[45] APA, *DSM-5,* 5.

[46] "Russell A. Barkley, Ph.D.," http://www.russellbarkley.org/; accessed 14 February 2016.

[47] Barkley, *NoSC,* 361.

Its core focus is on abnormal experience and behavior of persons that cause suffering for them or for others, or both. As physicians, our role is to diagnose and treat such abnormalities. *Yet what is considered abnormal changes over time and hence the boundaries of our field are fluid* [emphasis added].[48]

Chair of the *DSM-IV* task force, Allen Frances, also comments,

Our classification of mental disorders is no more than a collection of fallible and limited constructs that seeks but never finds the truth — but this remains our best current way of communicating about, treating, and researching mental disorders.[49]

Though psychiatrists' and humanistic psychologists' definitions of human nature and thus their psychiatric constructs are admittedly imprecise and ever-changing, they still expect society to accept their theory and labels as dogma. But accepting today's psychiatric theory about children will inevitably leave parents with wrong ideas about their children tomorrow. Not to mention, what parents allow to be done to their children today because it is claimed to be empirically sound may in the near future be viewed as barbaric and unsound. As will be seen in chapter four, the theories of genetic causes, chemical imbalances, and brain-dysfunction are already being abandoned by many leading theorists. Yet, these ideas were propagated for years as scientific dogma.

Not only do psychiatrists admit that their construct of ADHD is ever-changing, but the APA also asserts in the *DSM* that in order for them to maintain their authority over defining human nature, they must carefully speculate and change the *DSM* constructs:

The *DSM-5* Task Force overseeing the new edition recognized that research advances will require careful, iterative changes if *DSM* is to maintain its place as the touchstone classification of mental

---

[48] Z.J. Lipowski, "Psychiatry: Mindless or Brainless, Both or Neither?" *Canadian Journal of Psychiatry* 34 (3) (1989): 249-54.

[49] Frances, *Saving Normal*, 21.

disorders. Finding the right balance is critical. *Speculative results do not belong in an official nosology*, but at the same time, *DSM* must evolve in the context of other clinical research initiatives in the field [emphasis added].[50]

Admittedly, both speculation and continued changes are key components to maintaining the construct of ADHD and other proposed mental disorders. Because of this reality, the influential Dr. Francis shares his perception of the *DSM-IV* which he oversaw: "We saw *DSM-IV* as a guidebook, not a bible—*a collection of temporarily useful diagnostic constructs, not a catalog of 'real' diseases* [emphasis added]."[51] With every *DSM* revision, come new labels, new criteria, and new alterations to existing constructs. ADHD is not a true disease; it is an ever-changing construct which never arrives at precisely/objectively defining human nature.

Materialism

The construct of ADHD has morphed over the last century from a traditional worldview—which viewed humanity as psychosomatic and moral—to a materialistic/evolutionary worldview. Throughout the brief history of the construct, the various labels for the behaviors known today as ADHD have been descriptive—not always descriptive of the child, but always reflective of the social-moral views of their time.

In 1902, physician George Still designated the first label used to describe a child's bad and impairing behaviors as "a morbid defect in moral control."[52] Dr. Still explained the label as

---

[50] Frances, *Saving Normal*, 21. Nosology is a branch of medicine dedicated to the task of classifying disease.

[51] Ibid., 73.

[52] George Still, "Some Abnormal Physical Conditions in Children," *Lancet Medical Journal* 1 (1902): 1009.

representing children who were "aggressive, passionate, lawless, inattentive, impulsive, and overactive."[53] Though secular therapists generally view this nomenclature as puritanical,[54] the label accurately describes society's view in the early 1900s that all behavior was moral,[55] a view which is in line with Scripture. The original label—"morbid defect in moral control (*MDMC*)"— describes well the fallen condition of all people without Christ as being depraved and not just a small percentage of children who exhibit certain unacceptable behaviors. Scripture tells us that we are all naturally dead (morbid) in our trespasses and sins (mental states and behaviors; Eph 2:1). Since we are all in sin, we are defective or imperfect. This lack of holiness/perfection is moral in nature, and without the control of the Holy Spirit, we cannot meet God's moral standard and please Him. Romans 8:1-17 offers us the only antidote to our morbid defect in moral control –it is the work of God the Father, Son, and Holy Spirit that gives us life and moral control to please God and behave accordingly. Unlike secularists, however, Scripture focuses on the whole man (spiritual and physical natures) and not merely on the behaviors.

Twenty years later after the first label was suggested, psychiatrists changed the label to "post-encephalitic behaviors disorder."[56] This change revealed the shift in how psychiatrists

---

[53] Barkley, *NoSC*, 4.

[54] Hallowell and Ratey, *Driven to Distraction*, 166.

[55] John Wills Lloyd, Edward J. Kameenui, and David Chard, eds. *Issues in Educating Students with Disabilities* (Mahwah, NJ: Routledge, 1997), 30.

[56] Encephalitis is brain inflammation caused by viral infection.

and society in general viewed and approached behavior[57] —
through biology and specifically neurology rather than through
moral anthropology. Drs. Hallowell and Ratey explain this
sentiment:

> Where the story began is impossible to say. Certainly, the symptoms
> of ADD have been with us as long as history has been recorded.
> However, the modern story of ADD, the story of bringing those
> symptoms out of the realm of morality and punishment and into the
> realm of science and treatment, began somewhere around the turn of
> the century.[58]

They go on to write, "As clinicians began to speculate that
neurology, rather than the devil, was governing behavior, a
kinder, more effective approach to child-rearing emerged."[59]
From this point in psychiatric history, materialism became the
predominate philosophy that guided both psychiatric ideology
and eventually much of the American public. Dr. Eric Kandel,
one of the most outspoken materialists, explains:

> Indeed, the underlying precept of the new science of mind is that *all*
> mental processes are biological. . . . Therefore, any disorder or
> alteration of those processes must also have a biological basis.[60]

Atheistic psychiatrist Thomas Szasz also comments on the
necessity to believe both in materialism and to minimize or
disregard the executive moral control of the mind over the body,

> Having a healthy mind has been added to this value scheme by
> regarding the mind as if it were simply another part of the human

---

[57] Peter Gray, "The 'ADHD Personality': Its Cognitive, Biological, and
Evolutionary Foundations"; available from http://www.psychologytoday.com/
blog/freedom-learn/201008/the-adhd-personality-its-cognitive-biological-and-
evolutionary-foundations; accessed 3 October 2014.

[58] Hallowell and Ratey, *Driven to Distraction,* 270.

[59] Ibid, 272.

[60] Eric Kandel, *In Search of Memory: The Emergence of a New Science of Mind*
(New York: Norton Publishing Company, 2006), 336.

organism or body. In this view, the human being is endowed with a skeletal system, digestive system, circulatory system, nervous system, etc. — and a "mind." As the Romans had put it, *Mens sana in corpora sano:* "In a healthy body, a healthy mind." Curiously enough, much of modern psychiatry has been devoted to this ancient proposition. Psychiatrists who search for biochemical or genetic defects as the causes of mental illness are, whether they know it or not, committed to this perspective on human misery.[61]

In 1960, the third label "minimal brain dysfunction"[62] or "minimal cerebral dysfunction"[63] was assigned to ADHD behaviors and remained consistent with the psychiatric view that behavior is amoral,[64] that people are only biological animals, and that all human impairment, failure and fragility are biologically caused. Historian Ed Shorter remarks,

> Psychiatrists have an obvious self-interest in pathologizing human behavior and have been willing to draw the pathology line ever lower in their efforts to tear as much counseling as possible away from competing psychologists and social workers [not to mention Christian counselors and pastors]. Take, for example, the question of boyhood. Whereas once Tom-Sawyer-esque enthusiasm was seen as part of the natural spirits of ladhood, in the 1960s and after, a whole series of psychological diagnoses arrived to define such behavior as pathological. The bidding opened with "minimal cerebral dysfunction," as it was called in the 1950s and 1960s.

Shorter continues,

> Tom Sawyer, in other words, had brain damage. When this diagnosis was discarded as obviously absurd, hyperactivity and inattentiveness were zeroed in on because boys can sometimes be

---

[61] Thomas Szasz, *The Myth of Psychotherapy: Mental Healing as a Religion, Rhetoric, and Repression* (New York: Anchor Press, 1978), 195-96.

[62] Lloyd, Kameenui, and Chard, 31.

[63] Edward Shorter, *A History of Psychiatry: From the Era of the Asylum to the Age of the Prozac* (New York: John Wiley and Sons, 1997), 290.

[64] Barkley defines morality as a measurement of acceptable behavior as it relates to oneself (*NoSC*, 179-80). However, the Bible teaches that God judges people's thoughts, motives, and behaviors in relation to His holy character (1 Pet 1:13-17). Secularists still use the word *morality* in their writing, but their understanding of morality excludes any reference to God.

exasperating to deal with in the classroom. Ignoring the perils of school-teacher psychiatry, educational professionals grasped gratefully for this new pathologizing of boyhood.[65]

Likewise, highly regarded Harvard psychologist, Jerome Kagan states,

> Let's go back 50 years. We have a 7-year-old child who is bored in school and disrupts classes. Back then, he was called lazy. Today, he is said to suffer from ADHD (Attention Deficit Hyperactivity Disorder). That's why the numbers have soared.[66]

Robert Whitaker, as well, elaborates on how the perception and classification of children as being normal/abnormal has digressed over the last several decades:

> Not too long ago, goof-offs, cutups, bullies, nerds, shy kids, teachers' pets, and any number of other recognizable types filled the schoolyard, and all were considered more or less normal. Nobody really knew what to expect from such children as adults. That was part of the glorious uncertainty of life — the goof-off in the fifth grade might show up at his high school's twenty-year reunion as a wealthy entrepreneur, the shy girl as an accomplished actress. But today, children diagnosed with mental disorders — most notably, ADHD, depression, and bipolar illness — help populate the schoolyard. These children have been told that they have something wrong with their brains and that they may have to take psychiatric medications the rest of their lives, just like a "diabetic takes insulin." *That medical dictum teaches all of the children on the playground a lesson about the nature of humankind, and that lesson differs in a radical way from what children used to be taught* [emphasis added].[67]

Truly ADHD represents a new worldview — a radical new way to view children — and not a medical advancement.[68] For the last

---

[65] Shorter, *A History of Psychiatry*, 289-90.

[66] Jerome Kagan, "What about Tutoring Instead of Pills?" *Spiegel Online* (August 2, 2012): http://www.spiegel.de/international/world/child-psychologist-jerome-kagan-on-overprescibing-drugs-to-children-a-847500.html: accessed 2 February 2017.

[67] Whitaker, *Anatomy of an Epidemic*, 10.

[68] Children are by nature curious, which is large reason why the cartoon *Curious George* is liked by so many kids. As children explore and learn, their brains grow and neurological activity increases. This process stimulates the

century, biological psychiatrists have used labels and spurious claims to transform normal boyhood immaturity and foolishness into an alleged disease. Dr. Stephen Flora also comments:

> We have been led down a slippery slope of labels. What used to be called appropriately and simply a behavioral problem or difficulty came to be a labeled a 'behavioral disorder.' 'Disorders' are not very different from, or a result of, 'diseases.' Almost overnight, simple behavior problems became 'brain diseases.'[69]

Today, being an energetic boy with behavioral problems makes the chances of being diagnosed as having ADHD much higher.[70] These claims are not merely a few professionals' opinions; even the *DSM-5* acknowledges that boys are being diagnosed as having ADHD 2-1 over girls.[71]

In 1968 the label changed once again to "developmental hyperactivity" and "hyperkinetic reaction,"[72] which "supposedly manifest in restlessness and distractibility."[73] These labels formed the basis of the label assigned in 1980 as "attention-

---

senses and, in turn, increases their curiosity. But this normal tendency is regularly perceived as annoying, inconvenient, and detrimental.

[69] Stephen Flora, *Taking America off Drugs: Why Behavioral Therapy is More Effective for Treating ADHD, OCD, Depression, and Other Psychological Problems* (New York: State University of New York Press, 2007), 14.

[70] Children are by nature curious, which is a large reason why the cartoon *Curious George* is liked by so many kids. As children explore and learn, their brains grow and neurological activity increases. This process stimulates the senses and, in turn, increases their curiosity. But this normal tendency is regularly perceived as annoying, inconvenient, and detrimental.

[71] APA, *DSM-5*, 63.

[72] David Benner, ed., *Encyclopedia of Psychology* (Grand Rapids: Baker, 1985), 80.

[73] Shorter, *A History of Psychiatry*, 290.

deficit disorder" and eventually as "Attention-deficit Hyperactivity disorder."[74]

As with the ADHD criteria, society and psychotherapists and insurance companies in particular rely on the *DSM* to provide a common working label and a common language to describe the ADHD construct and categorize children. Secularists often think of the *DSM* as the "bible" of psychopathology; however, the National Institute of Mental Health (NIMH) sees it for what it is: "a dictionary, creating a set of labels and defining each."[75] ADHD, then, is just another label, which describes children's fallen but normal human nature. If the label possesses any value, it is in revealing secularist's anthropology and moral views rather than accurately describing or defining a child.

Determinism

Following closely to the philosophy of materialism is the idea of determinism. If people are not moral/spiritual beings, then they should not be held accountable for their actions. The way to assert this idea is through bio-determinism/neuro-determinism/genetic-determinism.[76] Psychiatrist Sally Satel and psychologist Scott Lilienfeld explain this common humanistic approach:

---

[74] Julian Haber, *ADHD: The Great Misdiagnosis* (New York: Taylor Trade, 2003), 30.

[75] Thomas Insel, "Transforming Diagnosis"; http://www.nimh.nih.gov /about/director/2013/transforming-diagnosis.shtml; accessed 23 October 2013.

[76] Lissa Rankin, *Mind over Medicine: Scientific Proof that You Can Heal Yourself* (New York: Hay House Inc., 2013), 25.

If "each act follows a cause," then all of us . . . are nature's victims. Bold as it was, however, the claim was not original. It drew on the ancient philosophical doctrine known as determinism, which states that every event is completely caused, or determined, by what happened leading up to it. Our decisions are inevitable products of a vast array of influences — our genes (and the evolutionary history they represent), the mechanisms of our brains, our upbringing, and the physical and social environments in which we live.[77]

In this evolutionary and deterministic thinking, humans are only amoral machines or animals that are not responsible for their actions. The construct of mental illness is not just a new anthropology but also a new suggested moral system which accommodates materialistic/deterministic ideology.

The construct of ADHD is an attempt to explain away one of the key aspects of human nature: morality. Neuropsychiatrist Richard Restak comments,

In reducing deviant behavior to brain dysfunction and the genetic, dietary, social and environmental factors that lead to it, neurologists *threaten to eliminate the humanistic concept of the person as a rational being endowed with rights and responsibilities.* The shift from the insanity defense to the neurological one would resolve the traditional tension between the mad and the bad by defining away the bad [emphasis added].[78]

Determinism is not only a major tenet of the evolutionary/humanistic moral system, but it also exploits the human desire to excuse away moral failure. From the fall (Genesis 3) of Adam and Eve to the present, excuses have become a common attempt to deal with guilt and human failure. The *DSM* and the idea of bio-determinism are mainstream in today's society because they seemingly provide an excuse to dismiss personal guilt and culpability. Former NIMH Consultant and professor of Psychiatry at Harvard Medical School, Peter Breggin, remarks,

---

[77] Sally Satel and Scott Lilienfeld, *Brainwashed: The Seductive Appeal of Mindless Neuroscience* (New York: Basic Books, 2013), 126-27.

[78] Richard Restak, *The Brain Has a Mind of Its Own: Insights from a Practicing Neurologist* (New York: Crown Publishers, 1991), 20.

> It's understandable that parents would prefer to think of their children as genetically defective rather than as resentful, rebellious, misunderstood, or even abused. But it's harder to see why people in despair would want to see themselves as innately defective, as some patients do. One reason is that they typically feel helpless. Genetic and biochemical theories confirm that helplessness and alleviate the need to overcome it. Often they feel frightened by the seemingly primitive impulses stirring within them, and genetic or biochemical theories help to explain those impulses away. Frequently they feel guilty about their passions and their problems – and especially about their resentment toward their parents – and biopsychiatry relieves them of facing these personal conflicts.[79]

As Breggin points out, deterministic theories/excuses are simply attempts to eliminate responsibility and to deal with guilt and responsibility. But Breggin does touch on one significant and common human condition: without God's grace, all people are helpless to resolve their guilt and morally provide righteousness/holiness as God requires. Nonetheless, we naturally understand culpability and attempt to frame it differently than God does. Some parents would rather take the blame for their child's human nature than to view them as naturally depraved and culpable for their behavior. Dr. David Allen writes,

> A patient's family members may be just as motivated to give a distorted view of a patient as is a patient. Parents, for example, may prefer to believe that their child has some sort of mental defect, so as not to experience as much of their own covert guilt about their parenting skills. Conversely, some may actually prefer to blame the child's behavior completely on themselves, in order to let their "perfect" child off the hook. Most mental health practitioners do not make home visits to watch patients and family members interact in their natural environment. Even if they did, unless they had a camera operating twenty four hours a day as in the movie *The Truman Show*, they could still be easily deceived.[80]

Moral failure and guilt must both be dealt with somehow, and determinism seemingly provides the secular means. However,

---

[79] Peter Breggin, *Toxic Psychiatry* (New York: St. Martin's Press, 1991), 94.

[80] David Allen, "Why Psychotherapy Efficacy Studies are Nearly Impossible," December 2012, https://www.psychologytoday.com/blog/matter-personality/201212/why-psychotherapy-efficacy-studies-are-nearly-impossible; accessed October 3 2014.

excuses — no matter how elaborate — do not change humanity's moral/ spiritual condition and culpability.

The construct of ADHD represents one elaborate excuse, which many secular clinicians have used in attempt to reshape the way society views behavior. Some psychiatrists, like Dr. Russell Barkley, have suggested that ADHD and Oppositional Defiant Disorder (ODD) be renamed or at least re-categorized as "Executive Function Disorders."[81] His suggested nomenclature stems from his deterministic beliefs that children cannot help thinking and behaving poorly, that bad choices and lack of self-control are the result of alleged brain-malfunction and chemical imbalances. He and others speculate that a child's "executive system" or "ES" has malfunctioned.[82] Drs. Sheik Hosenbocus and Raj Chahal explain,

> Damage to or dysfunction of the frontal lobe and disruption in fronto-subcortical pathways from chemical imbalances have been strongly associated with dysfunction of the ES as demonstrated through neuroimaging studies using PET and fMRI scanning (Elliott, 2003). Executive dysfunction indicates some malfunction in the circuits that connect the sub-cortical areas with the frontal lobes (Rosenblatt & Hopkins, 2006). *Both genetic and environmental factors can interfere with ES efficacy* [determinism].[83]

While these physicians clearly explain their deterministic beliefs, there are several problems with their assertions. First of all, the *DSM* admits that neuroimaging cannot assess why there seems to be a variance in the brain. In other words, cause and effect

---

[81] Russell Barkley, "The Important Role of Executive Functioning and Self-Regulation in ADHD," 2012, http://www.russellbarkley.org/content/ADHD_EF_and_SR.pdf.

[82] Sheik Hosenbocus and Raj Chahal, "A Review of Executive Function Deficits and Pharmacological Management in Children and Adolescents," *Journal of the Canadian Academy of Child and Adolescent Psychiatry* 21, no. 3 (2012): 223–29.

[83] Ibid.

cannot be discerned by simply observing fMRI or EEG images.[84]
Likewise, as will be observed in chapter 4, chemical imbalances
are widely dismissed as a valid etiology by informed
psychiatrists and neurologists. Furthermore, motive, intent,
guilt, fears, desire, and thoughts (to name a few) — which the
non-physical mind produces — can never be measured or
observed in the physical brain or with scientific observations.[85]
Determinists suggest that the brain is the cause of bad behavior,
but many others understand that the brain's atrophy can just as
easily be explained as an effect of poor thinking and wrong
choices. One should expect that poor thinking would negatively
impact the body. Secondly, executive dysfunction is not a
measurable scientific fact but a theory of materialism/
determinism and is entirely speculative. Neuroscientist Elliot
Valenstein comments,

> The many recent books on the so-called "pharmacological revolution
> in psychiatry" are another indication of how much our prevailing
> notions of mental illness have changed. These popularly written
> books use such phrases as "molecules of the mind" and "chemistry
> of mood" to convey the idea that all the important aspects of mental
> life are determined by brain chemistry . . . . Many recent books
> exaggerate and distort the connection between brain chemistry and
> psychological states.[86]

But the *DSM-5* recognizes that determining whether someone
could or could not help their moral behavior is not an objective
task:

> Even when diminished control over one's behavior is a feature of the
> disorder, having the diagnosis in itself does not demonstrate that a

---

[84] APA, *DSM-5*, 61.

[85] Berger, *Reality of the Physical Nature*, 52-60.

[86] Elliot Valenstein, *Blaming the Brain: The Truth about Drugs and Mental Health* (New York: Basic Books, 1998), 2.

particular individual is (or was) unable to control his or her behavior at a particular time.[87]

So what does demonstrate that someone could or could not help their moral actions? When it comes to mental problems, there does not exist such a measurement.

Determinism is the necessary conclusion of believing in materialism and denying humanity's spiritual nature. If children are only material products of their brains, chemicals, genes, and environments, then no child should be held accountable for his/her thoughts, desires, behaviors, or mindsets. Why then have an academic system that rewards effort, performance, and even good behavior?

A Reflection of One's Authority

Worldviews and their constructs about human nature are not amoral lenses through which to see the world or to judge children; worldviews always declare one's faith in an established authority. When it comes to ADHD, there are two possible authorities in which to place one's faith: a person can believe in the neo-Kraepelinian system — promoted and controlled by the American Psychiatric Association and presented in the *DSM-5*, or he/she can place faith in the Creator God as laid-out in the Bible. These two worldviews and established authorities are antithetical. Whichever authority is chosen reveals each individual's true faith/worldview.

The APA and their *DSM-5*

The *DSM-5* represents the APA's imposed authority over society and their imprecise anthropology. The APA has gained its power by reframing what it means to be human and offering

---

[87] APA, *DSM-5*, 25.

such labels and descriptions in a categorical system. Through the wide-acceptance of the *DSM*, psychiatry has convinced much of society to view children from the outlook of their humanistic worldview. Former president-elect of the APA, Jeffery Lieberman comments on the *DSM's* function:

> Psychiatry has become deeply ingrained within the fabric of our culture, winding through our most prominent social institutions and coloring our most mundane daily encounters. For better or worse, the *DSM* is not merely a compendium of medical diagnoses. *It has become a public document that helps define how we understand ourselves and how we live our lives* [emphasis added].[88]

In other words, the *DSM* is not really a book of medical nosology but a theory of anthropology that seeks to establish the APA as the authority over moral and social mindsets and activates.

The APA claims that the *DSM* provides both a precise explanation of human nature/abnormalities and that this precision gives it the authority to control, define, and address the human mind and behavior, Former APA president, Jeffrey Lieberman comments,

> This authoritative compendium of all known mental illnesses is known as the Bible of Psychiatry [*DSM*], and for good reason—each and every hallowed diagnosis of psychiatry is inscribed within its pages. *What you may not realize is that the DSM might just be the most influential book written in the past century.* Its contents directly affect how tens of millions of people work, learn, and live—and whether they go to jail. It serves as a career manual for millions of mental health professionals including psychiatrists, psychologists, social workers, and psychiatric nurses. It dictates the payment of hundreds of billions of dollars to hospitals, physicians, pharmacies, and laboratories by Medicare, Medicaid, and private insurance companies. . . . But the manual's greatest impact is on the lives of tens of millions of men and women who long for relief from the anguish of mental disorder, since first and foremost, *the book precisely defines every known mental illness. It is these detailed definitions that empower the DSM's unparalleled medical influence over society* [emphasis added].[89]

---

[88] Lieberman, *Shrinks*, 291.

[89] Ibid., 87-88.

34

While Lieberman claims that the APA's authority is empowered by the *DSM's* "precise definitions" of mental illness, the *DSM-5* (which Lieberman oversaw) reveals that the definitions of mental illness that it contains are neither exact nor encompassing. It states,

> The symptoms contained in the respective *diagnostic criteria sets do not constitute comprehensive definitions* of underlying disorders, which encompass cognitive, emotional, behavioral, and physiological processes that are far more complex than can be described in these brief summaries. *Rather, they are intended to summarize* characteristic syndromes of signs and symptoms that point to an underlying disorder with a characteristic developmental history, biological and environmental risk factors, neuropsychological and physiological correlates, and typical clinical course [emphasis added].[90]

Dr. Lieberman claims that psychiatry is the rightful authority over society because of its unique ability to precisely define and explain anthropology. But as his work overseeing the *DSM-5* reveals, the definitions and constructs that psychiatry offers are imprecise and simply incomprehensive summaries. As was also previously noted, the *DSM* and its constructs are always changing. According to Lieberman's logic, then, the APA should not have authority over society in discerning a child's behavior and mindsets or in forming social constructs of anthropology.

God and His Word

The Word of God claims to still be the authority over human mental and behavioral issues. But Scripture does not change its position or offer speculative ideas as its working definition for mankind. Instead, the timeless truth of Scripture offers lasting hope and reliability. This wonderful news is possible because Scripture is uniquely designed by God to reveal Himself, to perfectly describe all issues of life and human nature, and to

---

[90] APA, *DSM-5*, 19.

specifically address people's behavioral, spiritual/mental, and relational problems.

The Sufficiency of God's Word

The Bible's anthropology effectively explains the human mind and offers reliable ways to restore it to health. While this healing is a lifelong process that will be completed in eternity, it is a process that yields measurable — positive — temporal results.

Christ came to restore mankind to its created state of holiness through the true knowledge of Himself and the regeneration by the Holy Spirit. It is not surprising then, that God's revelation is perfect, sure, right, clear, pure, true, all-together righteous, and everlasting; it enables the restoration of man's soul, makes man wise, causes a glad heart, and provides enlightenment in all issues of life (Psalm 19:7-9). Second Peter 1:3-4 crystallizes the biblical claim that the true knowledge of God is sufficient to address all of life's issues, including the patterns of behaviors that secularists label as ADHD. Author and Christian counselor Ed Welch writes,

> Given the degree to which God has revealed himself and ourselves, we can assume that the Bible's counsel speaks with great breadth, addressing the gamut of problems in living. It is certainly able to speak to the common problems we all encounter, such as relationship conflicts, financial pressures, our responses to physical health or illness, parenting questions, and loneliness. But it also speaks to distinctly modern problems such as depression, anxiety, mania, schizophrenia and attention deficit disorder, just to name a few. Of course, the Bible doesn't speak to each of these problems as would an encyclopedia. It doesn't offer techniques for change that look like they came out of a cookbook.[91]

As will be discussed in the next two chapters, the Bible sufficiently addresses every aspect of what secularists describe in the construct of ADHD.

---

[91] Ed Welch, "What Is Biblical Counseling, Anyway?" *Journal of Biblical Counseling* 16, no. 1 (1997): 3.

The Reliability of God's Word

Not only is the Word of God sufficient to remedy the mind and meet the relational needs in each family, it is also reliable to accomplish this work across time, cultures, and familial circumstances. In contrast to the ever-changing secular views on ADHD, secular labels, and diagnostic criteria, God's declarations are immutable (Hebrews 6:17-18) and everlasting (Psalm 119:89) because their vantage point is His perfect knowledge (Proverbs 2:6). God's Word is the essential source of immutable truth that objectively provides reliable answers and is able to deliver us from our depraved heart and sinful behaviors. Furthermore, Scripture consistently discerns and addresses human behavior, morality, and motives (Hebrews 4:12-13). Commentator Donald Guthrie writes, "Nothing, not even our innermost thoughts, is shielded from the discernment of the message of God. It affects in a most comprehensive manner the whole man."[92] In light of the Scripture's sufficiency and reliability, parents', counselors, and educators' who are wise will depend upon the Bible's wisdom to explain and resolve their child's mental and behavioral problems.

The Hope in God's Word

Unlike secular theories of behavior, Scripture offers genuine hope of lasting change for each family. The apostle Paul writes, "For whatever was written in former days was written for our instruction, that through endurance and the encouragement of the Scriptures we might have hope" (Romans 15:4).[93] Paul, here,

---

[92] Donald Guthrie, *Hebrews: An Introduction and Commentary*, vol. 15 of Tyndale New Testament Commentaries (Downers Grove: InterVarsity, 1983), 122–23.

[93] The *ESV* is used throughout this book unless otherwise noted.

emphasizes that Scripture is both the revelation of God's instruction to believers as well as the source of genuine hope for now and eternity. He later states in verse 15:13, "May the God of hope fill you with all joy and peace in believing, so that by the power of the Holy Spirit you may abound in hope." God provides us not only with hope for joy and peace, but also with hope of positive changes.

One example of such biblical change is found in Titus 3:1-8, where Paul gives testimony of the power of God's goodness to save men from both eternal condemnation and sinful behaviors. Though Paul does not list specific ADHD behaviors in his letter, he does judge the church members' behaviors prior to conversion to be foolish, disobedient, deceived, lustful, and self-indulgent (Titus 3:3). Commentator F. F. Bruce emphasizes that Paul's use of the words *malice* and *envy* indicated the "anti-social nature" of the behaviors of their past lives prior to conversion.[94] Proverbs records similar wording in describing many of the same behaviors that secularists now label as criteria of ADHD. Paul's remedy for these heart conditions and outworking behaviors was not human ability or efforts, self-esteem, science, or mind-altering drugs; rather Paul declared the completed work of Christ on the cross to remedy the human soul/mind and immoral behavior (5-7). The believers' hearts on Crete changed according to their faith and produced behaviors that were not carnal or anti-social but rather "good works" that were "good and profitable unto men" (8). Scriptural examples such as this provide us with hope in the power of the Holy Spirit and the Word of God to produce similar changes in all of us.

---

[94] F.F. Bruce, *Romans: An Introduction and Commentary*, vol. 6 of Tyndale New Testament Commentaries (Downers Grove: InterVarsity, 1985), 254.

The discerning reader will be wise in honestly evaluating his/her presuppositional worldview and established authority. These issues are so important, that the remainder of the book compares and contrasts the two available worldviews/ authorities on human mindsets and behavior. As will also be observed throughout the book, this foundational faith will determine not only how one perceives their children and seeks to resolve their problems, but also how these children will most likely develop their own identity.

CHAPTER 2

ADHD REDEFINES NORMALCY

"Most of these changes [to the *DSM-5*] imply a more inclusive system of diagnoses where the pool of 'normality' shrinks to a mere puddle."[95] – Psychiatrists Til Wykes and Felicity Callard

There is one other, subtler aspect to this epidemic. Over the past twenty-five years, psychiatry has profoundly reshaped our society. Through its *Diagnostic and Statistical Manual*, psychiatry draws a line between what is "normal" and what is not.[96] – Journalist Robert Whitaker

All approaches to what is perceived to be ADHD behavior and to human nature in general require an anthropological presupposition; the psychiatric theory of ADHD is no exception. Deviances or abnormalities cannot exist without first establishing a fixed/objective standard of normalcy. Professor of psychiatry at the University of Texas Health Science Center, Steven Pliszka, states, "In mental health, we define disorders as "behavioral and psychological syndromes that deviate from some standard of normality" (Angold et al., 1999, p. 58)."[97] If

---

[95] Til Wykes and Felicity Callard, "Diagnosis, Diagnosis, Diagnosis: Towards *DSM-5*," *Journal of Mental Health* 19, no. 4 (2010).

[96] Robert Whitaker, *Anatomy of an Epidemic: Magic Bullets, Psychiatric Drugs, and the Astonishing Rise of Mental Illness in America* (New York: Broadway Books, 2015), 10.

[97] Steven R. Pliszka, *Treating ADHD and Comorbid Disorders: Psychosocial and Psychopharmacological Interventions* (New York: Guilford, 2009), 2.

standards cannot be established dogmatically, how then can there deviances be suggested logically? In truth, each time the APA creates a construct of abnormality in the *DSM*—such as ADHD—it reveals its anthropology and concept of normalcy. Dr. Barkley explains from a humanistic perspective:

> Any theory of child psychopathological condition such as ADHD will ultimately *have to be linked to larger theories of the nature of normal developmental* psychological processes and the neuropsychological processes that comprise them. . . . Consequently, any theory of ADHD is, of necessity, a theory of executive functions and self-regulation [emphasis added].[98]

Barkley emphasizes his own secular theory and coined terms, but his proposition exposes a larger foundational issue to every approach to the ADHD label and to self-control: one's view of the concept of ADHD (abnormality) is born out of his/her philosophical view of human nature (normality).

What does it mean, then, to be a normal child today, and how do we define normalcy? Most parents that I counsel recognize that something is wrong with their child, but they are unsure if their child's problems qualify him/her as abnormal or simply reveal his/her normal human nature to be impaired and problematic. Likewise, they are unsure if the problems are spiritual in nature or physically caused.

Secular Perspective

Today's psychiatrists assert that they are experts in defining, categorizing, and approaching human nature/the mind, but they also admit that defining normal human mindsets, emotions, and behaviors, is difficult if not impossible. While it may be difficult or impossible for secularists to define normalcy, they are insistent on their definitions of abnormalities laid out in the

---

[98] Barkley, *NoSC*, vii-viii.

DSM. Dr. Ed Tronick, a professor of developmental and brain sciences at the University of Massachusetts Boston, comments on the importance and yet difficulty of establishing a standard of normalcy: "There's this very narrow range of what people think the prototype child should look like [normal]."[99] Prominent psychiatrists and clinicians even admit that the 18 behaviors listed as criteria in the *DSM* are not abnormal but rather "fall within the normal range of human behavior."[100] Retired head of Psychiatry at Duke University Medical Center, Allen Frances — who oversaw the development of the *DSM-IV* criteria, explains, "Most of what passes for ADHD these days is really no more than normal variation or developmental difference."[101] Some psychologists and physicians perceive the normalcy of ADHD criteria as indicating an alarming subjectivity in the diagnostic process.

> We are convinced if a research team were able through some Orwellian act of Congress to assess every child in America between the ages of five and twelve, and said team adhered strictly to *DSM* guidelines, they would find that close to half of all elementary-age children in America qualify for at least one of these diagnoses. . . . The *DSM* criteria, when objectively and dispassionately applied, describe so many of today's kids is alarming, if not chilling.[102]

---

[99] Allen Schwarz, "Still in a Crib, Yet Being Given Antipsychotics," *New York Times,* December 10, 2015, http://mobile.nytimes.com/2015/12/11/us/psychiatric-drugs-are-being-prescribed-to-infants.html?referer=&_r=1; accessed 11 December 2015.

[100] Ellison, "Brain Scans Link ADHD to Biological Flaw Tied to Motivation."

[101] Allen Frances, "Most Active Kids Don't Have ADHD," *Psychology Today,* March 11, 2014, https://www.psychologytoday.com/blog/saving-normal/201403/most-active-kids-don-t-have-adhd; accessed 2 January 2017.

[102] John Rosemond and Bose Ravenel, *The Diseasing of America's Children: Exposing the ADHD Fiasco and Empowering Parents to Take Back Control* (Nashville: Thomas Nelson, 2008), 105-7.

Others suggest that the normalcy of ADHD behaviors seen in everyone reveals the culture to be disordered and not the people:

> American society tends to create ADD-like symptoms in us all. We live in an ADD-ogenic culture . . . the fast pace. The sound bite. The bottom line. Short takes, quick cuts. The TV remote-control clicker. High stimulation. Restlessness. Violence. Anxiety. Ingenuity. . . . *It is important to keep this in mind or you may start thinking that everybody you know has ADD*. The disorder is culturally syntonic — that is to say, it fits right in [emphasis added].[103]

Still, others argue that normalcy cannot be defined at all. Editor in Chief of the *Psychiatric Times*, Ronald Pies, exemplifies this position:

> Is normality a purely statistical term? Is it used in relation to a particular cultural subgroup, to the human species as a whole, or to the particular patient's usual state of affairs? Moreover, those who argue that psychiatry medicalizes normality while simultaneously asserting that there is no clear demarcation between normality and abnormality effectively refute their own argument. For if there are no absolute, categorical boundaries separating normal from abnormal, then the claim "psychiatry is medicalizing normality" cannot logically be sustained: the argument is devoured by its own premise. That is: if normality has no precise boundary in the realm of disease — including psychiatric disease — then there can be no verifiable medicalization of normality. Neither can there be a veridical demonstration of psychiatry's alleged diagnostic imperialism or its supposed creation of diagnostic false positives. Such claims are no more verifiable than a landowner's complaint that someone has impermissibly planted a tree on his property, when there are no clearly established property lines. But let's be clear: this doesn't mean that we can't make reasoned, empirically grounded judgments as to what conditions merit medical evaluation or treatment.[104]

Pies argues that critics of psychiatric theory are also unable to define normalcy or provide an absolute standard, but throughout Scripture, Jesus Christ is established as the clear standard of perfection and the source and goal of mental

---

[103] Hallowell and Ratey, *Driven to Distraction*, 191.

[104] Ronald W. Pies, "Psychiatry and the Myth of 'Medicalization,'" *Psychiatric Times*, April 18 2013, http://www.psychiatrictimes.com/depression/psychiatry-and-myth-"Medicalization"; accessed 10 July 2015.

restoration.[105] Christ alone provides the standard of normalcy of which we all fall short and to which we all need to be restored. Most psychiatrists deny this clear standard and seek to imprecisely define normalcy by creating constructs that define and categorize unwanted and detrimental human behavior as abnormalities in the *DSM* and by applying utilitarianism.[106] They feel sanguine about defining and standardizing alleged abnormalities but insist that normalcy is not absolute.

The APA has chosen to suggest a standard of normalcy by attempting to define what is abnormal. Yet, they concede that their definitions of what it means to be abnormal — as expressed in the *DSM-5* — are imprecise:

> In the absence of clear biological markers or clinically useful measurements of severity for many mental disorders, it has not been possible to completely separate normal and pathological symptom expressions [abnormal conditions] contained in the diagnostic criteria.[107]

One of the major problems with claiming the construct of ADHD as a biological illness — as we will observe in the chapters to come — is that no biological markers exist to diagnose children or to separate them as normal and abnormal.[108] Psychiatrists claim — as Dr. Pies exemplifies — that they make "empirically grounded judgments,"[109] but there exists no empirical evidence. Despite this fact, much of society has bought into this spurious belief system, which views normal children as biologically defective and mentally abnormal.

---

[105] Berger, *Necessity for Faith and Authority*, 30-44.

[106] Ibid., 5.

[107] APA, *DSM-5*, 21.

[108] Ibid., 61.

[109] Ronald W. Pies, "Psychiatry and the Myth of 'Medicalization.'"

If no biological markers exist and ADHD behaviors are normal, on what basis do clinicians claim a child has or does not have the alleged disorder of ADHD? Defining normal within psychiatric ideology amounts to applying two qualifiers created by the chair of the *DSM-III*, psychiatrist Bob Spitzer, in the early 1960s.[110] He first declared that if symptoms — for the construct of ADHD this mainly amounts to 18 behaviors — did not impair normal function or cause distress, then a person was not abnormal or diseased. Throughout the *DSM-5* this subjective qualification is referred to as "clinically significant disturbance/impairment,"[111] and the former APA president, Jeffery Lieberman, refers to it as "subjective distress."[112] Lieberman is correct: distress is a subjective opinion that considers human impairment — especially for a lengthy time — to be an abnormality within evolutionary ideology. It also assumes that humanity is by nature not impaired or distressed for any length of time.

If someone fully meets the criteria necessary to be diagnosed with ADHD, yet it is believed that the child is benefiting from his/her behavior, then according to Spitzer's theory (now the psychiatric theory), the child is not sick. Renowned secular authors on ADHD, Ed Hallowell and John Ratey, insist that "for many people, ADD is not a disorder but a trait, a way of being in the world." In their view, ADHD is a "positive character

---

[110] Berger, *Necessity for Faith and Authority*, 73-82.

[111] APA, *DSM-5*, 20.

[112] Jeffrey A. Lieberman, *Shrinks: The Untold Story of Psychiatry* (New York: Little, Brown and Company, 2015), 136.

quality" that provides many gifts and talents unless behavior becomes maladaptive, impairing, or distressful.[113]

Most parents, counselors, and educators, however, see a child's outburst, defiance, and attentional issues as always being maladaptive and impairing, and if not distressing to the child, these behaviors certainly distress the authority. So on what objective basis is a child considered to be "impaired?" As we will see in chapter four, the diagnostic process of ADHD is entirely subjective and many secularists feel that if parents seek help from a counselor or physician concerning their child's behavior, or schools insist that a child see a physician or therapist, then impairment is obvious. But what if human impairment and distress are normal?

What complicates matters further is that mental health professionals are required employees in most public schools today. If a child has a behavioral problem, there is already someone in place to interpret and label the behavior according to that person's worldview or the worldview learned through their education. There are even campaigns being launched — such as that proposed by the American Academy of Pediatrics Association — to impose mandatory annual screening of children for mental illnesses.[114] If children are forced to be evaluated for impairments and distress through a psychiatric lens, then the number of children being diagnosed as impaired and distressed and who fit into the psychiatric paradigm will surely increase

---

[113] Hallowell and Ratey, *Delivered from Distraction,* 4.

[114] American Academy of Pediatrics Association, "Updated Prevention Health Care Screening and Assessment for Children's Checkups," December 7, 2015, https://www.aap.org/en-us/about-the-aap/aap-press-room/pages/AAP-Releases-Summary-of-Updated-Preventive-Health-Care-Screening-and-Assessment-Schedule-for-Children's-Checkups.aspx; accessed 11 June 2016.

significantly. No child or adult lives without some impairment or distress.

The second criteria Spitzer imposed upon Kraepelin's system was to add the qualifying element of time or duration: the child being evaluated must behave according to the criteria listed in the *DSM* for a period of six months across various life settings. The *DSM* states this criterion as:

> Six (or more) of the following symptoms [behaviors] have persisted for at least 6 months to a degree that is inconsistent with developmental level and that negatively impacts directly on social and academic/occupational activities.[115]

Not only did Spitzer redefine Kraepelinian theory and the idea of mental illness with these two subjective qualifiers, but he also began the process of changing the way society in general views humanity.

Spitzer's changes to psychiatric theory reveal just how subjective the current secular constructs truly are. With ADHD, for example, a specific timeframe (such as six months) is an objective qualification, but a timeframe itself is subjective. Spitzer and his *DSM* committee could have subjectively chosen one, two, or twenty years for the prequalifying duration of ADHD. They also did not explain why a timeframe is objectively needed at all to separate whether someone has or does not have the alleged disease of ADHD. Spitzer's subjective time qualifications seemingly provided a much-needed demarcation line between normal and abnormal, but in truth, they only made the constructs of mental illness — such as ADHD — more subjective and skewed the philosophical boundaries between normal and abnormal.

Spitzer redefined mental illness, and in the process, he reframed the psychiatric perspective of normalcy. Former APA

---

[115] APA, *DSM-5*, 60.

president, Jeffery Lieberman, notes of Spitzer's redesign of the secular construct of mental illness:

> This was a definition of mental illness radically different from anything before. Not only was it far removed from the psychoanalytic view that a patient's mental illness could be hidden from the patient herself, but it also amended Emil Kraepelin's [the father of the current mental illness construct] definition, which made no reference to *subjective distress* and considered *short-lived conditions* to be illnesses too [emphasis added].[116]

These subjective qualifiers enabled constructs like ADHD to be believed. In the book, *Mental Illness, the Necessity for Faith and Authority*, I note that

> Spitzer's clinical distress/impairment makes mental illness a matter of a patient's and doctor's perceptions or beliefs. Equipped with this new distress qualification, clinicians could view any mindsets, behaviors, emotions, and desires that impair life as a disease rather than a normal human experience or even a character flaw. Such a reality also explains why almost any negative human emotion, behavior, desire, or mindset can be found in the ever-growing list of over 400 mental illnesses found in the *DSM*.[117]

Though some clinicians might attempt to deny that all human impairment and distress can easily be considered as mental illness or abnormality within current secular thinking, leading "mental health experts" and psychiatric ideologists do not view ongoing impairment or distress as part of the normal human nature; these common traits, instead, are framed as abnormalities. Take for example, the World Health Organization (WHO), which defines mental health — and thus normalcy — as "a state of complete physical, mental, and social well-being and not merely the absence of infirmity."[118] Many prominent psychiatrists deny the WHO's definition of normal/mental

---

[116] Lieberman, *Shrinks*, 136.

[117] Berger, *Necessity for Faith and Authority*, 77.

[118] World Health Organization, http://www.who.int/trade/glossary/story046/en/; accessed 21 December 2015.

health as being unrealistic, but the WHO's theory is, in truth, not much different from that of the APA's ideology. Whereas, the WHO chooses to define mental health precisely and directly, the APA states the same viewpoint indirectly by defining ongoing impairment as mental illness and refusing to disclose its standard of normalcy that precedes its ideas of abnormality. Both groups, however, are suggesting — stated or not — the same standard and evolutionary anthropology.

Evolutionary/psychiatric theorists cannot afford to view humanity as fragile or impaired let alone depraved and morally responsible. When something is morally wrong or a person is distressed, these common human traits must be recast within the framework of humanistic/utilitarian thinking. ADHD is not an illness, but it is not a psychiatric gimmick; it is a necessary theory for evolutionists to explain why children misbehave from a non-moral perspective.

Many of the most pressing issues surrounding the construct of ADHD are resolved simply by answering foundational questions concerning normalcy. For example, are children by nature self-controlled, or must they be taught to control their thoughts and bodies? Do they by nature make sacrifices now for future benefit, or do they naturally live for the moment? Are children naturally unselfish and altruistic, or are they ready — made to serve others? Do they normally give their attention rightly and on right things, or must they be taught how and to what to give attention? Do children regularly insist that they cannot obey, or do they naturally conform to parents' wishes? Are children born with right values/desires, or must they be taught what is worth pursuing in life? Is there a normative standard of development or a wide range of acceptable maturity? Answering these questions biblically will alone dismiss the ADHD construct as false and illogical.

Take for example the problems of self-control and future reward, which are central discussions within the construct of ADHD. Psychiatrists and humanistic psychologists seek to explain lack of self-control as an abnormality rather than as part of the normal human condition. They do so by suggesting that normal children are amoral beings born with the natural ability "to be organized, planful [sic], and goal-directed,"[119] and they view problems of self-control, struggles with focusing on future reward, and difficulties making right choices as abnormalities.[120] In fact, they theorize that children labeled as having ADHD are unable to regulate "long-term self-interest"[121] and incapable of self-control.[122] Barkley explains this anthropology:

> ADHD is a disturbance in a child's ability to inhibit immediate reactions to the moment so as to use self-control with regard to time and future. . . . What is not developing properly in your child is the capacity to shift from focusing on the here and now to focusing on the future. When all a child focuses on is the moment, acting impulsively makes sense. From the child's perspective, it is always "now." But this can be disastrous when the child is expected to be developing a focus on what lies ahead and what needs to be done to meet the future effectively.[123]

Barkley comments further, "For self-control to occur, the individual must have developed a preference for the long-term over the short-term outcomes of behavior."[124] This widely held

---

[119] Russell A. Barkley, *Taking Charge of ADHD: A Complete Authoritative Guide for Parents*. rev. ed. (New York: Guilford, 2000), xi. Hereafter referred to as *TCoA*.

[120] Ibid.

[121] Barkley, *NoSC*, 302.

[122] Ibid., 64.

[123] Barkley, *TCoA*, xi.

[124] Barkley, *NoSC*, 52.

hypothesis suggests that children diagnosed with ADHD have a biological defect in their neurological system that "inhibits" foreseeing future reward over immediate gratification, and therefore ADHD children are unable to maintain self-control.[125] In reality, this hypothesis has no scientific proof, and other than the alleged physical "inhibitors" that do not exist, the hypothesis describes almost all children and many adults. People, by nature, and especially children, struggle with self-control and have trouble trusting in things that are unseen or delayed. Part of the learning process that every individual must go through is to be taught the value of living in light of the future and not merely for immediate gratification.

Barkley's hypothesis of the nature of self-control in a child diagnosed with ADHD (abnormal) also describes his view of normalcy by indirectly suggesting that children by nature have self-control and can appreciate immediate sacrifices for future benefit. If his theory were accurate, then children diagnosed as ADHD are incapable of having eternal mindsets, placing their faith in God, or having self-control to behave in a way that pleases God.

Not only is the evolutionary theory and its new morality the foundational presupposition for the secular ADHD label, but the theory also governs the American educational system where the ADHD construct flourishes.[126] Though John Dewey is best known as the father of progressive education, he was also a prominent psychologist and the eighth president of the American Psychological Association who "felt the idea of God

---

[125] Ibid., 46.

[126] Robert Moss, *Why Johnny Can't Concentrate: Coping with Attention Deficit Problems* (New York: Bantam, 1990), 129, 142.

hindered creative intelligence."[127] America's acceptance of Dewey's ideologies in both education and psychology provided the ideal environment for the popularization of the ADHD construct.[128] As God was removed from the home and the school (cultural places of learning), American education became humanistic and harmful. Removing God, however, results in the natural foolish heart being better able to reveal itself in uninhibited foolish behavior: "The fool says in his heart, 'There is no God.' They are corrupt, they do abominable deeds, there is none who does good" (Psalm 14:1).[129] If society refuses to acknowledge the reality of humanity's depraved nature and refuses to teach right theological presuppositions in places of learning, we should expect people's moral behavior to further decline as it reflects societal rejection of God's goodness and wisdom.

Biblical Perspective

In contrast to the secular construct, Scripture clearly defines all children as impaired, distressed, and depraved from birth. Rather than theorize about what has gone wrong in the child, the

---

[127] David Benner and Peter Hill, eds., *Baker Encyclopedia of Psychology and Counseling*, 2nd ed. (Grand Rapids: Baker, 1999), 347.

[128] Thomas S. Szasz, *Pharmacracy: Medicine and Politics in America* (New York: Praeger, 2001), 212; James J. Chriss, *Social Control: An Introduction* (Cambridge: Polity, 2007), 230.

[129] Clarke writes, "The corruption of their *hearts* extends itself through all the actions of their *lives*. . . . Not *one of them does good*. He cannot, for he has no Divine influence, and he denies that such can be received" (Adam Clarke, *Psalms*, electronic ed., Clarke's Commentaries [Albany, OR: Ages Software, 1999], Ps 14:1).

Bible establishes that children begin disordered/depraved (See Appendix A) and struggling to pay attention. Proverbs 22:15a states, "Folly [foolishness; KJV] is bound up in the heart of a child." Foolishness/folly is an intricate part of everyone's character. The commentator, Tremper Longman points out that "to trust in one's own heart is the epitome of folly because the heart is limited in its knowledge and also, apart from a relationship with God, wicked."[130] *Foolishness* is a key biblical term that reflects all peoples' natural tendency to give attention to one's own wisdom and desires and to misplace one's values. Such misplaced attention results in corresponding foolish behavior.

If Jesus Christ is the standard of normalcy, and He was perfect as the Bible asserts, then everyone who morally fails falls short of God's moral mental and behavioral standards (Romans 3:23). When compared to Christ, we are all impaired, depraved, and in a desperate mental state from our beginning. It should be expected that children will struggle mentally to focus on right values and future rewards, that they will lack self-control, that they will need close supervision, and that they will struggle to behave in such a way that honors their parents and pleases God. All children — and adults alike — need to have their minds and behaviors transformed to reflect the mind of Christ (Romans 12:1-3; Philippians 2).

So how does the Bible answer the questions of normalcy? Scripture describes all children as naturally lacking self-control. In fact, moral self-control is a gift of the Holy Spirit; it is supernatural. Galatians 5:22-24 explains,

> But the fruit of the Spirit is love, joy, peace, patience, kindness, goodness, faithfulness, gentleness, *self-control*; against such things

---

[130] Tremper Longman III, *Proverbs,* Baker Commentary on the Old Testament Wisdom and Psalms (Grand Rapids: Baker, 2006), 496-97.

> there is no law. And those who belong to Christ Jesus have crucified
> the flesh with its passions and desires.

Self-control is not normal, yet, many Christians have accepted the secular theory that ADHD is a "developmental disorder of self-control."[131] Such a humanistic theory not only opposes God's wisdom, it also reshapes normal human depravity, fragility, and immaturity into a mental illness.

When psychiatrists dogmatically accept the medical model/evolutionary perspective, they tend to label odd or destructive behavior — which they are unable to fully explain or remedy — as abnormalities. This reality may be why the late respected neurologist and atheist, Norman Sacks, once stated, "Psychiatrists often invent ad hoc theories for curious syndromes, as if a bizarre condition requires an equally bizarre explanation."[132] However the presence of confusing, destructive, or enduring behavior is not an indication of disease or disorder.

In contrast to the secular perspective, the Bible insists that self-control is something that is obtained by the Holy Spirit's work through biblical teaching. John Piper explains that self-control, by nature, opposes natural human tendencies:

> The very concept of "self-control" implies a battle between a divided self. It implies that our "self" produces desires we should not satisfy but instead "control." We should "deny ourselves" and "take up our cross daily," Jesus says, and follow him (Luke 9:23). Daily our "self" produces desires that should be "denied" or "controlled."[133]

---

[131] Barkley, *TCoA*, 61.

[132] Oliver Sacks, *Hallucinations* (New York: Random House, 2012), 2.

[133] John Piper, "The Fierce Fruit of Self-Control," *Desiring God*, May 15, 2001, http://www.desiringgod.org/articles/the-fierce-fruit-of-self-control; accessed 2 December 2016.

The natural tendency of all people is to pursue what pleases them without regard to temporal and eternal consequences.

As we will observe in the next chapter in discussing the behaviors listed in the *DSM*, the Bible sees all children as not valuing future reward and living for the moment or for vanity, it understands that children are naturally born selfish and self-absorbed, it presents all children has misplacing attention, and it describes humanity's natural bent toward pursuing wrong, deceptive, and destructive desires and values. A child who lacks self-control, who struggles to work for future reward, who is selfish, disobedient, pursues wrong desires and vanity, and who struggles to honor his father and mother is, according to Scripture, a normal child.

The construct of ADHD (contained in the *DSM*) is not a harmless theory; it is a humanistic moral system that opposes God's wisdom and moral law. Constructs of mental illness are never free from moral values. Clinical psychologist Richard Bentall explains, "It is impossible to create a value-free theory of mental illness as hoped for by the neo-Kraepelinians."[134] In fact, psychiatrist and co-founder of the World Federation of Mental Health, Brock Chisholm, revealed in 1945 the underlying reason that evolutionists must form mental illness constructs like ADHD:

> The re-interpretation and eventually eradication of the concept of right and wrong which has been the basis of child training, the substitution of intelligent and rational thinking for faith . . . are the belated objectives of practically all effective psychotherapy.[135]

He later states,

---

[134] Richard Bentall, *Madness Explained: Psychosis and Human Nature* (New York: Penguin, 2003), 177.

[135] G. Brock Chisholm, stated at the UN World Health Organization in 1945.

> The pretense is made, as it has been made in relation to the finding of any extension of truth, that to do away with right and wrong would produce uncivilized people, immorality, lawlessness and social chaos. The fact is that most psychiatrists and psychologists and other respected people have escaped from moral chains and are able to think freely.[136]

Chisholm also insisted that psychiatry is the main organization which could eradicate such traditional parental morals: "If the race is to be freed from the crippling burden of good and evil, it must be psychiatrists who take the original responsibility."[137] The construct of ADHD represents one aspect of this new psychiatric moral system meant to deny God.

The most profitable and necessary discussion concerning the construct of ADHD is the discussion of both origins and human nature. Understanding where we came from and our true nature will fully explain what causes a child's wrong desires, misplaced attention, and behavior as well as how to positively change/ remedy the child's inward and outward problems. Holding to an evolutionary theory of origins and anthropology will lead people to trust in the construct of ADHD, whereas to believe in the biblical account of creation and accept God's description of human nature — normalcy — will mean that God's wisdom is the lens through which children are viewed.

While secularists reject the gospel and choose instead to construct their own anthropology and corresponding system of deliverance, they do understand that "effective treatment [of ADHD] often requires a radical rethinking of your view of yourself."[138] The most radical and necessary view — one which

---

[136] G. Brock Chisholm, "The Reestablishment of Peacetime Society," *Psychiatry: Journal of Biology and Pathology of Interpersonal Relations* 9, no. 1 (February 1946): 9.

[137] "Undermining Morals," http://www.cchr.org.uk/psychiatric-drugs/undermining-morals/; accessed 7 January 2016.

[138] Hallowell and Ratey, *Driven to Distraction*, 216.

completely opposes a child's natural estimation of himself/ herself—is Scripture's clearly presented anthropology and theology. How we perceive humanity—our worldview—is the most important discussion in understanding a child's maladaptive moral behavior and the construct of ADHD.

CHAPTER 3

ADHD DESCRIBES BEHAVIOR

"The epidemics of bipolar disorder and ADHD are largely artificial, brought about by the insensate drive to prove that all mental disorder is brain disorder, coupled with the total absence of anything that approximates a biological model of mental disorder. You know what they say: If the only tool you have is a hammer, then everything looks like a nail."[139] – Psychiatrist Niall McLaren

"It is worth reflecting whether the many attempts we have recently witnessed to discredit the concept of mental illness might not be a reaction to the equally absurd claims we have made that all unhappiness and all undesirable behaviour are manifestations of mental illness."[140] – Professor of Psychiatry at the University of Edinburgh, R. E. Kendell

While the ADHD label fails to discern children's nature or behavior accurately, the construct does identify eighteen potentially harmful behaviors that need to change. Throughout history, these behaviors have been troublesome to children and their families. Yet, the biblical analysis of these behaviors sheds tremendous light on the heart of a child and provides clear wisdom to address and remedy his/her genuine problems.

---

[139] Niall McLaren, "Flaws in the Serotonin Hypothesis of Depression," (January 3, 2015): http://www.futurepsychiatry.com/; accessed 12 March 2016.

[140] R. E. Kendell, "The Concept of Disease and Its Implications for Psychiatry," *British Journal of Psychiatry* 127 (1975): 305-15.

Proper attention certainly involves the physical eyes, ears, and brain, but it first demands that a child's heart incline unto authority. Our human tendency (what is normal), however, is to listen to our own way and to trust our natural perception of life. But doing so is incredibly destructive and impairing to both the child and those in significant relationships with him/her. The child's fundamental problem is not a deficit of attention, but misplaced attention. The construct of Attention Deficit-Hyperactivity Disorder (ADHD), then, is a misnomer. What the construct actually identifies is two problems with our fallen human nature: all children are born with both misplaced desires and with a wisdom deficit.

An Interest Deficit

Many of the behaviors presented in the *DSM-5* as criteria for ADHD reveal not an attention deficit, but an interest deficit. Unlike neurodevelopmental (e.g., autism or ASD) and neurodegenerative disorders (e.g., dementia), which constitute real biological diseases, the construct of ADHD describes children who are able to pay attention to things that interest them most. [141] The *DSM* acknowledges this reality by revealing that bad behavior "may be minimal or absent" when a child "is in a novel setting, is engaged in especially interesting activities, [and] has consistent external stimulation (e.g., via electronic screens)."[142] These *DSM* qualifications describe normal human

---

[141] The *DSM-5* lists ADHD as a neurodevelopmental disorder but it is not a biological disease.

[142] APA, *DSM-5*, 61. There is clear empirical evidence that what a child is exposed to at an early age shapes how they pay attention. Several studies reveal that a child's early interaction with electronics can shape not only how he/she

behavior and undermine the current theory that ADHD is "a deficit involving response inhibition."[143] Instead, the *DSM* and many clinicians accurately describe ADHD as a lack of right desire/values/interests/proper motivation:

> According to the theory, the trouble is a lack of motivation as well as a deficit of attention: People with the disorder can't generate the same degree of enthusiasm as other people for activities they don't automatically find appealing. "Parents always wonder why their children with ADHD can skateboard for hours and practice the same thing over and over but can't stay on task in school," said Swanson, who said he and fellow researchers have taken to calling the syndrome "*an interest deficit*" [emphasis added].[144]

Though Russell Barkley does not endorse *desire* as a key theoretical term, he is quoted often as stating, "There is no ADD while playing Nintendo."[145] Most children labeled as having ADHD can sit still and give full attention to their video games, remain quiet during their favorite movies, and participate in recreation that interests them for hours upon end without losing focus. This reality has led many professionals, such as Bruce Pennington, to conclude that the original label for ADHD (a morbid defect in moral control) actually reveals the child's true problem to be motivation: "Although these terms [*volitional inhibition* and a *defect in moral control*] sound quaint to our

---

pays attention, but can even affect how he/she perceives life. See http://science.sciencemag.org/ content/323/5910/69, and http://pediatrics.aappublications.org/content/ 113/4/708?sso=1&sso_redirect_count=1&n fstatus=401&nftoken =00000000-0000-0000-0000-000000000000 &nfstatusdescription= ERROR%3a+ No+local+token.

[143] Barkley, *NoSC*, 65.

[144] Katherine Ellison, "Brain Scans Link ADHD to Biological Flaw Tied to Motivation," http://www.washingtonpost.com/wpdyn/content/article/2009/09/21/ AR2009092103100.html; accessed 5 October 2012.

[145] Hallowell and Ratey, *Driven to Distraction,* 280.

modern ears, they capture the idea that motivation is inevitably an important input to the process of response selection."[146]

Scripture makes it clear that desires both reveal the spiritual heart and determine a person's behavior. Matthew 6:19-23 illustrates this truth:

> For where your treasure is, there your heart will be also. The eye is the lamp of the body. So, if your eye is healthy, your whole body will be full of light, but if your eye is bad, your whole body will be full of darkness. If then the light in you is darkness, how great is the darkness (21-23).

The commentators Hendriksen and Kistemaker explain these verses,

> Implication on the basis of verses 19–21: Just as a person has a natural eye (the *one* eye representing both eyes here) to illumine his physical existence and to bring him into contact with his earthly environment, so he has a spiritual eye, namely, the mind, to brighten his inner life, to guide him morally and spiritually, and to keep him in contact with the heavenly Father. . . . The impossibility of combining two opposite goals (glorifying God and satisfying the yearnings of the flesh) is stated very tersely and unambiguously in verse 24. No one can serve two masters; for either he will hate the one and love the other, or he will be devoted to one and look down on the other. You cannot serve God and Mammon. The man with the misplaced *heart* (verse 21) and misdirected *mind* (verses 22 and 23) also suffers from a misaligned *will,* a will not in line with God's will (verse 24). He imagines, perhaps, that he can give his full allegiance to the two goals of glorifying God and acquiring material possessions, but he errs. He will either hate the one and love the other, or vice versa.[147]

Adults or children who attempt to live according to the flesh and pursue natural desires cannot also pursue God's wisdom. What we treasure most will determine to whom or what we give our attention and how we behave morally. The desires/pursuits of

---

[146] Bruce Pennington, *Diagnosing Learning Disorders: A Neuropsychological Framework.* 2nd ed. New York: Guilford, 2009), 162.

[147] William Hendriksen and Simon J. Kistemaker, *Exposition of the Gospel According to Matthew*, vol. 9 of New Testament Commentary (Grand Rapids: Baker, 2012), 347–48.

the spiritual heart reveal a person's goals, determine his/her lifestyle, and ultimately determine his/her destination.

The book of Proverbs not only emphasizes all children's foolish nature, but it also establishes the value of pursuing God's wisdom. Much of the father's instruction in Proverbs is given to teaching his son to love, value, and pursue wisdom above all other things. For example, Proverbs 2:1-5 states,

> My son, if you receive my words and *treasure* up my commandments with you, *making your ear attentive* to wisdom and *inclining your heart to understanding*; yes, if you call out for insight and raise your voice for understanding, if you *seek it like silver* and search for it as for *hidden treasures, then you will understand* the fear of the Lord and find the knowledge of God [emphasis added].

In verse five the father also emphasizes that through valuing God's wisdom comes the fear of the Lord and understanding. There is a biblical pattern presented in this text that children need to learn and parents must teach: (1) value instruction (2) make the ear attentive (3) incline the heart to understand (4) then you will understand. Children who value or honor their parent's instruction will seek to understand what they are saying. The fact that a father must teach these things to his child, helps make it clear that the natural inclination of all children is to have misplaced values, which leads them to have misplaced attention and lack of understanding. Lack of understanding or foolishness—as clearly discussed in Proverbs as characteristic of every natural heart—produces foolish behavior.

The true problem that all children naturally have is a value system that fails to consider God's glory and their own destiny. Even secularists recognize that the nature of every child is to "want what he wants when he wants it. He acts without reflection or consideration of the consequences."[148] The heart of a child diagnosed with ADHD, like those of all unregenerate

---

[148] Wender, *ADHD*, 15.

children, rebels against right desires, right values, and right motives. Children labeled as ADHD are not abnormal or struggling with a deficit of attention, they are normal children who lack God-pleasing desires and who set their focus on vanity and pleasing self.

A Wisdom Deficit

Not only does Scripture—especially the book of Proverbs— make it clear that children are born with wrong desires and values, it also emphasizes that all children's hearts are foolish and lack God's wisdom (see appendix A). Likewise, the Bible teaches that naturally foolish hearts produce foolish behavior, which reveals character. Proverbs 13:16, for example, shows the connection between one's heart and his behavior. Kidner writes, "Here [Prov 13:16], character (whether one would hide it or not) is shown to be written all over one's conduct," [149] If all children's hearts are by nature foolish (Proverbs 22:15) and thus cause foolish actions, then the behaviors and human tendencies listed in the *DSM* explain normalcy and not an abnormality.

The New Testament discusses the same truth about human nature and reestablishes that foolish behavior always comes from the moral heart that lacks wisdom. Mark 7:20-23, for example says,

> And he said, "What comes out of a person is what defiles him. For from within, out of the heart of man, come evil thoughts, sexual immorality, theft, murder, adultery, coveting, wickedness, deceit, sensuality, envy, slander, pride, *foolishness*. All these evil things come from within, and they defile a person [emphasis added]."

---

[149] Derek Kidner, *Proverbs: An Introduction and Commentary*, Tyndale Old Testament Commentaries, ed. Donald J. Wiseman (Downers Grove: InterVarsity, 1977), 104.

Despite psychiatric attempts to assert that sometimes foolish behavior should be viewed as amoral, Scripture makes it clear that foolish behavior is always a reflection of a foolish heart.

As discussed in the previous chapter, all of the ADHD behaviors are normal, but as will be discussed in this chapter, not all the behaviors described in the ADHD construct are defined as foolishness in the Bible. Some of the normal behaviors described as ADHD criteria are simply amoral aspects of human nature (e.g., forgetting important things), which highlight our fragility rather than our depravity.

Despite the acknowledgement that the maladaptive behaviors framed as ADHD are not abnormalities, theorists still insist that the distinction between normal and abnormal is the degree to which the behavior impairs the child and those around him and the frequency and repetition of behavior.[150] Dr. Paul Wender—considered by many to be the "Dean of ADHD"[151]—stresses his own thinking that the frequency of behavior differentiates normalcy from abnormality: "Let me emphasize that the characteristics listed are not abnormal in themselves; they are only abnormal when they are excessive."[152] But who decides what should be considered excessive in order to make such a distinction?

Scripture, however, judges frequent and repetitive misbehavior to be expected from the foolish heart: "Like a dog that returns to his vomit is a fool who repeats his folly"

---

[150] Barkley, *TCoA*, 9.

[151] William Dodson, "We Owe a Lot to the 'Dean of ADHD,'" *ADDitude Magazine Online*, October 2016, http://www.additudemag.com/adhdblogs/28/12155.html; accessed 2 January 2017.

[152] Wender, *ADHD*, 9.

(Proverbs 26:11). By repeating foolish behavior, the fool "gives himself away."[153] The commentator Longman remarks, "One of the characteristics of fools is their unwillingness to listen to correction. They make mistakes, but since they will not listen to criticism, they are doomed to repeat those mistakes."[154] The more foolish a child's heart becomes, the more frequent will be his foolish behavior—even to the point that his life can eventually be dominated by his sin (Psalm 119:133; Romans 6:11-14).[155] Secularists often refer to this control as addiction. The repetition of foolishness does not identify a biological abnormality, but a foolish heart.

Children do not just need behavior therapy; they need to have their foolish hearts changed by receiving God's wisdom. Simply addressing behaviors, then, whether through behaviorism or medicine, will never remedy the child's core problem. The deficit that children truly have is a love and

---

[153] Kidner, *Proverbs*, 163. "In both the image and the topic, the body rejects the repulsive object (i.e., vomit and folly), but the debased spirit craves it!" (Bruce Waltke, *The Book of Proverbs: Chapters 1-15*. New International Commentary on the Old Testament, ed. R. K. Harrison and Robert L. Hubbard, Jr. [Grand Rapids: Eerdmans, 2004], 354).

[154] Longman, *Proverbs*, 467.

[155] Psychotherapists do not use the term *sin* but do recognize that pursuits and substances can dominate an individual's life and refer to those dominated by sin as *addicts*. All sin, not just addictive substances seeks to dominate and master mankind. Psalm 119:133, however, offers the remedy to repetition of foolishness. Boice writes, "Though sin is a master and seeks to destroy, the word of God can "give direction for [one's] footsteps, victory over sin, and salvation from those who have been trying to destroy him (vv. 133-4)" (James Montgomery Boice, *Psalms 107-50*, vol. 3 of *Psalms*, Expositional Commentary [Grand Rapids: Baker, 1998], 1043).

acceptance of God's wisdom which leads to sound desires and right attention.

The Visible Behavior

Clearly children's spiritual hearts are central to any discussion about their moral behavior and the construct of ADHD. Kids, however, are more than just spiritual beings — they are also physical in nature. It is important, then, to explore any valid physical maladies and possible environmental elements that may directly influence a child's behavior and not just assume that all attentional problems are spiritual issues. Though the whole person must be considered, behavior that is moral is never done apart from the spiritual heart and is never caused by physical damage or dysfunction. Therefore, before looking at the physical nature and considering valid physical impairments to a child's giving attention and communicating, it is vital to understand what behaviors the *DSM* lists as describing the child and compare it with Scripture's wisdom. Those behaviors which are moral will always be products of the child's depraved nature. In contrast, behaviors which are amoral (e.g., impaired motor skills, memory loss, and hindered social interactions) are regularly caused by physical disability or injury.

The Spiritual Nature

If God declares behavior to be morally wrong, then such behavior is not caused by genetic defects, faulty chemicals, dysfunctional brains, or trying/stressful/horrific circumstances. In other words, if God says that something is broken from birth because of Adam's original sin and our shared depravity, then there is no need to speculate about biological or environmental causes for human brokenness. Behaviors that are amoral highlight human fragility and can/often are caused by physical impairment or damage. The eighteen behaviors listed as criteria in the *DSM* are listed within three identified categories that characterize children diagnosed with ADHD: inattention, hyperactivity, and impulsivity.[156] Instead of viewing these behaviors through the APA's philosophical lens, believers must trust the wisdom of God to fully understand both the heart of children and how to genuinely remedy the destructive behavior. Likewise, they must take each behavior on its own — determining whether or not God declares it to be moral in nature.

ADHD- Inattention (ADHD-I)

Though the ADHD label suggests that attention is quantitative and a deficiency can exist,[157] secularists admit that "an actual deficit in attention in children with ADHD has not been found."[158] Rather than a hypothesis that claims attention is somehow a measurable neurological disposition,[159] Scripture reveals that giving attention rightly is a matter of learned obedience (Proverbs 1:5; 4:1-4, 20; 5:1). The commentator, Bruce Waltke, explains,

> [Hearing] signifies to give one's ear to the speaker's words externally and to obey them inwardly . . . . *Learning (leqah;* see 4:2) represents the same Hebrew root rendered 'accept' in 1:3 and means 'getting a grasp on what the teacher wishes to convey.[160]

---

[156] APA, *DSM*, 59-66.

[157] Barkley, *NOSC*, viii.

[158] Ibid., 79.

[159] Wender, *ADHD*, 35-36.

[160] Waltke, *Proverbs 1-15*, 177-79.

Biblically, a child's attention is the beginning of his/her obedience. The Bible also stresses that giving attention is an indicator of one's values (Proverbs 7:1-4; 8:10-11).[161] Both of these truths are developed further in the book *Teaching a Child to Pay Attention*.[162]

Biblical View of Attention

The Old Testament establishes attention as a child's responsibility: "Hear, O sons, a father's instruction, and be attentive, that you may gain insight" (Proverbs 4:1).[163] These

---

[161] Kidner sees the logical connection of hearing, valuing, and obedience (*Proverbs*, 75). He views the metaphor of binding the father's words in verse 3 (and also in 3:3) to reflect the child's response of "glorying" in them, "meditating" upon them, and "acting by them" (ibid., 63, 77). Giving attention to authority is not merely the intake of information, but treasuring it, repeating it, and then acting upon it. Even parental commands that may lack value to the child are based upon a value system of the father/son relationship. In other words, a child who values his relationship with his parents (and with God) will value his parent's instructions. A child should treasure his godly parent's wisdom and instructions (based on and founded on divine commands) above even rare treasure (Proverbs 8:10) (ibid., 77). Waltke, like Kidner, sees the father in 8:10 desiring his son to listen to him and make his wisdom the affection of his heart (*Proverbs 1-15*, 399). Proverbs implies that the value the son should find in the commands comes from the value he finds in the relationship with his authority—the father's authority comes from God. Longman writes, "At the very least, we can say that the words the father is urging on the son come with a great deal of authority" (119). Thus, the commands of God are written as the father's own (ibid., 119-20). Ultimately, the value in parental commands and instructions comes from the authority and creative order of God.

[162] Daniel R. Berger II, *Teaching a Child to Pay Attention: Proverbs 4:20-26* (Greenville, SC: Alethia International Publications, 2014).

[163] The father's imperative command to his son to pay attention is repeated ten times in chapters 1-9 of Proverbs (R. N. Whybray, *Proverbs* [New Century Bible Commentary. Grand Rapids: Eerdmans, 1994], 23-30).

injunctions reveal that attention is volitional and thus a spiritual matter that requires both the child's obedience to parental instructions and his learning of valuable wisdom. Scripture assumes that he who has an ear to hear, according to God's natural design (Proverbs 20:12),[164] should willfully offer his/her attention to his/her authority (Matthew 11:15).[165] But the Bible does not assume that children naturally give their attention to an authority or to wisdom.

With the exception of valid physical hindrances that impair the senses, God has made children fully capable of giving attention and holds them responsible to do so. Waltke emphasizes that the

> responsibility to respond to instruction lies squarely on the child's shoulders; he must listen to it (Proverbs 1:8), accept it (1:3; 19:20; 23:23), love it (12:1), prize it more highly than money (4:7; 23:23), and not let go of it (4:13).

Both maturity and responsibility are developmental, and believing parents must start teaching their children at an early age the importance of paying attention and valuing their instructions.[166] This teaching, of course, must be age-appropriate

---

[164] Longman suggests that this proverb not only shows Yahweh's goodness in providing man with hearing and seeing, but he implies that the proverb gives deeper insight by directing the reader's attention toward grace. Physically and spiritually "there is no seeing or hearing apart from his good gift" (*Proverbs,* 380). Similarly, Waltke sees the same usages throughout Proverbs. He writes that "hearing (or listen) almost always connotes 'to listen and obey,'" but he points out that the eye is used to refer to "moral discernment" and not just physical sight (*Proverbs 15-31,* 140-41). God designed the eyes and ears for the specific purposes of education and relationship.

[165] "A proverbial expression to evoke attention" (John Peter Lange and Philip Schaff, *A Commentary on the Holy Scriptures: Matthew* [Bellingham, WA: Logos Bible Software, 2008], 206).

[166] Waltke writes that within the historical context of Proverbs a father began "stern teaching" after the child had been weaned/after three years of age

and must include training children to have right desires as well as how to use their eyes and ears in a way that pleases God. Learning to pay attention rightly is a vital skill that children can begin to learn from an early age.

Not only does Scripture teach that children are responsible to give attention correctly, but it also emphasizes that the object of their attention reveals their heart's affections (Proverbs 8:10-21)[167] and thus their life's direction (8:32-36). Scripture describes attention as one's willful act of using the senses to receive information that is deemed important (Proverbs 2:1-6).[168] Stated

---

(*Proverbs 1-15*, 277). Since each child is different, parents should assess their children individually and approach their education according to how God has created them (*Proverbs 15-31*, 205).

[167] Waltke writes: "*Those who love me* [wisdom] implicitly states the heart's affections for receiving her communicable virtues" (*Proverbs 1-15*, 404). In discussing Proverbs 8:35, Waltke connects the mature son's paying close attention (35) with his doing the will and pleasure of another. As he listens to wisdom and receives it ("involving one's desire"), he in turn receives God's pleasure—"acceptance, approval, delight of another" (*Proverbs 1-15*, 425). To whom or what one gives attention not only reveals that person's desires but determines if the anticipated hearer is approved and an object of delight to the teacher. This is true not only on a vertical plane with God and man, but also in human relationships (e.g., father/son). The child who does not listen to (delight in) his father and mother will bring them shame and sorrow compared to the joy and delight of the child who learns to listen (Proverbs 10:1; 17:21). *Proverbs 15-31*, 60.

[168] One example is the hearing ear, which Waltke notes, without its use, memorization and ultimately heart changes will not occur in the child's life (ibid., 220-21). He also states, "According to [Prov] 2:2 the ear (4:20) is the key to the heart (v. 23)" (ibid., 295). Unfortunately, the naturally foolish heart chooses to use the senses to live according to his own wisdom instead of pleasing God (Waltke, *Proverbs 15-31*, 140-41). Kidner also points out that the process of education (he speaks of moral education) must involve both the child exploring teachings and instructions as well as treasuring them (*Proverbs*, 61).

differently, people express their value system/reveal their pursuits through the focus of their eyes, ears, and hearts (Proverbs 4:20-27). The naturally depraved and deceived heart, however, esteems its own wisdom above God's and thus embraces a self-centered lifestyle (Proverbs 3:7-8), focuses its attention toward self (pride), and focuses on things that lack actual value (worldliness/vanity). A child's tendency to disregard the instructions of his/her authority is the result of his/her naturally proud heart and misplaced desires: the default position.

CHILDREN'S DEFAULT SETTINGS
PARENTS
OFF
MY WAY & AMUSEMENT

This tendency explains why children choose to esteem their own desires and thoughts as more valuable than those of their parents, teachers, and friends and consequently, direct their attention accordingly (Proverbs 18:1-2).[169] Proverbs 18:1 also teaches that those who shun valuable relationships do so unwisely in order to pursue their own desires; the verse describes "those who are internally focused on their own desires, but such a focus would naturally separate them from the community."[170]

Whereas the Old Testament provides us with the foundation for understanding God's design and function of the physical anatomy of attention, the natural tendency of the spiritual heart/mind to misplace attention, and an attentional value

---

[169] Murphy also recognizes the logical conclusion—the individual who is antisocial and who seeks his own desires and blurts out his own opinions is a "fool (Prov 12:16, 23; 13:16)" (134–35).

[170] Longman, *Proverbs,* 354.

system to follow and teach to our children (e.g., Proverbs), the New Testament assumes God's design and thus commands children to obey their parents (Ephesians 6:1) and to honor or esteem them as valuable (Ephesians 6:2).[171] Both obedience and honor are volitional, and they reflect and depend upon a child's right focus. Children who learn to value divine wisdom (Proverbs 4:7)[172] will also highly esteem their God-fearing parents' instructions, warnings, rules, values, and corrections, and this right value system will lead them to obedient behavior[173] set on pleasing the Lord (Colossians 3:20). If a child

---

[171] *Honor* (τιμάω) usually means to value, to set a price on, or to greatly esteem. John MacArthur writes, "The right *attitude* behind the right act of obedience is honor (τιμάω), which means to value highly, to hold in the highest regard and respect" (John MacArthur, *Ephesians,* MacArthur New Testament Commentary [Chicago: Moody, 1986], 312). "Honor refers to the public acknowledgment of a person's worth, granted on the basis of how fully that individual embodies qualities and behaviors valued by the group" (Stanley E. Porter and Craig A. Evans, *Dictionary of New Testament Background: A Compendium of Contemporary Biblical Scholarship* [Downers Grove: InterVarsity, 2000], 518). "While honor is an internal attitude of respect, courtesy, and reverence, it should be accompanied by appropriate attention or even obedience. Honor without such action is incomplete; it is lip service (Isa. 29:13). God the Father, for example, is honored when people do the things that please him (1 Cor. 6:20). Parents are honored through the obedience of their children" (Sam Hamstra Jr., "Honor," *Evangelical Dictionary of Biblical Theology,* ed. Walter A. Elwell [Grand Rapids: Baker, 1996]). In summary, honor is a two-directional mindset that (1) fixes one's attention and (2) produces obedience that pleases the Lord. Right attention (eyes and ears) produces a right mindset which in turn produces right motives, desires, and directions. A child's obedience without a right heart change falls short of pleasing the Lord (it is not done "in the Lord" [Eph 6:1]).

[172] Clarke says of this verse, "Let [wisdom] be thy chief property" (*Proverbs,* Proverbs 4:7).

[173] Ephesians 6:1 states that a child's obedience is *right,* which is a judicial term indicating that the child's behaviors should be just. Solomon also stated in

chooses to esteem something more highly than God (idolatry), then his/her attention will be misdirected and behavior will reflect his/her unrestraint and disobedience (Proverbs 29:18).[174] This tendency exposes that idolatry is the natural bent of everyone's heart.

Alleged *ADHD-I*, then, is not a biological deficiency in one's ability to give attention, but rather a child's natural inclination to value his/her own desires over the instructions of his/her authority and to choose the path which he/she perceives is most convenient. This natural tendency reveals the commonality of immature and foolish children who believe that their own opinions, desires, and perceptions of life are more valuable than pleasing God and listening to their authorities' instructions. It means that these children are normal, and normal human nature, unfortunately, is impairing and ultimately leads to destruction.

Proverbs 1:2-4 that the result of parental teaching and application of wisdom leads children to just and equitable behavior. Waltke emphasizes that the child's wise behaviors are *"right* [or 'righteous,' *sedq*], and *just* [or 'justice,' *mispat*], and *fair* [or 'upright,' *mesarim*]" (*Proverbs 1-15*, 177). Cohen writes, "The reader [of Proverbs] will be taught how to acquire the discipline which will enable him to perceive the line of conduct that is just and right" (Abraham Cohen, *Proverbs* [London: Soncino Press, 1973], 2).

[174] "Instruction [based on divine wisdom] is now said to effect *prudent behavior* (*haskel*, i.e., 'wise behavior,' 'good sense'; see p. 94) as the first of its benefits. This changed behavior is not maladaptive or destructive to the community, but 'that which serves and heals the community.'" One's true attention both reveals the heart and ultimately determines one's behaviors (Waltke, *Proverbs 1-15*, 177).

Biblical View of the *DSM* Inattentive Behaviors

Similarly, children diagnosed with ADHD-*I* will exhibit behaviors found under the category of inattention. Secularists list the child's behaviors as: (1) "often *fails to give close attention* [emphasis added] to details or makes careless mistakes in schoolwork, work, or during other activities," and "often *does not seem to listen* [emphasis added] when spoken to directly."[175] As previously stated, the object of a person's attention reflects desires and values. If children "fail" (as the *DSM* states) to listen to their parents, they reveal their desire to get their own way and to honor themselves above others. These behaviors are not abnormal, but normal childish actions that require parents to teach and supervise their children from the earliest of years. If a child cannot give attention across all life's environments, then he/she does not fit the ADHD description.

Secularists also describe the child diagnosed with ADHD as one who "often does not follow through on instructions and *fails to finish schoolwork, chores, or duties in the workplace* [emphasis added]."[176] Scripture addresses this behavior in numerous passages such as Proverbs 6:6-11, which reveals that the natural heart of the child is slothful, and if left alone, the child will grow to become a sluggard. The first section of this passage (6-8) directs the learner to obtain wisdom from the ant, which, without supervision, takes initiative and shows responsibility to complete its tasks. The second portion warns the child that laziness is counterproductive to success and that he/she is accountable (9-11). Whether the APA realizes it or not, they assert in the *DSM* that not following through with

---

[175] APA, *DSM-5*, 59.

[176] Ibid., 59.

74

instructions is the child's "failure." Both sections of Proverbs 6:6-11, as well as 10:4-5, judge the individual who is capable of understanding but who neglects responsibilities, lacks diligence, and leaves tasks incomplete to be slothful. Derek Kidner notes in his commentary on Proverbs four common characteristics of the sluggard: (1) he will not start tasks on his own initiative, (2) he will not finish things without supervision, (3) he will not take responsibility for his failures, and (4) "consequently he is *restless* with unsatisfied desire [emphasis added]."[177] Kidner's description of the nature of slothfulness is almost identical to the APA's description of children with behavioral problems. The sluggard or slothful child of Proverbs is not abnormal; he/she is simply following his/her natural tendencies to pay attention to that which is easy, convenient, and momentarily intriguing.

As described in the *DSM* definition of ADHD, children who are slothful need constant supervision to complete tasks, since they lack the diligence and self-motivation exemplified by the ant: "Signs of the disorder [ADHD] may be minimal or absent when the individual receiving frequent rewards for appropriate behavior, is under close supervision . . ."[178] This explanation does not describe an abnormality, since by nature, all children need supervision to accomplish tasks until parents can cultivate maturity, right motivation, self-control, and right values in their children's lives. To assume otherwise is to assume that children do not naturally need supervision. Some children, however, need more supervision than others until maturity and self-control are learned.

In his discussion on the sluggard, Kidner also concludes that the sluggard is not abnormal:

---

177 Kidner, *Proverbs*, 43.

178 APA, *DSM-5*, 61.

> [The wise man] knows that the sluggard is no freak, but, as often as not, an ordinary man who has made too many excuses, too many refusals and too many postponements. It has all been as imperceptible, and as pleasant, as falling asleep.[179]

The young child who is given excuses for his self-centered nature and his disobedience — who is not taught right pursuits and motives — is on his way to forming a lifestyle of slothfulness (becoming a sluggard).[180] Longman remarks on Proverbs 12:11: "Perhaps it may be said that those who lack substance (heart) pursue that which lacks substance ('emptiness')."[181] Though Proverbs views a sluggard as one who never learned the value of self-discipline and self-motivation, being slothful is a common condition of humanity — easily observed in children.[182]

Not only is the foolish heart naturally slothful, but it is likewise naturally disobedient. Assuming that the child understands instructions and that the instructions are age-appropriate, the child's failure to follow instructions can reveal a heart that does not value his authorities' wisdom and lacks the desire to please the Lord (Colossians 3:20). The child may desire better academic success, better relationships, parental praise, and better experiential outcomes in life, but his/her excuses and lack of parental honor and obedience will result in unrealized desires, incomplete work, and lack of success (Proverbs 13:4; 20:4). This reality is why the Father strongly warned his son about being

---

[179] Kidner, *Proverbs*, 43.

[180] He is a sluggard because of his depraved "habits" which most often begin in his childhood (ibid., 42-43).

[181] Longman, *Proverbs*, 274.

[182] Kidner shows that the simple fool, like the sluggard, chases after vanities (12:11) and is characterized by "lazy thoughtlessness" (Kidner, *Proverbs*, 39).

lazy: "Proverbs is intolerant of lazy people; they are considered the epitome of folly."[183]

The *DSM* also describes the ADHD child as one who "often avoids, dislikes, or is reluctant to engage in tasks ["doesn't want to do things" – from the *DSM-IV*, 92] that require sustained mental effort."[184] Proverbs 28:19 describes this unwise characteristic: "Whoever works his land will have plenty of bread, but he who follows worthless pursuits will have plenty of poverty."[185] By nature, children (and adults) want the easiest way, and, in pursuit of amusement and immediate self-indulgence, they regularly avoid what requires sustained effort.

Even secular clinicians recognize that children base their immature value systems on what best pleases them now, rather than on future reward.[186] This tendency is evidenced in children labeled as ADHD who lack maturity and desire to complete their homework, yet they are able to sustain uninterrupted mental

---

[183] Longman, *Proverbs*, 561-62. Waltke sees the same comparison and explains, "A foolish son shows his moral degeneracy by his laziness (cf. Eccl 10:18). In 6:6 the sluggard is admonished to 'become wise,' the antithesis of being a fool; in 24:30 the sluggard is said to 'lack sense'; and in 26:12-16 the sluggard is said to be more despicable than a fool. In other words, this partial subunit escalates his being a fool (19:13) to his being a sluggard (19:15)" (Waltke, *Proverbs 15-31*, 109).

[184] APA, *DSM-5*, 59.

[185] This proverb contrasts the diligent worker who will have his needs met, with the foolish who pursues vanity and will always be in need. Kidner recognizes the symmetry of 28:19 and 12:11: the sluggard does not lack energy, but discrimination in what is worth following (*Proverbs*, 96-97). Some translations see the one lacking discernment as pursuing vain people, but as Steveson notes, "vain things" is more likely in mind (Peter A. Steveson, *A Commentary on Proverbs* [Greenville, SC: Bob Jones University Press, 2001], 398).

[186] Barkley, *NoSC*, 58-63.

effort as they play video games for hours. In contrast, Proverbs 17:24 describes the discerning person as one who diligently sets his/her attention on wisdom instead of vanity. That Proverbs 17:24 mentions the eyes of the fool is important because it indicates that the object of the fool's attention is vanity rather than wisdom.[187] The child who avoids responsibilities in pursuit of pleasure is living according to the foolishness that is bound in his/her natural heart.

Two other behavioral patterns of inattention are listed in the *DSM:* a child is prone to lose important things, and he/she is often forgetful.[188] Although Scripture does not identify these common behaviors as sin/moral behavior, these behaviors do describe the fallen condition of everyone since people tend to forget and lose things — even things of value. One commentator notes, "We remember what is most important to us. The son who often forgets his homework never forgets his soccer game."[189] Like giving attention, forgetfulness and losing possessions are matters of a child's value system, maturity, and focus in life.

People are forgetful when they fail to see enough value in prioritizing and retaining information. Proverbs 4:4-10 conveys the truth that remembering requires sustained effort, willful

---

[187] Waltke notes, "The imprecision suggests that the eyes of the wise focus on wisdom, which in turn serves him well, but the fool's focus flits from one godless, unattainable thing to another that does not profit him" *(Proverbs 15-31,* 62).

[188] APA, *DSM-5,* 59.

[189] Jim Newheiser, *Opening Up Proverbs* (Leominster, England: Day One Publications, 2008), 59.

obedience (4-5),[190] and a discovery of value (6-10). Waltke writes concerning Proverbs 2:2,

> "Accept" is escalated to store up (treasure), which means, with the accusative of thing, to hide or conceal for a definite purpose (cf. Ps 119:11). That notion entails that one treasures that which he stores (see 2:4; 10:14; Job 15:20; 21:19; Hos 13:12). The metaphor signifies to memorize with religious affection Solomon's "sound bites" in order to have them ready when the occasion demands them (cf. 5:2; 7:1; 22:18; cf. Job 23:12; Ps 119:11).[191]

The principles that apply to remembering the most important parental instructions (divine wisdom) also apply to temporal instructions. For example, as children esteem amusing activities more desirable than responsibilities or obedience, they can lose focus and forget to complete tasks or forget important possessions at school. Though the *DSM* portrays *ADHD-I* children as often forgetful, these activities are selective, since most children diagnosed with ADHD remember daily activities such as how to operate their MP3 players, their favorite video

---

[190] To remember or not forget something assumes that it has been first acquired. The son was commanded to "acquire wisdom" and to "not forget nor turn away" from wisdom (Longman, *Proverbs,* 149-50). Waltke also notes the two metaphors that are used in the father's (grandfather's) commands: (1) the metaphor of economy — the son was to use all his resources to buy wisdom (2) the metaphor of love or marriage — the son was to value and be intimate with wisdom, forsaking all others. This would not be a one-time decision, but a lifelong dedication that would cost him everything (*Proverbs 1-15,* 279). Longman also states of Proverbs 3:1: "Not to forget is to remember; and to remember something in the OT means more than mere cognitive retention. To remember, or not to forget, means to obey. That the son's obedience is to be more than a superficial matter is specified in the second colon, where it is his heart, standing for his core personality, [*sic*] that is to protect the commands. Again, protection means to observe the commands that are to be deeply embedded in the son" (*Proverbs,* 131).

[191] "Its method is not one of free speculation, but of treasuring and exploring received teachings so as to penetrate to their principles" (Kidner, *Proverbs,* 61). See also Waltke, *1-15,* 220.

game's logins and passwords, and lines from their favorite movies. Remembering and paying attention are closely linked since remembering is the willful and ongoing act of committing one's attention to something of value.[192] Being distracted, losing necessary items, and forgetting things are characteristics of all children.

Wise children — and adults alike — diligently work to remember and treasure important possessions just as God expects His children to remember His covenants, commands, character, and works. Though forgetfulness may not be a sin of commission, it can reveal one's value system and a child's immaturity.

Adults also regularly forget significant dates, things, and ideas, which may explain why God repeats commands and truths throughout His Word. One illustration is a husband who highly esteems his wife; he makes every effort to remember things that she cherishes or are important to her (e.g., anniversary).

Additionally, God's plan of evangelism through the work of the Holy Spirit is also accomplished through communication that requires an instructor and a hearer (Romans 10:14-18). In like manner, sanctification requires that the hearer obey God's Word (as he is able to understand) rather than forget it (James 1:22-27). Derek Kidner comments on the repetition of the father's call to his son to give him his attention as deliberate and important since it reveals that "a major part of godliness lies in

---

[192] Waltke's view is consistent with that of the philosopher of science Michael Polanyi who said, "True knowledge flows from personal commitment to a set of particulars, as tools or clues, to shape a skillful achievement, not from detached observation of them." Remembering is the act of committing one's mind to a set of particulars (ibid., 219).

dogged attentiveness to familiar truths."[193] Attention is foundational to the gospel, discipleship, parenting, education, counseling, and every important human relationship. Attempts to redefine attention apart from God's design are deceptive and destructive, and ultimately these human theories attack God's plan for social, familial, and ecclesiastical structure and progress.

There are a few other criteria listed under inattention in the *DSM*, but Scripture explains these behaviors to be common human nature rather than indicators of abnormality. The Bible describes many of these behaviors to be products of a heart that is naturally foolish, slothful, unwise, and lacking self-control. These are the reliable judgments of God which describe the child who naturally — whether volitionally or ignorantly — chooses to value himself over God's will and whom secularists label as *ADHD-I*.

It is important to understand that if your child is struggling to pay attention as described in the ADHD construct, he/she is not abnormal. Though it may feel as though you are alone in your struggles and no one else is dealing with your problems, you are not alone. Simply look at how rapidly the number of people identifying their children as behaving in an impairing way and struggling to give attention is expanding.

ADHD – Hyperactivity (Part of ADHD-HI)

Hyperactivity is one of the key behaviors that leads many children to be stigmatized with the ADHD label. But what exactly is hyperactivity and is it an abnormality? It must first of

---

[193] Kidner, *Proverbs*, 68. "'Hearing and doing' God's will, with the corollary that believers should not be quick to follow their own desires and designs, is a common theme in the Wisdom literature: see Proverbs 10:9; 13:3; 15:1; 29:20; Eccl 7:9; 9:18," (Ralph P. Martin, *James*, vol. 48 of Word Biblical Commentary [Dallas: Word, 1998], 47).

all be explained that no standard of normalcy exists for children's energy levels. The idea of hyperactivity is an attempt to create abnormality where none exists — viewing high energy as a disorder. In fact, having an abundance of energy is highly sought after. With children, though, high energy is regularly perceived as negative. This reality is most likely due to the fact that high energy children inconvenience caretakers and educators and demand more time and attention. But high-energy (or hyper-activity) is a positive and highly sought after quality. What is destructive is high energy without self-control.

Scripture does not regard hyperactivity to be sin against

God, yet it does declare uncontrolled thoughts, emotions, and behaviors to be foolish and destructive. High energy and continuous movement are positive qualities in God's design for specific people when controlled, and believers should not consider these traits counterproductive or sinful. Yet, Scripture compares the person who lacks control over his/her spirit to a city without walls that is open to destruction (Proverbs 25:28).[194]

---

[194] Waltke writes that lack of self-control characterizes the fool and is illustrated in Proverbs 25:28 by the absence of walls (*Proverbs 15-31*, 344). Waltke explains the depth of this metaphor in describing three parallels to the

Biblical View of Hyperactivity

The Bible does not view hyperactivity to be a medical illness, a moral issue, or an abnormality. More and more secular professionals are coming to the same conclusion. In fact, highly regarded psychiatrists and psychologists are now attempting to "demedicalize hyperactivity."[195] Renowned psychiatrist Allen Frances offers one example: "We mustn't jump to the assumption that every active kid is mentally disordered."[196] Others, such as the highly respected Drs. Ed Hallowell and John Ratey argue, "Although ADD can generate a host of problems, there are also advantages to having it . . . such as high energy, intuitiveness, creativity, and enthusiasm, and they are completely overlooked by the 'disorder' model."[197] Dr. Laura Batstra also suggests that parents "try to relabel hyperactive behavior as enthusiastic and energetic."[198] Society has learned to consider high-energy children to be problematic, but in reality, the child's high energy is part of God's design and may be necessary for future occupation or life-calling. Pastors, teachers, policemen, firefighters, educators, counselors, politicians,

---

defenseless city without walls and the fool: (1) Without self-control, sin will master him. He states: "Freud may have first articulated psychologically that we are not masters in our house, ruled as we are by unruly passions, but he is not the first to discern it. Proverbs knows the power of sin that drives one to death" (344). (2) The fool is open to society's retributions for his unrestrained folly that have hurt them. (3) Last, he is an easy target for the wicked who wish to destroy him (Waltke, *Proverbs 15-31*, 344).

[195] Frances, "Most Active Kids."

[196] Ibid.

[197] Hallowell and Ratey, *Driven to Distraction*, xi.

[198] Laura Batstra quoted by Frances, "Most Active Kids."

doctors, counselors, health technicians, artists, athletes, and salesmen are just some of the many career choices in which high-energy individuals often excel.[199] These personality traits please God when they are directed and Spirit-controlled for God's purpose and glory.

In retrospect, some clinicians have diagnosed some of the most successful high-energy athletes to have had ADHD (e.g., Michael Jordan and Michael Phelps),[200] and they also consider many well-known world leaders and prominent figures throughout history to have had ADHD.[201] The vast majority of these individuals were successful in their respected areas without the use of psychostimulants or the stigma of the ADHD label. Being highly driven and full of energy is simply not a malady. High energy, especially when it is controlled and directed toward pleasing God, should be viewed as a tremendous advantage in life and usually necessary to achieve goals and to be successful.

Biblical View of the *DSM* Hyperactivity Behaviors

Though Scripture does not specifically address the traditional understanding of hyperactivity ("highly energetic or excessively active"),[202] it does address the *DSM's* definition which combines a child's expected obedience with his lack of

---

[199] Hallowell and Ratey, *Delivered from Distraction,* 4.

[200] "Famous People with ADHD," http://adhdandmore.blogspot.com /2009/ 01/famous-people-with-adhd.html.

[201] Ibid.

[202] "Hyperactivity," http://www.merriam-webster.com/dictionary /hyperactivity.

84

self-control. To understand this subtype, it is helpful to divide the six criteria (behaviors) under hyperactivity into two separate groups. The first two *DSM* behaviors under hyperactivity pertain to a child's behavior in relation to the expectations and rules of his/her authority, and the second group of four behaviors describes lack of self-control.

The first two criteria in the *DSM* list are "often leaves seat in situations *when remaining seated is expected* [emphasis added]" and "often runs about or climbs *in situations where it is inappropriate* [emphasis added]."[203] Though the APA classifies these two criteria as hyperactivity, they, in truth, describe a child's disobedience toward authority. The APA and many clinicians suggest that this disobedience should be excused since, they theorize, ADHD children are physically and mentally incapable of obedience.[204] In their view, "ADHD impairs the human will and volition,"[205] so authorities should not expect the child to obey. In other words, disobedience and rebellion — whether blatant or passive — are not viewed as normal characteristics of children's hearts within psychiatric theory.

If, however, authorities are responsible and establish clear and appropriate boundaries, and if the child understands the expectations, then Scripture judges the child who violates these rules to be disobedient and not merely hyperactive as the *DSM* suggests. Scripture pronounces these behaviors as injustice to both God and the parent (Ephesians 6:1)[206] to the extent that in

---

[203] APA, *DSM-5*, 60.

[204] Barkley, *NoSC*, 315.

[205] Ibid.

[206] Charles Hodge writes, "Children, obey your parents. The nature of character of this obedience is expressed by the words in the Lord . . . . In the following verses also Lord constantly has this reference and therefore must have

the Old Testament excessive disobedience (rejection of parental authority or rebellion) was punishable by death (Deuteronomy 21:18).[207] Though God's grace is longsuffering toward rebellious children, rebellion remains a serious sin against God and man (Romans 1:30-32). It is no wonder, then, that children whose disobedience is excused away will many times be also diagnosed from the *DSM* as having Oppositional Defiant Disorder (ODD) to explain away their outright rebellion. When parents do not require their children to give their attention to their authority, then sooner or later defiance will be the inevitable result.

A note of caution is in order: parents and educators should consider the possibility that they may not always be clearly communicating their expectations to the children in their care, as Joseph and Mary illustrate. Christ was not in sin for remaining in Jerusalem, since He was always obedient to God (Luke 2:49) and always submissive to His parents (2:51):

> Joseph and Mary *were astonished*. Clearly they had expected nothing like this. There is reproach in Mary's question, *Son, why have you treated us so?* and in her reference to their anxious search. For Jesus it

---

it here. The ground of the obligation to filial obedience is expressed in the words, for this is right. It is not because of the personal character of the parent, nor because of his kindness, nor on the ground of expediency but because it is right—an obligation arising out of the nature of the relationship between parents and children, and which must exist wherever the relationship itself exists" (Charles Hodge, *Ephesians*, vol. 7 of Crossway Classic Commentaries, ed. Alister McGrath and J. I. Packer [Wheaton: Crossway, 1994], 202).

[207] "We may have here another example of a penalty stated in an extreme form in order to underline the serious nature of the crime. . . . While no example of the carrying out of this sentence occurs in the pages of the Old Testament, the prescriptions underlined the seriousness of the offence." (J. A. Thompson, *Deuteronomy: An Introduction and Commentary*, vol. 5 of Tyndale Old Testament Commentaries, ed. Donald J. Wiseman [Downers Grove: InterVarsity, 1974], 253).

was a matter of surprise that there should have been any difficulty. The natural place for him to be was *in my Father's house.*[208]

Clear instruction is essential for children to understand and to be obedient to their authorities' expectations.

Whereas the first two behaviors under hyperactivity are disobedience, the last four behaviors are matters of self-control and immaturity. They describe a child who "often fidgets with or taps hands or feet or squirms in seat," "often unable to play or engage in leisure activities quietly," "often talks excessively," and "is often 'on the go,' acting as if 'driven by a motor.'"[209] Two of the behaviors pertain to a child who lacks control of his mouth (see Proverbs 21:23) and whose speech is loud and excessive. Scripture consistently contrasts the foolish individual who is loud (Proverbs 9:13) with the wise individual who is quiet, controlled, and pleasing to God and his/her society. Kidner points out that "the sparing use of words is commended as a mark of a cool spirit', which denotes 'a man of understanding.'"[210] The Bible—especially in the wisdom literature—consistently contrasts a foolish man who lacks control of his tongue with a wise man who strives with the Spirit's help to control his words. The commentator Douglas Moo explains this truth from James 1:19:

> The importance of controlling one's speech is a popular theme in wisdom literature (cf. Prov 10:19; 15:1; 17:27-28 . . .). Significantly, looseness in speech is often linked with unrestrained anger.

---

[208] Leon Morris, *Luke: An Introduction and Commentary*, vol. 3 of Tyndale New Testament Commentaries (Downers Grove: InterVarsity, 1988), 108–9.

[209] APA, *DSM-5*, 60.

[210] Kidner also gives three reasons why a controlled tongue is a wise choice: (1) "it allows time for a fair hearing (18:13; verse 17)" (2) "it allows tempers to cool (15:1)" (3) "its influence is potent: 'a soft tongue breaketh the bone' (25:15)" (*Proverbs*, 48).

> According to Proverbs 17:27, "He who restrains his words has knowledge, and he who has a cool spirit is a man of understanding."[211]

It is common sense to realize that children who cannot learn to control their tongues will also fail to control their tempers. What is also true, is that children who are always concerned about their viewpoint and gaining others' attention has not learned to value the counsel and directives of those in authority or his/her peers. Running the mouth is a clear indicator of a child who is self-focused.

Not only does Scripture address behaviors of the mouth which proceed from the heart, the Bible also addresses the last criterion under hyperactivity, calling it hastiness which leads to eventual poverty and deeper sin (Proverbs 19:2).[212] The secularists' description of the child "driven by a motor" does not merely mean high energy, but also a child who has "a tendency not to plan ahead" and is, instead, hasty.[213] Scripture declares hastiness to be characteristic of an immature individual who lacks right focus in life and subsequently lacks plans to achieve success (Proverbs 21:5).[214] Waltke writes,

> The hasty act without moral reflection to avoid the hard discipline of diligence. We should assume that the diligent creatively plan within

---

[211] Douglas J. Moo, *James: An Introduction and Commentary*, vol. 16 of Tyndale New Testament Commentaries (Downers Grove: InterVarsity, 1985), 82.

[212] "A person who 'hasteth with his feet' is one who acts without knowing his goal. He hurries into mindless activity with no clear end in mind" (Steveson, *Proverbs*, 253).

[213] Wender, *ADHD*, 27.

[214] Whereas the lazy lack motivation (right desires) to do what is right, the hasty lack discernment (right thoughts) (Waltke, *Proverbs 15-31*, 172).

the framework of God's revealed will and by nature act accordingly.[215]

The child who is hasty naturally goes through life motivated by his/her wrong desires and behaves accordingly, which is why Kidner recognizes "restlessness" to stem from "unsatisfied desires."[216] This understanding defines most immature children and not an abnormality.

Though Scripture pronounces the behaviors framed as hyperactivity in the *DSM* to be simple foolishness in some cases and direct disobedience in others, high energy, enthusiasm, and intuitiveness are not sinful, undesirable, or abnormal personality traits. Barkley admits,

> It is commonplace for children, especially young preschool children, to be active, energetic, and exuberant and to flit from one activity to another as they explore their environment and its novelties.[217]

A discerning parent or teacher will be careful to separate a child's normal high energy, lack of self-control, and curiosity from willful rebellion.

The *DSM* characteristics of hyperactivity reveal the child's heart to be disobedient, uncontrolled, and indicative of the problematic direction of his/her life's course. These behaviors are issues of obedience, Spirit-filled self-control, and maturity which believing parents are responsible to exemplify and to

---

[215] Waltke, *15-31*, 172; although the verse refers to an older child (or adult) being hasty to become rich, the problem of hastiness is a problem of the natural heart even seen in younger children. The idea behind hastiness is that one trusts in his own way in order to get what he wants, and this individual contrasts the one who trusts in the Lord and is diligent in his work while he waits patiently for God's will to be accomplished.

[216] *Proverbs*, 43.

[217] Barkley, *NoSC*, 1.

cultivate in their children's hearts while depending on the work of the Holy Spirit.

ADHD – Impulsivity (Part of ADHD-HI)

Just as the APA misnamed the second group of *DSM* criteria *hyperactivity*, they also misuse *impulsivity* to describe the third group of behavior. All three behaviors under *impulsivity* reveal a heart that is naturally consumed with getting its way over loving others, and as must be understood, this tendency reveals the natural bent of all children.

The Biblical View of Impulsivity

According to the Bible, the *DSM* behaviors collectively depicted as *impulsivity*, in actuality, describe self-centeredness rather than mere impulsivity. These behaviors reflect the natural human heart which esteems itself as more important than others. Philippians 2:3-5 describes this tendency and the need for it to change:

> Do nothing from selfish ambition or conceit, but in humility count others more significant than yourselves. Let each of you look not only on his own interests, but also to the interests of others. Have this mind among yourselves, which is yours in Christ Jesus.[218]

The *DSM* criteria for impulsivity (which should be labeled as self-centeredness) expose a child's need for the Word of God to renew him/her with the mind of Christ and to instill in him/her

---

[218] MacArthur states that selfish ambitions (personal goals) are the roots of all sin and an exaggerated self-view (personal glorification) is the root of relational problems. In essence, this defines someone who is a proverbial fool. Here Christ (true wisdom) is the antithesis of the fool, and Christians are to renew their mind in this wisdom (Christ) (John F. MacArthur Jr., *Philippians*, MacArthur New Testament Commentary [Chicago: Moody, 2001], 110–11).

a loving value system that esteems God and others as more important (Matthew 22:36-40).

The Biblical View of the *DSM* Impulsivity Behaviors

The three criteria which comprise the impulsivity grouping in the *DSM* reveal a child's naturally self-centered heart: "often blurts out an answer before a question has been completed," "often interrupts or intrudes on others (e.g., butts into conversations, games, or activities . . .)," and "often has difficulty waiting his or her turn."[219]

As with hyperactivity, two of the criteria under impulsivity relate to the child's control over his mouth. Scripture points out that lack of control over the mouth is characteristic of the naturally foolish and shameful nature of humanity (Proverbs 29:20).[220] For example, Proverbs 18:13 conveys this truth: "If one gives an answer before he hears, it is folly and shame." The *DSM* criterion under impulsivity is almost verbatim to Proverbs 18:13's description of human folly. Scripture also considers an individual's frequent interruptions and lack of control of his mouth to be evidence of his self-focus and natural foolishness. Waltke states it as such: "This introductory proverb typically pertains to being teachable. Its subject is implicitly the fool who, before the wise has finished speaking, boorishly interrupts him to spout his own opinion (see 18:2)."[221] Proverbs 17:28 also states, "Even a fool who keeps silent is considered wise; when he closes

---

[219] APA, *DSM-5*, 60.

[220] This is speech that is not considered before it is delivered (Waltke, *Proverbs 15-31*, 447-48).

[221] Waltke, *Proverbs 15-31*, 79.

his lips, he is deemed intelligent."[222] The fool's uncontrolled desire to make his/her opinion known and his/her inability to control his/her emotions reveal the natural heart.

Because of their hasty words, angry reactions, and self-centeredness, children diagnosed with ADHD often lack good friends.[223] In contrast to the naturally selfish heart, patience and self-control describe the mature believer (Titus 2:2).[224] Children who behave according to the *DSM*'s criteria for impulsivity live from a natural heart that esteems itself more highly than it should and that needs to be renewed with the mind of Christ (Romans 12:1-3; Philippians 2:3-10) and controlled by the Holy Spirit (Romans 12:6-21; Galatians 5:19-26).

ADHD - Comorbidity

When clinicians diagnose a child to be ADHD, they more often than not, also diagnose a comorbid disorder.[225] What further confounds such a diagnosis is the fact that all of the behaviors that are qualified as ADHD criteria in the *DSM* are found in other psychiatric disorders and even in some valid diseases. The most frequent comorbid diagnosis of ADHD appearing in approximately half all diagnoses is Oppositional-

---

[222] "Using humor . . . the sages suggest that the best chance a fool has for being thought intelligent is to avoid speaking" (Longman, *Proverbs*, 351).

[223] Wender, *ADHD*, 26.

[224] "The first practical outworking of such sound doctrine will be an insistence that behaviour should tally with belief" (Donald Guthrie, *Pastoral Epistles: An Introduction and Commentary*, vol. 14 of Tyndale New Testament Commentaries [Downers Grove: InterVarsity, 1990], 213).

[225] Pennington, *Diagnosing Learning Disorders*, 155.

Defiant Disorder (ODD).[226] In fact, many believe ADHD and
ODD are inseparable diagnoses:

> Most hyperactive children manifest interpersonal behavior that has
> several distinct characteristics: (1) a considerable resistance to social
> demands, a resistance to "do's" and "don'ts," to "shoulds" and
> "shouldn'ts"; (2) increased independence; (3) domineering behavior
> with other children. *Probably the single most disturbing feature of
> ADHD children's behavior, and the one most frequently responsible for
> their referral for treatment is the difficulty many of these children have in
> complying with requests and prohibitions of parents and teachers*
> [emphasis added]. Some ADHD children may appear almost
> impossible to discipline. In some respects they seem to remain two
> years old.[227]

Barkley informs parents to expect ODD behaviors with ADHD
and describes what parents should watch for:

> [the child] often loses control of temper, often disputes or argues
> with adults, often actively rebels against or refuses adults' rules or
> requests, often deliberately does things that annoy other people,
> often blames others for own misdeeds, often easily irked or annoyed
> by others, often resentful and angry, and often spiteful or
> revengeful.[228]

Barkley's description of ODD and ADHD accurately depicts the
biblical understanding of the "ordinary fool"[229] and, in some
older children, the definition describes Proverbs' depiction of a
scoffer. Though most children diagnosed with ADHD may not
be ordinary fools or scoffers, all children begin as simple fools in
need of divine wisdom (refer to appendix A). When left to their
naturally foolish way of thinking apart from the gospel, these
children will become full-fledged fools and even scoffers.

No matter how secularists attempt to categorize and label
children, God's remedy for people's sinful nature is the same

---

[226] APA, *DSM-IV-TR*, 88.

[227] Wender, *ADHD*, 24-25.

[228] Barkley, *TCoA*, 169.

[229] Kidner, *Proverbs*, 39-41.

across all humanity. Though the depraved hearts of children labeled with ADHD are not peculiar, these children express their foolish hearts in more frequent and observable behaviors. While it is difficult and extremely frustrating to have a child who expresses himself/herself without restraint, in some ways their behavior provides an advantage to parents — since behavior can supply insight as to the child's greatest spiritual needs.

Physical Impairments

All Christian parents, of course, must address the child's spiritual nature. But parents should also consider physical impairment that can influence a child's ability to pay attention and to cultivate right relationships. Biology and environment can *influence* a child's behavior but genetics and environment do not *cause* children to act foolishly; their own spiritual hearts are to blame.[230] This distinction changes who/what is responsible for behavior and is significant. We must keep in mind that by nature we are all born with foolishness interwoven into our spiritual hearts.

Though the nature of children's giving attention is volitional, valid biological hindrances to paying attention do exist. Partial blindness or deafness, for example — which hinder children's ability to offer attention — are problems sourced in the eyes, ears and or neurological system. Similarly, brain damage or sensory impairment/ processing issues,[231] ear and sinus infections,[232]

---

[230] Alleged etiologies will be discussed in chapter four.

[231] Moss, *Why Johnny Can't Concentrate,* 3-4.

[232] Priscilla L. Vail, *Learning Styles: Food for Thought and 130 Practical Tips for Teachers K-4* (Rosemont, NJ: Modern Learning Press, 1992), 24-25.

allergies,[233] thyroid disease,[234] mental disabilities, syndromes, and physical injuries can also influence one's ability to give attention. These are valid biological impairments that can influence moral behavior and cause amoral behavior, yet leading secular theorists deny that these maladies cause the construct of ADHD.[235] Most of these issues are best examined by a physician (ideally a believer) who can determine any valid medical issues and give counsel on psychoactive drugs.

Injuries or Defects

When pediatricians examine a child prior to diagnosing him/her as having ADHD, they typically first give the child a physical that evaluates the eyes and ears for injuries or defects — looking for potential influences to behavior that would eliminate ADHD as explaining the child's maladaptive behavior.[236] Children who show impaired sight or hearing in all circumstances in life and not just in uninteresting or undesirable activities should definitely be examined by a medical doctor.

---

[233] Haber, *ADHD*, 72-73.

[234] Hallowell and Ratey, *Driven to Distraction*, 120.

[235] Barkley argues, "No doubt you've encountered claims that factors other than those just discussed cause ADHD. Some of these were originally founded in sound hypotheses but have since been disproven. Others are sheer falsehoods; there is not now and never has been any scientific support for them. As we continue to make conclusive findings about ADHD, let us hope that quackery surrounding the subject will vanish. In the meantime, use what you know about the scientific method to sort fact from fiction" (*TCoA*, 75).

[236] Haber, *ADHD*, 47-48.

Autism Spectrum Disorder

Autism (Autism Spectrum Disorder or ASD) is a prominent example of valid physical impairment that hinders children's ability to communicate and pay attention. The construct of autism should not be considered to be a mental illness, since it is a description of symptoms resulting from physical malady and not foundationally a spiritual/mental problem as ADHD is. It is listed as a mental illness in the *DSM* because the psychiatrist, Eugene Bleuler (who created the term *schizophrenia*) first coined the term *autism* to describe people's "withdrawal from reality."[237] From this definition, the term was eventually applied to children who struggled to communicate and were seemingly withdrawn from society or important relationships. Dr. Peter Breggin comments, "The pioneering work of Leo Kanner, described in his 1948 textbook *Child Psychiatry*, first defined autism as a distinct syndrome of early childhood withdrawal."[238] But not all autistic children — even the most severe or profound cases — are actually withdrawn from reality; they are simply imprisoned by their nervous system, and their intelligence can even measure above normal. Those with the disorder previously referred to as Asperger's, for example, have a high degree of intelligence,[239] and many eventually become leaders in their chosen occupational fields.[240]

---

[237] Joanna Moncrieff, *The Bitterest Pills: The Troubling Story of Antipsychotic Drugs* (London: Palgrave Macmillan, 2013), 13.

[238] Breggin, *Toxic Psychiatry*, 288.

[239] Frances, *Saving Normal*, 147-49.

[240] See the documentary "A Mother's Courage" for examples of children with autism who were able to write detailed books, become leading innovators, and teach at the university level (http://www.amotherscourage.org/).

Autism, like ADHD, is a construct. But autism is a construct created to describe non-moral behavior/impairment. As previously noted, ADHD is a construct that seeks to describe a child's moral tendency or inclination to listen to one's own natural thinking, to follow one's own interests/desires without respect to authority or wisdom, and to act/live accordingly. In contrast to ADHD, ASD seeks to describe amoral behavior caused by valid impairment or damage to the nervous system. More specifically, ASD describes symptoms relating to biological defects or damage which are explained as a neurodevelopmental disorder; the nervous system is not able to develop as it should or is delayed. (ADHD is speculated to also be a neurodevelopmental disorder, yet no empirical evidence exists to justify such a claim.)

ASD is best understood as a construct that attempts to explain symptoms created by valid physical diseases. The *DSM* acknowledges that autism is regularly associated with "known medical or genetic condition[s]."[241] For example, autism is a key characteristic of children with genetic syndromes such as Rett, Fragile X, Duplication 15q, and Down Syndrome.[242] Autism is also associated with other medical conditions such as epilepsy.[243] These are real biological syndromes or diseases with clear biological-diagnostic markers.[244] Likewise, the *DSM* also states,

---

[241] Ibid., 53.

[242] Ibid.

[243] Ibid.

[244] "Chromosome 15q11.2-13.1 duplication syndrome (dup15q syndrome) is a clinically identifiable syndrome which results from duplications of chromosome 15q11.2-13.1" (http://www.dup15q.org/understanding-dup15q/what-is-dup15q-syndrome/).

The neurodevelopmental disorders frequently co-occur; for example, individuals with autism spectrum disorder often have intellectual disability (Intellectual developmental disorder [what was once called "mental retardation"])."[245]

If a child has problems described in the construct of autism, he/she has a physical problem which creates the symptoms of poor communication, attention, relationships, motor skills, repetitive amoral behavior, and intellectual impairment.

Today's *DSM* construct of *Autism Spectrum Disorder* (ASD) seeks to identify children who have some degree of sensory impairment or heightened senses, which affect their social interactions. Although it is clear that the construct of autism describes some type of valid neurological or genetic impairment that directly affects a child's ability to communicate and offer their attention, the construct, as psychiatrist Joanna Moncrieff notes, is highly controversial.[246]

There are four reasons why the construct of autism is controversial. (1) First of all, as was established, autism is a construct that describes problems of communication, relationships, attention, motor skills, intellect, and obsessive behavior.[247] In other words, the construct of autism best explains symptoms of valid syndromes, diseases, or neurological damage rather than being a disease itself. Contrary to popular thinking, autism is not the child's underlying problem; it represents biologically caused symptoms. The *DSM's* lack of clarity on this matter causes a great deal of confusion to many and explains in large part why autism is controversial.

---

[245] APA, *DSM-5*, 31.

[246] Moncrieff, *Bitterest Pills*, 13.

[247] APA, *DSM-5*, 32; 50-59.

This lack of clarity not only enables autism to be broadly defined but also facilitates problems with communication and relationships — which are not related to physical problems — to be considered a disease. With both strong advocacy groups marketing the construct and the increase in academic benefits/ assistance from receiving a diagnosis, the labeling of children as autistic has escalated significantly in recent years. Psychiatrist Allen Frances recognizes the epidemic that the APA created in how they constructed ASD in the *DSM-IV*:

> *DSM-IV* may have started the autism epidemic, but other powerful engines drove it forward beyond all expectation. Probably most important was the positive feedback loop between spirited patient advocacy and the provision of school and therapeutic programs that require an autism diagnosis.[248]

Without clearly defining autism as being symptoms and not itself a disease, many children who have no physical problem are regularly diagnosed as falling on the Autism spectrum.

(2) Another reason that autism is controversial and why so many children are being misdiagnosed is that it is a construct represented by an imprecise spectrum, with imprecise standards of normal neurodevelopment, and imprecise boundaries of sensory variances. Without precise qualifiers, many children who are simply struggling with behavioral issues or are socially "late bloomers" can easily be labeled as autistic. Dr. Allen Frances explains,

> The twentyfold increase in just twenty years occurred because diagnostic habits had changed radically, not because kids were suddenly becoming more autistic . . . . But rates have artificially swelled because *many people within the range of normal variability (or with other mental disorders) have been misidentified as autistic* — especially when the diagnosis is made in primary care, in school systems, and by parents and patients [emphasis added].[249]

---

[248] Frances, *Saving Normal*, 148.

[249] Ibid., 147-48.

Harvard psychologist Jerome Kagan also comments,

> The Centers for Disease Control and Prevention in Atlanta recently announced that one in 88 American children has autism. That's absurd. It means that psychiatrists are calling any child who is socially awkward autistic. If you claim that anyone who can't walk a mile in 10 minutes has a serious locomotor disability, then you will trigger an epidemic of serious locomotor disabilities among older people. It may sound funny, but that's exactly what's going on in psychiatry today.[250]

A good number of children are considered autistic simply because what defines normal social communication, attention, and intellect are not objectively established.

The construct also does not objectively consider sensory impairment, processing, and overstimulation as normative among all children. Most people have dominant senses while they are at the same time weak in other areas. For example, in the spectrum of vision, many children need prescription glasses, while others have above 20/20 vision. As is often the case, children who have poor eyesight typically have heightened hearing or other senses (e.g., touch). Sensory variances are normal among people and age groups. When these variances pertain to the child's senses vital to communication, the child can easily fall behind what is considered by some to be normal development for the child's age group and thus qualify him/her as having ASD.[251] Still, a standard of normalcy for neurological/sensory development and processing is non-existent to clearly define the autism spectrum.[252]

---

[250] Jerome Kagan, "What about Tutoring Instead of Pills?" *Spiegel Online* (August 2, 2012): http://www.spiegel.de/international/world/child-psychologist-jerome-kagan-on-overprescibing-drugs-to-children-a-847500.html: accessed 2 February 2017.

[251] APA, *DSM-5*, 53.

[252] When it comes to children who genuinely struggle from physical impairment, touch is sometimes the predominant way they communicate,

(3) Autism is also controversial because physicians regularly diagnose it along with ADHD. While the autism spectrum is a broad concept, what is well-defined and is considered to be a clear diagnostic marker for ASD is a child's consistent problem communicating across all of life's settings and in all relationships. Likewise, the problems described in ASD are not considered in Scripture to be moral issues, whereas the Bible explicitly states the majority of the ADHD behaviors to be products of the depraved human nature and characteristic of all people.

When it comes to attentional issues, the *DSM* makes a distinction between the two constructs. The APA describes the child with ADHD as having the ability to pay attention when there is enough interest, desire, supervision, or reward.[253] In other words, the construct of ADHD describes a child whose giving attention is selective and based on self-control. In contrast, children diagnosed on the autism spectrum are unable to give attention properly across life's various environments. The *DSM* explains that those with ASD exhibit "persistent deficits in social communication and social interactions across multiple contexts."[254] Playing video games or watching movies will not hold the attention for any length of time of a child who has a valid physical syndrome — such as Fragile X syndrome — in the same way they will with a child labeled with ADHD. Unless, of

---

whereas the normal attentional senses — seeing and hearing — are impaired or weak. This impairment causes incredible frustration for parents who, like most others, are accustomed to communicating with the eyes, ears, and mouth. Furthermore, stimulation of the senses can either be heightened or impaired within the definition of ASD, and degrees of sensory stimulation, perception, and processing also lack a standard definition of normalcy.

[253] Ibid., 61.

[254] Ibid., 50.

course, the child labeled as autistic has no valid physical impairment or injuries.

Despite the clear distinction made in the *DSM* between ADHD and autism, these constructs are regularly diagnosed together.[255] But when psychiatrists and other clinicians label children as both having autism and ADHD, they create a logical fallacy; either the child cannot pay attention across all life's environments or he/she can. Typically, the label of ADHD is assigned to autistic children when they express high energy or "hyperactivity."[256] If a child consistently struggles to pay attention and to communicate, and it is not selective — showing self-control when it is convenient or desirable, then according to the *DSM*, the child is autistic.

Some children, who are diagnosed as having ADHD, in actuality, fall on the autism spectrum. What has been identified by physicians and those in the child's life is a problem with giving attention, with communicating, and with "developing, maintaining, and understanding relationships"[257] in all areas of life. This impairment is not due to the depraved nature as God explains it to be, but to valid biological causes.

While the relational, communicable, and attentional problems that autism describes are clearly physical rather than spiritual issues, the child who can understand is still depraved like all children, and he/she also requires guidance and godly wisdom. Children who are "highly functional" often express their hearts' desires clearly, and much of the time, even those with severe or profound disability express their desires in

---

[255] "When criteria for both ADHD and autism spectrum disorder are met, both diagnoses should be given" (ibid., 58).

[256] Ibid., 58.

[257] Ibid., 54.

repetitive behavior or through an expressed obsession.[258] It is not uncommon for autistic children to be obsessed with touching a family pet, fixating on objects like water or food, climbing or jumping, and exhibiting repetitive motor skills like twitching or flailing the arms for stimulation. The *DSM* states, "In addition to the social communication deficits, the diagnosis of autism spectrum disorder requires the presence of restricted, repetitive patterns of behavior, interests, or activities."[259] Not all autistic children express their interests, but many do.

Furthermore, many children overcome their impairment and/or sensory processing issues through physical, cognitive, and speech therapies.[260] Autism is a neurodevelopmental disorder and not a neurodegenerative disorder; that is, the child's nervous system is not getting worse and can improve/heal. Repetition is one of the keys to improvement, just as it is in any education—even when valid physical impairments obstruct learning. Planned and supervised repetition can heal the nervous system through the process known as neuroplasticity,[261] which helps many children minimize their impairment and some to even "grow out of" their problems.[262]

---

[258] Repetitive or obsessive behavior can also better reveal how the child processes sensory stimulation or reveal his/her sensory strengths and weaknesses (ibid.).

[259] Ibid., 31.

[260] Jennifer Richler, "Is it Possible to Recover from Autism?" *Scientific America Online*, July 1, 2013, https://www.scientificamerican.com/article/is-it-possible-to-recover-from-autism/; accessed 2 January 2017.

[261] Daniel R. Berger II, *Reality of the Physical Nature* (Taylors, SC: Alethia International Publications, 2016), 97-109.

[262] Richler, "Is it Possible to Recover from Autism?"

(4) Another reason that autism is controversial stems from the fact that the etiology of autism is controversial and widely claimed to be unknown. For the last decade, there have been numerous studies which indicate a correlation between vaccinations and autism. But the prevalent belief among professionals is that these studies provide correlations and not causation. Many experts assert that they lack concrete answers as to why some children have significant degrees of sensory impairment or processing issues; they are unsure what exactly causes autism. However, as previously noted from the *DSM*, autism is already widely recognized to be a symptom of valid biological syndromes or genetic and medical disorders. In addition to genetic disorders (e.g., down syndrome), recent studies reveal strong correlations between mothers who take Selective Serotonin Reuptake Inhibitors (SSRIs or "antidepressants") — which by nature and name impair and perturb the nervous system — before conceiving or during pregnancy and their children being born with neurological/ sensory impairment or processing issues.[263] Other psychoactive substances consumed by mothers are already understood to attack the nervous system and create neurodevelopmental problems in the children. "Fetal alcohol syndrome," for example, is listed in the *DSM* as causative for autism.[264] These causes (etiologies), of course, do not explain every case of autism, but they do provide further evidence that autism is a symptom of physical diseases, defects, or damage. Likewise, this knowledge

---

[263] Daniel R. Berger II, "The Link between Autism and Antidepressants," December 26, 2016, http://www.drdaniel berger.com/single-post/2016/12/26/The-Link-between-Autism-and-Antidepressants-A-Growing-Amount-of-Research-Reveals-the-Connection.

[264] APA, *DSM-5*, 53.

provides a direction for future studies to explore what is damaging the nervous system in these children.

Still, autism remains controversial because it is a construct, its exact mechanisms are unknown, its definition is somewhat imprecise (allowing children without physical impairment to be labeled) and describes symptoms rather than a disease, and it is regularly confused with the construct of ADHD. Parents whose child clearly struggles to communicate and to pay attention in all of life's situations — not just selective environments — should see a physician who is knowledgeable about genetic syndromes and other medical conditions which produce the behaviors and impairment described as ASD. Though autism is a construct, it is a valid biologically caused description of amoral behavioral/ attentional/social problems.

Environmental Influences

Romantic psychiatrists argue that "nurture" or environment determines a child's mindsets, choices, and behavior, but Scripture declares that no matter the circumstance, people are still responsible for their moral behavior. Though environments do not cause children to misbehave, environments do regularly influence choices and actions. Circumstances can also reveal the human nature more readily.

Difficult Environments

Physical and emotional trauma regularly and negatively influences many children's thinking, attention, and behavior. Harvard psychiatrist, Peter Breggin, insists that parents and teachers who desire "to help a child should be willing to look to the conduct of the parents and other potential abusers in the

child's environment."[265] In 2014, the Childhood Domestic
Violence Association reported that on average five million
children were abused every year.[266] Abused or neglected
children will understandably focus on the pain and confusion
that others have caused in their lives.[267] Many times, these
children become frustrated, anxious, and act out over the wrong
being done to them. Even while addressing the child's
responsibility for his/her own behavior and value system,
anyone who seeks to help such children must guide and love
them as well as acknowledge that they may be victims of others'
sinful behavior. Unfortunately, these difficulties in life describe
far too many children sitting in our classrooms.

Other times a child will struggle giving attention to
academic pursuits and meaningful relationships because of their
parents' divorce, fighting, or anger, and such turmoil can lead
the child to misbehave in school, daydream, and be preoccupied
with the poor relationships in his/her home.[268] Authorities in the
child's life should not assume that all inattention is entirely due
to a heart that lacks wisdom and right desires. There may be
strong influences that add to a child's tendency to be distracted
and misplace attention. It is understandable, for example, that a
child would value his/her home situation more than academic
success. When there is turmoil in the home, the child can easily

---

[265] Breggin, *Toxic Psychiatry*, 274.

[266] "10 Startling Statistics about Children of Domestic Violence," *Childhood Domestic Violence Association,* February 21, 2014, http://cdv.org/2014/02/10-startling-domestic-violence-statistics-for-children/: accessed 7 June 2014.

[267] Haber, *ADHD*, 67-68.

[268] Andrew Root, "Fading from the Family Portrait," *Christianity Today*, July/August 2012, 70-73. See also Breggin, *Toxic Psychiatry*, 273.

be distracted in school and let his/her mind wander to the point that academic and social successes are impaired. Likewise a bully at school can create anxiety and greatly distract a child. All facets of a child's life must be examined in order to administer God's grace effectively and to avoid foolishly causing further emotional damage to the child's heart.

Sleep Patterns

Similarly, quality and quantity of sleep are major factors in giving attention rightly. A child's sleep habits will help or hinder his/her physical growth as well as mental, spiritual, and social development.[269] There is clear evidence that sleep influences one's ability to pay attention. Psychiatrist Judith Owens remarks,

> There is substantial empirical evidence supporting an overlap in those central nervous system centers that regulate sleep and those that regulate attention/arousal, suggesting disruptions in one system might well have parallel effects on the other. Furthermore, similar perturbations in neurotransmitter pathways, particularly noradrenergic and dopaminergic systems, are found in both ADHD and sleep disturbances.[270]

What Dr. Owens' statement reveals is that what may appear to be attentional problems in neuroimages may actually be a physical sign of sleep disturbances. Pictures of the brain cannot explain causality or take pictures of the mind, but they can allow comparisons to be made about the brain. Not surprisingly, parents whose children have been diagnosed as having ADHD commonly report that their children have difficulty sleeping.[271]

---

[269] Monastra, *Parenting Children with ADHD,* 75.

[270] Judith Owens, "A Clinical Overview of Sleep and Attention-Deficit/Hyperactivity Disorder in Children and Adolescents," *Journal of the Canadian Academy of Child and Adolescent Psychiatry* 18, no. 2, (2009): 92–102.

[271] WebMD, *"ADHD and Sleep Disorders,"* http://www.webmd.com/add-adhd/guide/adhd-sleep-disorders; accessed 14 August 2012.

Problems sleeping and problems paying attention are typically correlates, and lack of sleep often leads to relational and behavioral problems. The National Institute of Neurological Disorders explains:

> Sleep appears necessary for our nervous systems to work properly. Too little sleep leaves us drowsy and unable to concentrate the next day. It also leads to impaired memory and physical performance and reduced ability to carry out math calculations. If sleep deprivation continues, hallucinations and mood swings may develop. Some experts believe sleep gives neurons used while we are awake a chance to shut down and repair themselves. Without sleep, neurons may become so depleted in energy or so polluted with byproducts of normal cellular activities that they begin to malfunction. Sleep also may give the brain a chance to exercise important neuronal connections that might otherwise deteriorate from lack of activity.[272]

Dr. Richard Saul also points out that 100 percent of his patients who struggle to pay attention, to remain focused, and to have self-control also have problems sleeping.[273] A child's lack of sleep or poor quality of sleep can influence his/her ability to think clearly, to learn,[274] to control emotions,[275] and to choose wise behavior.[276]

The Mayo clinic suggests that children from infancy to adulthood require nine to eleven hours of sleep each night, and

---

[272] National Institute of Neurological Disorders and Strokes, "Brain Basics: Understanding Sleep," http://www.ninds.nih.gov/disorders/brain_basics/understanding_sleep.htm; accessed 2 June 2016.

[273] Ibid., 59.

[274] Jennifer Warner, "The Fight for Adequate Sleep . . . in Preschool?" http://www.everydayhealth.com/news/fight-for-adequate-sleep-preschool/?xid=aol_eh-sleep_1_20140224_&aolcat=AJA&icid=maing-grid7%7Cmain5%7Cdl17%7Csec1_ lnk3%26pLid%3D449822; accessed 2 June 2016.

[275] Higbee, "'Tony' and Bipolar Disorder," 174.

[276] Saul, ADHD Does Not Exist, 51-63.

they recommend an additional three-hour nap for younger children to maintain proper health.[277] Other research, such as that conducted by *Harvard Medical School Journal,* also concludes that naps "provide measurable cognitive benefits" even for adults.[278] Still other studies show "that people who sleep so little over many nights don't perform as well on complex mental tasks as do people who get closer to seven hours of sleep a night,"[279] and chronic poor sleep results in daytime tiredness, difficulties in focusing attention, behavioral self-control, emotional self-control, and increases impulsive activity.[280] Additionally, anxiety, antisocial behavior, and expressed anger are found to be increased in children when sleep deprivation is present.[281] If research is correct, then an increase in quality sleep should positively enhance a child's academic performance, cognitive abilities, and behavior. It must be made clear, though, that sleep deprivation does not cause moral failure and misplaced focus; rather, that lack of sleep influences one's ability to self-regulate as God intends. It is fairly safe to say that some children who are diagnosed as having ADHD are deprived of sleep, and this

---

[277] Timothy Morganthaler, "How Many Hours of Sleep Are Enough for Good Health?" http://www.mayoclinic.org/healthy-living/adult-health/expert-answers/how-many-hours-of-sleep-are-enough/faq-20057898; accessed 2 June 2016.

[278] "Napping Boosts Sleep and Cognitive Function in Healthy Older Adults," *Harvard Women's Health Watch* 19, no. 1 (September 2011): 6.

[279] Ibid.

[280] R.E. Dahl, "The Impact of Inadequate Sleep on Children's Daytime Cognitive Function," *Seminars in Pediatric Neurology* 1 (Mar 3, 1996): 44-50.

[281] Kathryn Turnbull, Graham J. Reid, and J. Bruce Morton, "Behavioral Sleep Problems and their Potential Impact on Developing Executive Function in Children," *Sleep* 36, no. 7 (July 1, 2013): 1077-84.

deprivation both impairs normal neurological function and exposes the depraved nature more easily.

Psychostimulants

Lack of sleep represents a major hindrance to a child's attentional abilities as well as to his/her behavior. Yet, psychostimulants — which allegedly treat ADHD — are known to cause sleep deprivation.[282] Ritalin and Dexedrine, for example, are known to inhibit sleep in children. Research indicates that children taking these drugs are two to three times more likely to have problems sleeping, a significant percentage by anyone's standard.[283] Physicians explain this common occurrence in the *Journal of Pediatric Psychology*: "In both acute and long-term clinical trials, parents have listed sleep problems as one of the most common and persistent side-effects of stimulant medication."[284] The reason is simple: psychostimulants "enhance the levels of arousal in the central nervous system (CNS) and autonomic nervous system (ANS)."[285] Normally, people are stimulated through their senses/nerves,[286] but these powerful

---

[282] Owens, "A Clinical Overview of Sleep," 92–102.

[283] Reut Gruber, et al., "Performance on the Continuous Performance Test in Children with ADHD Is Associated with Sleep Efficiency," *Sleep* 30, no. 8 (Aug 1, 2007): 1003–9.

[284] Penny Corkum, et al., "Acute Impact of Immediate Release Methylphenidate Administered Three Times a Day on Sleep in Children with Attention-Deficit/Hyperactivity Disorder," *Journal of Pediatric Psychology* 33, no. 4 (October 9, 2008): 368-79.

[285] Gruber, et al., "Sleep Efficiency," 1003–9.

[286] "Peripheral Neuropathy: Potentially Disabling Nerve Problems," *Mayo Clinic Health Letter* 29, no. 10, (October 2011): 1-3.

drugs overtake normal functions of the nervous system and do not shut off when a person tries to sleep. The drug's action results in the child remaining in a heightened/aroused state as long as the drugs are in his/her system.

This reality poses a logical and ethical problem for physicians to use a drug that knowingly hinders sleep and which in turn hinders attention:

> The relationship between sleep problems and ADHD is hardly a straightforward one, and may present clinically in a number of different guises. For example, psychotropic medications used to treat ADHD or comorbid psychiatric conditions associated with ADHD (i.e., mood disorders, anxiety) may themselves result in sleep problems in some patients, daytime manifestations of primary sleep disorders such as obstructive sleep apnea may "mimic" ADHD symptomatology in others, comorbid sleep problems may exacerbate ADHD symptoms, and/or sleep problems may in some cases represent an "intrinsic" dysregulation of sleep and wakefulness associated with ADHD-related CNS dysfunction.[287]

When psychostimulants are prescribed — which knowingly perturb a child's sleep — to allegedly treat the problem of inattention, the drugs may actually exacerbate the child's problems and create a self-fulfilling prophecy. When children stop taking their stimulants, they often sleep in excessive amounts as their bodies reset themselves. It is quite possible that many highly energetic children labeled as having ADHD and subsequently prescribed psychostimulants are being hindered and impaired by lack of sleep. All people, when they do not receive an appropriate amount of sleep, will more easily expose their impairing human nature.

---

[287] Owens, "A Clinical Overview of Sleep," 92–102.

Dietary Habits

Although no food in itself causes what secularists claim is ADHD,[288] chemicals, sugars, monosodium glutamate, and caffeine are widely regarded as substances that can negatively influence a child's decisions and behaviors.[289] The body relies on amino acids, iron, zinc, magnesium, and fatty acids to replenish brain cells and promote cell growth within the body.[290] This design makes it imperative that a child have foods that maintain physical health, allow clear thinking, and better enable self-control.

Whereas some clinicians theorize that wrong diets or malnutrition can cause bad behavior,[291] food in itself does not control a person's will unless it contains a controlling substance such as alcohol. Likewise, malnutrition, sugar, and caffeine (by themselves) never cause sinful behavior. Yet, they can influence a child's and an adult's abilities to make good decisions.

One thing that can be agreed upon by all approaches to the construct of ADHD is that the child is behaving in an impairing and destructive way. How the eighteen behaviors are interpreted, labeled, and attempted to be remedied, though, are matters of great disagreement. In truth, however, these varied approaches and contested remedies are simply matters of one's presuppositional faith/worldview.

---

[288] WebMD, "ADHD Diets," http://www.webmd.com/add-adhd/guide/adhd-diets?page=2; accessed 14 August 2012.

[289] Keith Low, "ADHD and Diet: Improving ADHD Symptoms with Diet," http://add.about.com/od/childrenandteens/a/Nutrition.htm; accessed 14 August 2012.

[290] Monastra, *Parenting Children with ADHD*, 76.

[291] Haber, *ADHD*, 135-39.

CHAPTER 4

ADHD IS NOT A MEDICAL CONDITION

"[ADHD] is an invention. Every child who's not doing well in school is sent to see a pediatrician, and the pediatrician says: 'It's ADHD; here's Ritalin.' In fact, 90 percent of these 5.4 million kids don't have an abnormal dopamine metabolism. The problem is, if a drug is available to doctors, they'll make the corresponding diagnosis."[292] – Former Harvard Psychologist, Jerome Kagan

"This [the ADHD construct] is a concoction to justify the giving out of medication at unprecedented and unjustifiable levels."[293] – Psychologist and Professor Emeritus at Duke University Medical School, Keith Conners

Materialists have tried to reduce the mind and moral behavior to matters of science and medicine, but there exists no empirical evidence to support such spurious claims. Dr. Allen Frances comments on how the construct of ADHD has been medicalized:

ADHD is spreading like wildfire. It used to be confined to a small percentage of kids who had clear-cut problems that started at a very early age and caused them unmistakable difficulties in many

---

[292] Jerome Kagan, "What about Tutoring Instead of Pills?" *Spiegel Online* (August 2, 2012): http://www.spiegel.de/international/world/child-psychologist-jerome-kagan-on-overprescibing-drugs-to-children-a-847500.html: accessed 2 February 2017.

[293] Keith Conners quoted by Alan Schwarz, "The Selling of Attention Deficit Disorder," *New York Times Online* (December 14, 2013): http://www.nytimes.com/2013/12/15/health/the-selling-of-attention-deficit-disorder.html?action=click&contentCollection=Health&module=RelatedCoverage&pgtype=article&region=Marginalia&utm_campaign=Constant+Contact&utm_medium=email&utm_source=January+2015&_r=0; accessed 2 January 2017.

situations. *Then all manner of classroom disruption was medicalized and ADHD was applied so promiscuously that an amazing 10 percent of kids now qualify.* Every classroom now has at least one or two kids on medication. And increasingly, ADHD is becoming an explain-all for all sorts of performance problems in adults as well [emphasis added].[294]

As we have seen, "the clear-cut problems" Dr. Frances describes are normal human nature. More children are getting diagnosed as ADHD and perceived to be diseased because society's worldview has changed to filter children through psychiatric thinking. Having a fluid construct, such as ADHD, allows for both the medicalization of behavior and the promiscuous and subjective application of the theory.

As noted in chapter one, materialism is the underlying philosophy on which the current construct of ADHD was created and is maintained. Belief in materialism demands that every human mindset, behavior, and emotion fit into biological explanations and terminology. But perceiving human problems through materialism still requires that valid and reliable solutions/remedies be offered for human problems.

Naturally, biological psychiatrists and other physicians — who hold to materialism and determinism — theorize and search endlessly for biological remedies to a child's inattention and impairing behavior. Clinicians and theorists with their expertise in medicine and their belief in materialism treat and explain the construct of ADHD as if it were a medical disease. Yet, no objective biological etiology, marker, or remedy exists to apply a disease model to children's maladaptive behavior. Still, in order to maintain the construct of ADHD as valid, psychiatrists and other clinicians must continue to claim the construct as a neurological disease or genetic defect and hope that someday a biological connection will be found.

---

[294] Frances, *Saving Normal*, 141.

115

There are four main reasons why ADHD is believed by many to be a medical issue: (1) the *DSM* and diagnostic process, (2) etiological claims (causes), (3) psychostimulants, (4) and the new claims of neuroimaging. As will be observed in this chapter, none of these psychiatric claims have yielded empirical evidence/objective reasons to consider the construct of ADHD as a medical disorder.

The DSM and the Diagnostic Process

The *DSM* descriptions of ADHD and its diagnostic process are not objective, reliable, or scientific. It is worth repeating that there exist no biological markers to validate the construct of ADHD as a biological abnormality or enable objective diagnoses. The *DSM* states,

> In the absence of clear biological markers or clinically useful measurements of severity for many mental disorders, it has not been possible to completely separate normal and pathological symptom [abnormal] expressions contained in the diagnostic criteria.[295]

The *DSM* later acknowledges that "no biological marker is diagnostic for ADHD."[296] What parents, doctors, and educators must realize is that the *DSM* and the diagnostic process cannot distinguish normal children from abnormal or alleged diseased children from the well using real medical procedures and the child's observable biology. Within the APA's standardized framework, clinicians have only the child's behavior and other's testimony both to draw conclusions about the child's condition and to figure out a solution. But no one is arguing against the fact that the child is misbehaving — only how bad behavior should be interpreted and remedied.

---

[295] APA, *DSM-5*, 21.

[296] Ibid., 61.

Though psychiatrists admit that "problems and critical issues still remain,"[297] they continue to claim scientific validity for the *DSM* and its proposed diagnostic process.[298] The *DSM* does not discuss any actual biological problem, and anyone can "identify it" without ever having studied neurology, medicine, or biology. This is true, because the construct of ADHD is only a subjective interpretation of children's common impairing behavior.[299]

Today's society has in general learned to view behavior through the psychiatric lens. When children enter a doctor's office to be evaluated for their behavior, physicians do not have objective tests available to discover anything new; they simply affirm or deny that the child's behavior fits the APA's descriptions. Former director of the National Institute of Mental Health and Harvard professor of neurobiology, Steven Hyman comments in a Harvard publication:

> Despite major advances in the treatment of psychiatric symptoms in recent years, there are still no definitive clinical tests to determine whether someone has a given disorder or not. "We have no equivalent of a blood-pressure cuff or blood test or brain scan that is diagnostic." . . . The genetics of mental illness are also "fiendishly complex," [Hyman] says; although there is evidence that many conditions run in families, science has yet to identify the particular genes responsible for any disorder.[300]

---

[297] Barkley, *NoSC*, 14.

[298] Russell A. Barkley, Kevin R. Murphy, and Mariellen Fischer, *ADHD in Adults: What the Science Says* (New York: Guilford, 2008), 38-39.

[299] Carol Tavris, *Psychobabble and Biobunk: Using Psychological Science to Think Critically about Popular Psychology* (Upper Saddle, NJ: Prentice Hall, 2001), 102.

[300] Ashley Pettus, "Psychiatry by Prescription: Do Psychotropic Drugs Blur the Boundaries between Illness and Health?" *Harvard Magazine Online* (July-August, 2006):http://harvardmagazine.com/2006/07/psychiatry-by-prescripti.html; accessed 21 January 2017.

When educators insist that a child has ADHD, they are really saying that a child tends to behave in impairing and difficult ways similar to millions of other children. When scientists say behaviors run in families, they are merely identifying that behavior is learned (e.g., internationally adopted children learn the language of their new family/culture — what they are taught — rather than the language of their origin).

While chapter one discussed the subjective criteria imposed upon the construct of mental illness by Dr. Bob Spitzer, it is good to visit these subjective criteria once more in this chapter as they directly apply to the diagnostic process. The *DSM* lists two seemingly objective qualifications in regard to duration or time that allegedly determine abnormality: symptoms must be present for at least six months (the time qualifier), and some behaviors must be present prior to the age of twelve.[301] In the *DSM-IV*, the age qualifier was seven years old, so even this criterion is non-essential and subject to change.[302] Some therapists dismiss the latter qualification as nebulous since almost all children exhibit hyperactivity and impulsivity prior to age seven (now twelve).[303] The other seemingly objective qualification is the persistence of six of the nine criteria for at least six months. Yet, within this assessment, clinicians must subjectively determine what qualifies as persistent, and one must question why six months is the designated time frame and not five months or even ten years.

The *DSM* verbiage ensures that diagnoses be subjective by qualifying each criterion with the word *often*. Every behavior

---

[301] APA, *DSM-5*, 60.

[302] APA, *DSM-IV*, 92-93.

[303] Rosemond and Ravenel, *Diseasing of America's Children*, 107.

listed in the *DSM* begins with this qualification, and its presence undermines validity as

> dependence on the word 'often' to define 'symptoms' of ADHD reduces the disorder to one of personal taste, having nothing to do with any scientific, medical, or objective criteria.[304]

Furthermore, the "often" qualifier highlights the APA's pattern of imprecisely defining normalcy and failing to distinguish it from abnormality. It also highlights the fluidity and subjective nature of the construct of ADHD.

Reliable standards of measurement in the diagnostic process simply cannot exist because of how the APA created and defined the construct of ADHD. Opinions regularly vacillate and conflict, compromising the claim that the ADHD construct is a scientific fact and a reliable explanation of behavior.[305] This reality also explains why so many children qualify as having ADHD. The very nature of the educational system demands that children sit still, keep quiet, obey authority, and constantly learn new material and retain it. A teacher's idea of "often" can easily consist of one distressful situation, a couple of outbursts, or a consistent expression of his/her natural lack of self-control or "high energy." With the "often" qualifier, utilitarianism or one's subjective opinion becomes the gold-standard of normalcy/abnormality in the home, classroom, and clinician's office.

Not only are the individual criteria written subjectively, but so also are the main classifications of behavior. For example, the therapist must determine when a child has persistent inattention, hyperactivity, or impulsivity *"to a degree that is maladaptive and inconsistent with developmental level."*[306] In other words, if a

---

[304] Flora, *Taking America off Drugs*, 77.

[305] Rosemond and Ravenel, *Diseasing of America's Children*, 17.

[306] APA, *DSM-IV*, 85.

child's behavior is impairing, then according to Bob Spitzer's theory, it should be considered as a mental disorder. As with the time qualifier, this phraseology assumes both the existence of a normative measurement of age-appropriate behavior and a presuppositional view that children are not naturally impaired or distressed. Since a standard of normalcy is non-existent, the therapist must subjectively judge how a child compares to others his/her age.

What is regularly identified as abnormalities in children said to have ADHD is actually varying degrees of immaturity and foolishness. When children are compared to other children of the same age, there will inevitably be differences in their rate of maturation. But research indicates that it is the youngest children in the classroom—compared to others in the same classroom—who are said to have ADHD:

> Several earlier studies have also found a higher incidence of ADHD among the youngest children in classrooms, suggesting that less mature children may be inappropriately labeled and treated for ADHD. "It certainly appears that in some cases lack of maturity is being misinterpreted as ADHD, and it raises alarms about over-diagnosis," says researcher Richard L. Morrow of the University of British Columbia.[307]

Similarly, Dr. Frances comments,

> Another startling study showed that a good predictor of a child getting tagged with ADHD is his date of birth. The youngest kid in the class is almost twice as likely to be diagnosed as the oldest. We have turned immaturity into a disease.[308]

Though Paul Wender believes ADHD is under-diagnosed, he concedes that immaturity describes ADHD well: "Immaturity is

---

[307] Salynn Boyles, "Immaturity Mistaken for ADHD?: Youngest Kids in the Classroom More Likely to Be Diagnosed," http://children.webmd.com/news/20120305/is-immaturity-being-mistaken-adhd?ecd=wnl_prg_031112. Accessed 2 2013 April.

[308] Frances, "Most Active Kids."

neither a very scientific nor a very specific word, but it often does accurately describe the behavior of ADHD children."[309] Immaturity, personality, youth, and developmental differences in children, however, do not equal diseases or abnormalities. Likewise, not performing well academically or fitting into the academic system are not indicators that a child has a neurodevelopmental disorder. The variance in normal developmental rates of children adds to the diagnostic complexity of alleged ADHD and renders its validity and objectivity impossible.[310]

The *DSM* further reveals or rather opens the door for more subjectivity in the final criterion for ADHD, which states that therapists should evaluate thoroughly whether the observed behaviors might be attributable to another disorder or influence. Clinicians must subjectively assess whether a child's behaviors are signs of alleged ADHD or have another cause. Of this qualification, Dr. Monastra writes,

> In my opinion, the final criterion for ADHD is often ignored or minimized by health care professionals. It requires that the doctor diagnosing ADHD ensure that the symptoms of inattention, impulsivity, or hyperactivity are not caused by another mental or physical disorder.[311]

Monastra also states that in conducting over 10,000 patient evaluations, rarely did he find that other physicians previously tested ADHD patients for sleep apnea, allergies, thyroid disorders, or other physical influences.[312] Some professionals

---

[309] Wender, *ADHD*, 28.

[310] Pennington, *Diagnosing Learning Disorders*, 4.

[311] Monastra, *Parenting Children with ADHD*, 23.

[312] Ibid.

recognize that ADHD does not objectively describe or explain a child's behavior, so they create new unofficial labels to describe children who behave according to the *DSM's* description of ADHD but allegedly do not have the "disease." These children are said to have "faux-ADHD"[313] or "pseudo–ADHD."[314] This determination is not made on objective facts or biological markers, but made on the basis of subjective opinion.

Subjectivity in the diagnostic process likewise results from the absence of reliable tests to measure the presence of ADHD. The *DSM-IV* states, "There are no laboratory tests, neurological assessments, or attentional assessments that have been established as diagnostic in the clinical assessment of Attention-Deficit/Hyperactivity Disorder."[315] The absence of an objective diagnostic test results in unreliable diagnoses and reliance on therapists' perception.

> The diagnosis of ADHD is difficult, both because of the number of confounding conditions that must be excluded, and because objective tests of ADHD are less well developed than those for dyslexia or other learning disorders. So clinicians should be duly cautious in making this diagnosis.[316]

---

[313] Robert Pressman and Steve Imber, "Relationship of Children's Daytime Behavior Problems with Bedtime Routines/Practices: A Family Context and the Consideration of Faux-ADHD," http://www.pedipsyc.com/abstract_Faux ADHD.php; accessed 21 September 2011; Daniel DeNoon, "Kids' Poor Bedtime Habits May Bring ADHD Misdiagnosis," http://www.webmd. com/add-adhd/news/20110919/kids-poor-bedtime-habits-may-bring-adhd-misdiagnosis.

[314] Edward Hallowell, "Dr. Hallowell's Response to NY Times Piece 'Ritalin Gone Wrong,'" http://www.drhallowell.com/blog/dr-hallowells-response-to-ny-times-piece-ritalin-gone-wrong/.

[315] APA, *DSM-IV*, 88-89.

[316] Pennington, *Diagnosing Learning Disorders*, 166.

Biomedical journalist Karen Barrow quotes psychiatrist Joel Nigg:

> It is not easy to diagnose ADHD. Unlike diabetes or heart disease, ADHD can't be detected with a blood test or scan. "Like other psychiatric diagnoses, the boundaries of ADHD are fuzzy, so clinicians' judgments play a big role," says Joel Nigg, Ph.D., a professor of psychiatry, pediatrics, and behavioral neuroscience at Oregon Health and Science University.[317]

Harvard psychologist, Jerome Kagan also recognizes that diagnosing ADHD is "fuzzy."[318] The diagnostic subjectivity or "fuzziness" leads to confusion and differing opinions on rates of ADHD in society. Since no objective test exists,[319] therapists have only subjective evaluations to apply, and disagreement on who has ADHD is prevalent.

> Diagnosing ADHD takes good clinical detective work," says child psychiatrist Ismail Sendi of Michigan's Henry Ford Health System. Sendi tested 388 Michigan children who were taking Ritalin. He found that only sixty-seven had been correctly diagnosed. "The other 82 percent should have been getting treatment for another disorder.[320]

The difficulty and probable impossibility of proper diagnoses — if ADHD were actually a disease — has led many professionals to form strong opinions about the rate of ADHD diagnoses. Some

---

[317] Karen Barrow, "Why ADHD is a "Fuzzy Diagnosis?" *ADDitude Online,* http://www.additudemag.com/adhd/article/10597.html.

[318] Jerome Kagan, "What about Tutoring Instead of Pills?" *Spiegel Online* (August 2, 2012): http://www.spiegel.de/international/world/child-psychologist-jerome-kagan-on-overprescibing-drugs-to-children-a-847500.html: accessed 2 February 2017.

[319] Petersen, *Our Daily Meds,* 98.

[320] Francha Roffé Menhard, *Drugs: The Facts about Ritalin* (New York: Marshall Cavendish Benchmark, 2007), 26.

insist that ADHD is under-diagnosed,[321] while others argue that it is assigned to children way too often.[322] The American Academy of Pediatrics (AAP) published a clinical guideline for diagnosing ADHD in which it expresses this concern for proper diagnoses: "The *DSM* system does not specifically provide for developmental-level differences and might lead to some misdiagnoses."[323] These alleged misdiagnoses are an unavoidable product of the subjective nature of the *DSM* and the diagnostic system it espouses. But because the construct and diagnostic process are so subjective, what is a misdiagnosis, what is faux-ADHD, and what is a good diagnosis are all convoluted and matters of one's opinion.

The subjective diagnosis of children's behavior is not limited to trained clinicians. The current diagnostic system requires the parents,[324] teachers,[325] and other authorities to evaluate, compare, and identify children through measurement systems such as the "Behavioral Rating Scales" (BRS). Psychotherapy bases this rating system on a standardized form, yet the BRS relies on the subjective opinions and observations of the administrator,[326] and

---

[321] Marie Hartwell-Walker, "It May Not Be ADHD," http://psychcentral.com/lib/2010/it-may-not-be-adhd.

[322] Haber, *ADHD*, 2-3.

[323] "Clinical Practice Guideline for the Diagnosis, Evaluation, and Treatment of Attention-Deficit/Hyperactivity Disorder in Children and Adolescents," http://pediatrics.aappublications.org/content/early/2011/10/14/peds.2011-2654.

[324] Monastra, *Parenting Children with ADHD*, 17.

[325] Rosemond and Ravenel, *Diseasing of America's Children*, 69.

[326] Pennington, *Diagnosing Learning Disorders*, 166.

as we have already mentioned, the very construct it allegedly measures has no objective or validating determiners. Many ADHD theorists admit that these rating scales are circular in reasoning, but they argue that external measurements somehow eliminate circularity.[327]

Finally, subjectivity exists in the selection of criteria for the *DSM*. When psychiatrists selected the current system of measurement, they included only eighteen behaviors. No standard of exclusion/inclusion existed for determining ADHD criteria. The *DSM-III* (1987) contained different criteria for the ADHD construct than does the *DSM-IV* (1996) and *DSM-5* (2000).[328] The *DSM-III* also required the existence of eight of fourteen symptomatic behaviors in a child compared to six of nine in the *DSM-IV* and 5. In both editions, committees subjectively chose which behaviors (and the quantity) should compose the criteria for diagnosing ADHD – a benefit of creating a construct. Since therapists have observed the label's limitation in describing the spectrum of behaviors associated with the label,

> Many behavioral scientists, neurologists, parents, educators, and pediatricians would like to see a name for the disorder that would better capture all of the varied problems these children have.[329]

Therapists who were not on the *DSM* selection committee sometimes assert that the *DSM* qualifications are inadequate in describing the true nature of the child's problem.[330] Which

---

[327] Barkley, *NoSC*, 66.

[328] Haber, *ADHD*, 32.

[329] Ibid., 35.

[330] Hallowell and Ratey, *Driven to Distraction*, 9.

behavior should or should not be considered a criterion in the construct of ADHD is entirely subjective.

Additionally, the majority of individuals who exhibit ADHD behaviors also exhibit behaviors found in other *DSM* disorders.[331] One example is oppositional-defiant disorder (ODD), which according to the *DSM-IV* is diagnosed in approximately half of ADHD children.[332] Since secularists closely link ADHD and ODD, it is possible that these constructs are not separate problems, but part of the same larger problem the *DSM* committee and secularism has overlooked or even denied.

According to some clinicians, the ADHD construct is even more fluid than the *DSM* presents it to be. For example, Robert Moss takes issue with not only limiting the definition of ADHD symptoms, but also in classifying these criteria as a disorder:

> The term "disorder" implies that this is a disease with specifically defined characteristics that appear in every case. ADD does not have a list of distinct symptoms that will be present with each child. As we have seen, this condition encompasses a broad range of manifestations, and no two patients exhibit the same exact characteristics.[333]

---

[331] Elissa P. Benedek, review of *ADHD in Adults: What the Science Says,* by Russell A. Barkley, Kevin Murphy, and Mariellen Fischer, *Bulletin of the Menninger Clinic* 73, no. 1 (Winter 2009): 69-74. The *DSM* provides what it refers to as *Differential Diagnoses* in which other disorders such as low self-esteem, anxiety disorders, conduct disorders, obsessive compulsive disorder, and or substance abuse are allegedly considered prior to the clinician assigning the diagnosis of ADHD to a child or adult (*DSM*, 87-89).

[332] APA, *DSM-IV-TR*, 88; Barkley, *NoSC*, 307.

[333] Moss, *Why Johnny Can't Concentrate*, 3.

Psychiatrists rationalize the inclusion and exclusion of behavior through comorbidity,[334] which allows them to diagnose children with unlimited numbers of disorders in order to describe fully all maladaptive behavior. In any given school there will be children diagnosed as having two or three different psychiatric disorders at the same time.

Further compromising the legitimacy of the diagnostic process and really undermining the entire ADHD construct presented in the *DSM* is a category of fourth and fifth types of ADHD listed as "Other Specified Attention-Deficit/ Hyperactivity Disorder" and "Unspecified Attention-Deficit/ Hyperactivity Disorder":[335]

> This category applies to presentations in which symptoms characteristic of attention deficit/hyperactivity disorder that cause clinically significant distress or impairment in social, occupational or other important areas of functioning predominate *but do not meet the full criteria for attention-deficit/hyperactivity disorder* . . . [emphasis added].[336]

While the *DSM* states that the criteria must be met for proper diagnoses to be made, this description provides a catch-all subtype for what clinicians might feel fits their idea of the disorder. With the exception of behavior (inattention, hyperactivity, or impulsivity), the "Not Otherwise Specified" subtype eliminates all previous criteria as the basis for diagnosing ADHD and establishes the therapist's subjective opinion as the true system of measurement for ADHD. Considering the existence and definition of these two ADHD

---

[334] Gabrielle Weiss and Lily Trokenberg Hechtman, *Hyperactive Children Grown Up: ADHD in Children, Adolescents, and Adults*, 2nd ed. (New York: Guilford, 1993), 346.

[335] APA, *DSM-5*, 65-66.

[336] Ibid., 65.

subtypes in the *DSM* leaves the discerning individual understanding that everyone with any common behavioral struggles qualifies as having ADHD.

The "Other Specified" and "Unspecified" subtypes expose that ADHD is a construct that anyone can apply with or without a medical degree, medical training, or understanding of the human body. In fact, the construct is so fluid that some well-respected psychiatrists assert that not all ADHD behaviors are actually observable:

> ADD comes in many shapes and sizes. In many people, particularly adults, the symptoms of ADD are masked by more obvious problems such as depression or gambling or drinking, and the underlying ADD is never detected. In other people the symptoms take on a particular cast, congruent with the person's personality as it evolves over time, so that the symptoms are never really noticed the way symptoms of a cold or flu might be but rather are dismissed as being part of 'just the way he is,' not warranting medical or psychiatric intervention. And within the domain of properly diagnosed ADD, there is also much variability.[337]

Drs. Hallowell and Ratey's suggestion not only reveals the subjective nature of the diagnostic process, but clearly defines ADHD as an abstract idea that is unobservable and unapproachable with scientific tools. In truth, they assert that the clinician's opinion supersedes the *DSM*.

Since the construct of ADHD, as presented in the *DSM*, is overwhelmingly subjective and therefore lacks validity and reliability, therapists must diagnose children based on subjective hypotheses which are attempts to explain behaviors.[338] This realization led Thomas Insel, the former director of the National Institute of Mental Health (NIMH), to withdraw support for future revisions of the *DSM*:

---

[337] Hallowell and Ratey, *Driven to Distraction*, 9.

[338] Barkley, *NoSC*, vii-viii.

> The weakness [of the *DSM*] is its lack of validity. Unlike our definitions of ischemic heart disease, lymphoma, or AIDS, the *DSM* diagnoses are based on a consensus about clusters of clinical symptoms, not any objective laboratory measure.[339]

In place of the *DSM*, the NIMH is proposing a more biological and empirical approach to mental disorders, which they call "Research Domain Criteria (RDoC)."[340] Still, secularists are already questioning the validity of this newly proposed system of measurement as it attempts to describe the same invisible "diseases."[341]

Evidence simply does not exist by which secularists can empirically claim ADHD as an objective construct or as a valid disease.[342] As we previously remarked but worth revisiting, is the chair of the *DSM-IV* task force, Allen Frances explanation of what psychiatric disorders truly are: "We saw *DSM-IV* as a guidebook, not a bible—*a collection of temporarily useful diagnostic constructs, not a catalog of 'real' diseases* [emphasis added]."[343] ADHD, like all the other psychiatric constructs, is not a real disease.

The Etiological Claims

What actually causes a child to get out of his seat when he is expected to remain seated or to cut in line when it is clearly not

---

[339] Insel, "Transforming Diagnosis."

[340] Ibid.

[341] Christopher Lane, "The NIMH Withdrawals Support for the DSM-5," http://www.psychologytoday.com/blog/side-effects/201305/the-nimh-withdraws-support-dsm-5.

[342] Stein, *Ritalin Is Not the Answer*, 22-23.

[343] Frances, *Saving Normal*, 73.

his turn? Finding out why children behave as they do is imperative to finding out why they misbehave. This is precisely the reason the construct of ADHD is maintained and defended. In order for materialism/evolutionary thinking to be accepted as the best anthropology and explanation of children's common bad behavior, a biological etiology (cause) must be realized. Otherwise, many of the behaviors listed as criteria for ADHD will be exposed as moral in nature.

The APA and Scripture differ considerably on how they perceive the origin of a child's moral behavior. Evolutionists/ materialists speculate that a child's biology and environment are to blame for bad behavior, whereas Scripture declares that all moral behavior is sourced in the child's spiritual heart/mind and directly affects his/her physical nature. These two views are antithetical.

The Secular Perspective

While secular theorists speculate about what causes a child to behave according to the *DSM* description of ADHD, there exists no empirical evidence to prove any biological etiology. Many prominent clinicians admit that "the precise causes of ADHD are unknown."[344] Despite this fact, theorists speculate about two "potentially causative factors"[345]: (1) abnormal and chemically imbalanced brains[346] and (2) genetic flaws.[347]

---

[344] Barkley, *NoSC*, 29.

[345] Ibid.

[346] Monastra, *Parenting Children with ADHD*, 29.

[347] Barkley, *NoSC*, 37.

Seemingly substantiated theories suggest that ADHD is caused by abnormal or immature brains in those labeled as having ADHD. In fact, the construct of ADHD is listed as a neurodevelopmental disorder in the *DSM*.[348] These claims are based on results of neuroimaging of ADHD brains compared to those of so-called normal individuals. Though many clinicians have widely accepted this research as hard evidence for ADHD etiology, researchers admit that these studies do "not prove that ADHD arises from these particular brain structures."[349] Psychopharmacologists and pharmaceutical companies have conducted thousands of studies attempting to prove their etiological hypotheses.[350] Still, no solid empirical evidence exists to validate their claims.[351] Furthermore, many researchers arrive at different conclusions about the same studies. Brain scans, for example, can expose various correlations that yield different interpretations:

> The study, which appeared in the proceedings of the National Academy of Sciences, used medical imaging techniques to examine the brains of children with and without ADHD symptoms. Researchers did not find any permanent flaws or deficits in the brains of the ADHD children, but did discover that parts of the ADHD children's brains were developing more slowly than those of other children . . . Dr. Philip Shaw told the *New York Times* (11-13-07), "I think this is pretty strong evidence we're talking about a delay, and not an abnormal brain."[352]

---

[348] APA, *DSM-5*, 59.

[349] Barkley, *NoSC*, 35.

[350] ADHD is one of the most researched theories (Barkley, *NoSC*, 29-46).

[351] Petersen, *Our Daily Meds,* 106.

[352] Education Reporter, *Newspaper of Education Rights* no. 263 (Dec. 2007): 1.

But if the youngest children in the classroom are the most diagnosed as having ADHD,[353] then one should expect the youngest children's brains to be "underdeveloped" compared with his/her older classmates.

Despite this fact, studies are continually published that make it seem as though ADHD is a valid neurological disorder. The largest and most recent study done to date — which evaluated brain volume in thousands of children — was published in the prestigious medical journal, *The Lancet*,[354] and immediately after, articles were written across the world claiming that the "smaller brain theory for ADHD had been confirmed." *Medscape*, for example, asserted:

> The structure of the brain of children with attention-deficit/hyperactivity disorder (ADHD) differs from that of normally developing children — a difference that is clearly visible on MRI. This suggests that ADHD should be considered a neurologic disorder, researchers say. In the largest imaging study of ADHD conducted to date, investigators found that five regions of the brain were slightly smaller in children with ADHD compared to children without the disorder.[355]

At least the author of this particular entry admits that the study is not actually conclusive. The problem described is immaturity and not neurological impairment as is "suggested." The *Lancet* specifically states,

---

[353] Frances, "Most Active Kids."

[354] Martin Hoogman, et al., "Subcortical brain volume differences in participants with attention deficit hyperactivity disorder in children and adults: a cross-sectional mega-analysis," *The Lancet* (February February 15, 2017): http://www.thelancet.com/pdfs/journals/lanpsy/PIIS2215-0366(17)30049-4.pdf: accessed 24 February 2017.

[355] Megan Brooks, "Confirmed: ADHD Brain is Different," *Medscape Online* (February 23, 2017): http://www.medscape.com/viewarticle/876133?nlid= 113034_2051&src=WNL_mdplsnews_170224_mscpedit_psyc&uac=264124BV&spon=12&impID=1296964&faf=1: accessed 24 February 2017.

> Exploratory lifespan modeling suggested a delay of maturation and a delay of degeneration, as effect sizes were highest in most subgroups of children (<15 years) versus adults.[356]

In other words, as a child matures so too does his/her brain.

But it is widely understood that children mature at different rates and that neurological variances are expected:

> Although brain development is subject to significant individual variation, most experts suggest that the brain is fully developed by age 25. For some people, brain development may be complete prior to age 25, while for others it may end after age 25. The mid-20s or "25" is just an average age given as checkpoint for when the brain has likely become mature.[357]

Add to this fact that, according to the *DSM-5*, most children diagnosed as having ADHD are boys who mature at a slower pace than girls.[358] This research does not prove in any way that there exists a valid brain malfunction. Those who make such claims and label children as having ADHD should at least wait until a boy turns 25 and his brain reaches maturity.

Brain scans may in fact show that there is a problem in the brain, but they are unable to offer an explanation of what caused the brain's atrophy, impairment, or variances. Psychiatrist Peter Breggin remarks,

> Common sense and experimental evidence indicate that certain passionate states are associated with corresponding changes in brain

---

[356] Hoogman, "Subcortical brain volume differences," *The Lancet*.

[357] "At what Age is the Brain Fully Developed?" *Mental Health Daily* (February 2, 2015): http://mentalhealthdaily.com/2015/02/18/at-what-age-is-the-brain-fully-developed/: accessed 24 February 2017.

[358] "ADHD is more frequent in males than in females . . . with a ratio of approximately 2:1" (APA, *DSM-5*, 63). "Female brains develop about on average two years earlier than male brains, so you're more likely to have a late developing male brain than female" (Brain Maturity Extends Well Beyond Teen Years," *NPR Online* (October 10, 2011): http://www.npr.org/templates/story/story.php?storyId=141164708: accessed 24 February 2017.

function. Prolonged mental stresses of almost any kind, as well as psychical trauma or stress, cause the brain to stimulate increased production of certain hormones, such as steroids. Conversely, if you are relaxing right now, your steroid output may decline. *In each of these instances the mental state influenced the brain, rather than vice versa.* We find the same results examining brain waves. If you are excited with intense focus of your attention, your brain is likely to generate fast low-amplitude electrical waves on the electroencephalogram (EEG). If you then relax, the EEG will show alpha waves — slower, with a higher amplitude in each case, *the mental state influenced how the brain reacted, not vice versa* [emphasis added].[359]

These researchers have chosen to ignore the empirical evidence showing that a child's negative thoughts and responses to experiences can and do regularly impair and atrophy the brain.

Furthermore, as discussed in the previous chapter, the brains of sleep deprived children and those with who struggle holding their attention look exactly the same in brain scans.[360] Likewise, the study admits that a good portion of the children in the study were taking psychoactive substances,[361] which are known to cause brain atrophy. There is simply no way to know objectively what causes the brain to be smaller or show impairment in a brain scan. Materialists, though, still insist that the brain is the fundamental cause of attentional problems.

Not only do the current neurological studies fail to prove causality of differentials in both brain development and brain size, but the studies are also replete with invalidating factors. One such invalidating factor is the presence of stimulant medications in the children tested:

Neuroscientists have made much-touted progress in understanding the brain, but still that understanding is extremely superficial. We have no idea, really, how the brain does any of the amazing things it

[359] Breggin, *Toxic Psychiatry*, 112.

[360] Judith Owens, "A Clinical Overview of Sleep and Attention-Deficit/Hyperactivity Disorder in Children and Adolescents," *Journal of the Canadian Academy of Child and Adolescent Psychiatry* 18, no. 2, (2009): 92–102.

[361] Hoogman, "Subcortical brain volume differences," *The Lancet*.

does (beyond the simplest reflexes), but we do have some ideas about which parts of the brain are most involved in which functions. . . . Not surprisingly, therefore, researchers looking for brain correlates of ADHD have focused on the prefrontal cortex and on dopamine. The results of such research are highly variable from lab to lab, with much controversy resulting. Also, the results are often confounded because most of the people in the ADHD groups have been treated with stimulant drugs, either at the time of study or in the past, so it is not clear if any brain difference observed is a correlate of the ADHD itself or is caused by long-term effects of the drug.[362]

Gray further explains that psychotropic drugs affect both the physicality of the brain and the results of the studies[363] and concludes his findings by stating,

> So far no biological marker of ADHD has been found that is sufficiently reliable to be used as an aid in diagnosis. The studies of brain differences are interesting, but they have no bearing at all on the question of whether ADHD is a disorder or a normal personality variation. All personality variations have a basis in the brain. Of course they do. The brain controls all of behavior, so any difference that is reflected in behavior must exist in the brain.[364]

Brain scans do not prove ADHD's existence, but rather they provide evidence that all behavior physically manifests first in the brain—a point on which all sides agree. Renowned pediatrician William Carey also sees the lack of empirical guidelines in research as a problem that must be addressed to validate claims that ADHD is caused by brain malfunctions. He insists that there exists

> an absence of clear evidence that the ADHD symptoms are related to brain malfunction. . . . Chemical testing and brain imaging techniques have not proven anything. The associations

---

[362] Gray, "ADHD Personality."

[363] Similar studies show that Ritalin physically atrophies rats' brains (Menhard, *Facts about Ritalin,* 53).

[364] Gray, "ADHD Personality."

demonstrated so far have been inconsistent and are not clear as to cause, association, or consequence of the symptoms.[365]

Though scientists search for biological answers in neurochemistry, many clinicians acknowledge that being human consists of more than mere brain sizes or measurable chemicals.[366] Alvin Poussaint, professor of psychiatry at Harvard University, frankly admits, "I don't think anything is ever going to be strictly biological that has to do with the brain."[367] People are more than biological animals or mere material masses, and their moral behaviors are more than mere products of brainwaves that can be pharmaceutically adjusted.

Chemical Imbalances

Another popular claim associated with neuropsychology is that ADHD is caused by a chemical imbalance. This popular secular theory is based on the cause/effect principle; as Dr. Paul Wender — known as the "Dean of ADHD"[368] since he was one of the first psychiatrists (in 1971) to theorize that the child's maladaptive behaviors were genetically caused — notes: "Medication can be regarded as a form of replacement therapy; that is, it *apparently* [emphasis added] supplies chemicals that are lacking or causes the body to create more of the missing

---

[365] "What to Do about the ADHD Epidemic," *American Academy of Pediatrics: Developmental and Behavioral Pediatrics Newsletter* (Autumn 2003): 6-7; http://www.ahrp.org/children/CareyADHD0603.php.

[366] Stephen Post in *Generation RX*, DVD, directed by Kevin P. Miller (Vancouver: Common Radius Films, 2008), 5:40.

[367] Ibid., 5:07.

[368] Http://www.webmd.com/paul-h-wender; accessed 5 July 2012.

chemicals. "[369] The presumed chemical imbalance is also the major argument for why secularists consider psychotropic drugs necessary to treat ADHD.[370] Dr. Wender explains the logic that many clinicians use to arrive at this conclusion:

> The widespread effect of stimulant medication on various psychological functions has led child psychiatrists to believe that the brain chemistry of people with ADHD is in some ways different from that of others.[371]

By claiming that an ADHD child's brain and its associated neuro-chemicals are somehow abnormal, psychopharmacologists can seemingly turn a non-physical problem into a biological disease[372] and sell an alleged biological remedy.

Though psychiatry once asserted that the chemical imbalance theory was a valid etiology, the lack of empirical evidence, the complexity of the brain, the absence of a measurable standard of normal chemical levels, and the failed attempts to balance the brain have left most prominent psychiatrists disowning such a fraudulent idea. In fact, Ronald Pies, editor in chief of the prestigious *Psychiatric Times*, explains how so many people have been deceived into thinking mental illnesses — like ADHD — are caused by missing or imbalanced chemicals:

> I am not one who easily loses his temper, but I confess to experiencing markedly increased limbic activity whenever I hear someone proclaim, "Psychiatrists think all mental disorders are due to a chemical imbalance!" In the past 30 years, I don't believe I have ever heard a knowledgeable, well-trained psychiatrist make such a

---

[369] Wender, *ADHD*, 69.

[370] Ibid., 65.

[371] Ibid., 72-75.

[372] Gray, "ADHD Personality."

preposterous claim, except perhaps to mock it. On the other hand, the "chemical imbalance" trope has been tossed around a great deal by opponents of psychiatry, who mendaciously attribute the phrase to psychiatrists themselves. And yes — the "chemical imbalance" image has been vigorously promoted by some pharmaceutical companies, often to the detriment of our patients' understanding. In truth, the "chemical imbalance" notion was always a kind of urban legend — never a theory seriously propounded by well-informed psychiatrists.[373]

While he shifts the blame off of psychiatrists, he later admits that many psychiatrists purposely spread this false claim to their patients in order to "best help them."[374]

The chemical imbalance theory has no validity. Just as secularism applies a non-existent standard of normal development to each diagnosis of ADHD, it also applies a non-existent standard of chemical levels in the brain (i.e., "chemical imbalances," specifically in the neurotransmitters, e.g., dopamine) as a potential etiology of ADHD. Not only do brain chemical levels differ between individuals — rendering a standard level of each brain chemical impossible, but chemicals also fluctuate at high levels in each person (between different emotions, activities, and mental processes) and make so-called normal levels of brain chemicals immeasurable.[375] David Burns of Stanford University, as quoted by Petersen, stresses that,

---

[373] Ronald Pies, "Psychiatry's New Brain-Mind and the Legend of the 'Chemical Imbalance,'" *Psychiatric Times*, July 11, 2011, http://www.psychictrictimes.com/blogs/psychiatry-new-brain-mind-and-legend-chemical-imbalance. It is widely understood within psychiatry that the chemical imbalance theory is false, yet for decades, the theory was spread as dogma. For further study on the theory of chemical imbalance, see Daniel R. Berger II, *Mental Illness: The Necessity for Dependence* (Taylors, SC: Alethia International Publications, 2016), 27-3.

[374] Ronald Pies, "Doctor, Is My Mood Disorder Due to a Chemical Imbalance?" *Psych Central*, http://psychcentral.com/blog/archives/2011/08/04/doctor-is-my-mood-disorder-due-to-a-chemical-imbalance/.

[375] Rosemond and Ravenel, *Diseasing of America's Children*, 64-65.

We cannot measure brain serotonin levels in living human beings, so there is no way to test this theory. Some neuroscientists would question whether the theory of chemical imbalance is even viable, since the brain does not function in this way, as a hydraulic system.[376]

In the documentary, *Generation RX*, psychiatrist Peter Breggin also reveals his concern with psychiatry's claim of chemical imbalance:

> It's quite ironic actually, because the only imbalances that we know of in the brains of people called mental patients are the ones inflicted on them by the psychiatric drugs. How ironic: we make a false claim that they have chemical imbalances and then we give them chemical imbalances.[377]

Doctors and scientists simply cannot know if or when a chemical is imbalanced, and a growing number are abandoning the false theory. Despite this fact, many pediatricians are still explaining a child's bad behavior with the worn-out and disproven chemical imbalance theory.[378]

Abnormal Genes

Besides the neurological/chemical etiological claims, there also exists the popular genetic claim.[379] Though Barkley leads the way in pronouncing ADHD to be both neurological and genetic, he also acknowledges that "far more research is needed before we can be as sanguine about the biological nature of ADHD as we might like to be."[380] He further admits that "no evidence

---

[376] Petersen, *Our Daily Meds*, 105.

[377] *Generation RX*, 7:10.

[378] See Berger, *Mental Illness: The Necessity for Dependence*.

[379] Monastra, *Parenting a Child with ADHD*, 39.

[380] Barkley, *NoSC*, 32.

exists to show that ADHD is the result of abnormal chromosomal structures," yet he insists that heredity is a validated etiology for ADHD.[381]

Other prominent psychiatrists, though, admit that no single gene will ever be linked to any mental impairment. Former APA president, Jeffery Lieberman (who oversaw the *DSM-5*), recognizes that claiming a defective gene as a valid etiology for mental illness is not scientifically sound:

> One of the most promising arenas of research is genetics. It is virtually certain that no single gene alone is responsible for any particular mental illness, but through increasingly powerful genetic techniques we are starting to understand how certain patterns or networks of genes confer levels of risk.[382]

The single gene theory — which has been claimed by secularists for centuries as determining one's thoughts and causing mental illness — is now admitted to be false. In its place, psychiatrists speculate about a new theory of genetic patterns — hoping still to someday find a way to link mental processes with genetic variances. But many psychiatrists are admitting that genes have nothing to do with what is being called ADHD. Highly regarded psychologist Jerome Kagan — who began research on the construct of ADHD in the 1960s — offers a useful analogy:

> There's a place in a large city with very bad drinking water, and kids are always getting sick with dysentery. So you keep treating the dysentery, but meanwhile it would be much better to clean up the drinking water....The drugs work on the dysentery for about 48 hours, but you're not treating the problem. *And the problem is not genetic* [emphasis added].[383]

---

[381] Ibid., 37.

[382] Lieberman, *Shrinks*, 306.

[383] Pettus, "Psychiatry by Prescription: Do Psychotropic Drugs Blur the Boundaries between Illness and Health?" *Harvard Magazine Online*.

Despite clear statements to the contrary, many people choose to believe the false idea that the construct of ADHD is a genetic problem.

Neuroscientist Niall McLaren emphasizes that the dramatic increase in diagnoses of ADHD over the last twenty years (if ADHD were truly genetically caused) indicates either a serious genetic flaw in the population or exposes ADHD to simply be a fluid construct — nothing more than a created idea. McLaren later states that the dramatic rise of children diagnosed as having ADHD exposes just how easy it is for psychiatrists to create "a new disease" out of normal behavior and blame it on an invisible connection between the mind and a person's genes:

> In fact, genetic diseases don't increase by 900% in one generation, so something else is happening. For an example of that "something else," look no further than this gem: a New Disease. Not satisfied with snagging 15% of the juvenile population and putting them on drugs, at a national cost of about $9billion a year, the bounds of pathology are to be stretched again, further eroding the concept of normality. Psychiatrists and psychologists have decided that the quiet little day-dreamers in school are mentally ill: "Called sluggish cognitive tempo, the condition is said to be characterized by lethargy, daydreaming and slow mental processing. By some researchers' estimates, it is present in perhaps two million children."[384]

Without normalcy objectively defined, genetic variances can be blamed for all types of human behavior and mindsets, and every child — whether hyper, calm, or somewhere in between — can be fit into one or more of the psychiatric constructs.

Genetic studies could potentially link genes to neurological patterns and brain variances, but scientific tools can never study the invisible aspects of attention sourced in the heart. There is no scientific means nor will there ever be to objectively link a gene or cluster of genes with desire, faith, motive, fear, or selfishness to name a few. Genes/chromosomes are physical, whereas the

---

[384] McLaren, "Serotonin Hypothesis of Depression."

mind and thoughts are spiritual. Just as materialists have failed to explain the brain-mind connection, the gene-mind connection poses an equally failing effort to explain mental impairment and distress. There is also a great amount of evidence in the field of epigenetics, which shows that genes are not fixed and can be turned on and off by one's thoughts.[385] Proverbs 3:7-8 states the same truth: "Be not wise in your own eyes; fear the LORD, and turn away from evil. It will be healing to your flesh and refreshment to your bones." Even if ADHD were hypothetically shown to be a valid biological disorder, both Scripture and science make it clear that changing one's faith (thoughts) will directly alter that person's physical nature. The potential scientific discovery of damaged genes, atrophied brains, and diminished neuronal activity can just as easily be attributed to a child's poor thinking as they can be claimed as causes of bad behavior.

What the genetic theory amounts to, then, is a new form of eugenics, which is not as much interested in people's physical characteristics and heritage as it is in their character traits and impairing mindsets, emotions, and behavior.[386] In spite of researchers' failure to discover an ADHD gene or specific chromosome, some psychiatrists are sure it exists and continue to market their spurious claim.

Alternative Theories

In addition to these widely held hypotheses, less-accepted theories of ADHD etiology also exist such as dietary causes,[387]

---

[385] Berger, *Reality of the Physical Nature*, 110-15.

[386] Ibid., 113-19.

[387] Elaine Fletcher-Janzen and Cecil Reynolds, *Disorders Diagnostic Desk Reference* (Hoboken, NJ: John Wiley and Sons, Inc., 2003), 74.

exposure to lead at an early age,[388] maternal smoking,[389] over-stimulation (e.g., excessive TV viewing),[390] premature births,[391] and theories such as "symmetric tonic neck reflex."[392] The *DSM* acknowledges that a history of child abuse, drug exposure, lead poisoning, infections, or low birth weight could all be present in these children's lives, yet the *DSM* does not hold that these conditions cause ADHD. Psychiatry's claim to know what does not cause ADHD (environmental issues, medical issues, diets, sleep patterns, etc.)[393] implies that they are sure of its cause. Clinicians admit, however, that empirical evidence to prove ADHD etiology still eludes them:[394]

> The exact mechanism underlying ADD remains unknown. There is no single lesion of the brain, no single neurotransmitter system, no

---

[388] J.M. Braun et al., "Exposures to Environmental Toxicants and Attention Deficit Hyperactivity Disorder in U.S. Children," *Environmental Health Perspectives* 12 (December 2006): 114.

[389] "Bad Behavior 'Linked to Smoking,'" BBC News, http://news.bbc.co.uk/2/hi/health/4727197.stm.

[390] Weiss, "Babies and TV."

[391] Christian Nordqvist, "Premature Babies Much More Likely to Have ADHD," http://www.medicalnewstoday.com/articles/ 44574.php; accessed 18 September 2010.

[392] Nancy E. O'Dell and Patricia A. Cook, *Stopping ADHD: A Unique and Proven Drug-Free Program for Treating ADHD Children and Adults* (New York: Avery Publishers, 2004). Their entire book proposes a theory which states that children who did not learn to crawl lack control over their bodies and behaviors, and thus ADHD is the result. This theory promotes a form of behavior modification.

[393] Ibid.

[394] Barkley, *NoSC*, 29.

single gene we have identified that triggers ADD. The precise workings of the brain that underlie ADD have so far escaped us, in part due to the extraordinary complexity of the attentional system.[395]

Scientists must continue to search for causes of maladaptive behavior,[396] since many believe that justification of the construct's continued existence depends on this discovery — or at least the never-ending search to make the construct appear scientific. When it comes to etiologies of ADHD, determining what causes the alleged disease is not a matter of science but of faith.

The Biblical Perspective

Unlike secular theories based on evolutionary thought, Scripture declares that a person's spiritual heart/mind controls his/her moral behavior; the spiritual heart is the foundational problem.[397] Solomon emphasized to his son the need to diligently guard his heart since from the heart proceed the issues of life (Proverbs 4:23).[398] Solomon's deliberate choice of words depicts a city gate which controls traffic and illustrates how the

---

[395] Hallowell and Ratey, *Driven to Distraction*, 269.

[396] Barkley, *NoSC*, 37-41.

[397] Peter Steveson writes about guarding the heart (Proverbs 4:23) that "the concern for the keeping of one's own mind [heart] should transcend any other self-protecting act. This is so because the mind is the source of every thought, every word, and every action of man" (*Proverbs*, 63).

[398] Longman sees the comparison between Proverbs 4:23 and 3:1. The child is to protect or guard his heart. This is not merely a defensive position against wrong doctrine, but a protection of the stored wisdom (to ponder). He states, "Protection means to observe the commands that are to be deeply embedded in the son." This also reveals that guarding or protecting the heart means to remember or keep in mind to the point of obedience (*Proverbs*, 131).

spiritual mind controls moral behavior (Proverbs 4:23-27).[399] The gate of the heart controls the mouth (24), the eyes (21, 25), the feet (26-27), and the ears (20) – the very anatomy over which those diagnosed as having ADHD lack self-control. Yet, while the heart controls behavior, behavior also controls the mind. In other words, the afore-mentioned behavior of giving attention — namely guarding the heart, seeing, and hearing when coupled with desire and faith — shapes a person's character. Waltke recognizes this paradox:

> Since the heart is the center of all the person's emotional-intellectual-religious-moral activity, it must be safe-guarded above all things (4:23). Paradoxically, the eye and ear are gates to the heart and shape it (see 2:2; 4:21-23;), but at the same time the heart decides what they will hear and see (4:25-26).[400]

The New Testament also recognizes the spiritual heart as responsible for and the source of all its own behaviors: "what comes out of the mouth proceeds from the heart, and this defiles a person" (Matthew 15:18). Ryle emphasizes, "With respect to the human heart our Lord declares in these verses that it is the true source of all sin and defilement."[401] The Bible indicates that moral behavior always comes from a person's spiritual heart/mind rather than biology.

---

[399] Waltke notes that cartographers used the same phrase to describe "'exits' of a city" such as in Ezekiel 48:30, and he also recognizes other usages such as the psalmist's use in describing his escape in Psalm 68:20 which lead him to conclude: "The point here is that the heart is the source of the body's activities" (1-15, 298). Similarly, Whybray translates "from it flow the springs" as "literally, 'the outgoings' of life" (R.N. Whybray, *Proverbs*, New Century Bible Commentary [Grand Rapids: InterVarsity, 1996], 82). Kidner also notes that the issues of life are those things which both enter the man (20-22) and flow out of the man ("'the outgoings'; RSV: *the springs*") (*Proverbs*, 68).

[400] Waltke, *1-15*, 92.

[401] Ryle, *Matthew*, 128.

Children are not born paying attention rightly and must have their eyes, ears, and values trained to do so. That children struggle with giving attention and behaving in a way that is self-centered, uncontrolled, and maladaptive is not indicative of a biological illness, and there is no need to desperately search for a biological etiology to explain such behavior apart from God's precise explanation. These moral behaviors, as Scripture clearly explains, are prominent characteristics of all children's depraved/foolish and spiritual minds.

The Psychostimulant Prescriptions

The claim that psychotropic drugs enable a child to have self-control and to behave better, coupled with a noticeable change in behavior and academic performance when psychostimulants are consumed has convinced many people that ADHD is a valid disease and that drugs provide the best treatment/therapy. The case has already been made that ADHD is a construct and not an illness, disorder, or an abnormality, but the seemingly positive changes from consuming psychoactive substances has led many people to believe that ADHD is a medical condition and that psychostimulants are medicines that heal or reverse biological impairments/defects. But are psychostimulants actually medicines that treat a disease, or are they substances that perturb/attack normal (even healthy) neurological functions in the consumer to bring about the observable effects? Many clinicians have come to realize that being able to control behavior with chemicals in no way validates behavior as a disease:

> Chemical remedies thus play a role in measuring and defining mental disorders . . . . if clinicians' mere ability to treat symptoms identifies something as illness, disease categories will continue to

146

expand while doctors' understanding of what they are treating will remain imprecise.[402]

The fact that drugs — whether illicit or prescribed — blunt, restrain, and change behavior with powerful drugs does not prove ADHD to be a disease.

There are two main types of psychostimulants which are regularly given to children said to have ADHD: methylphenidates and amphetamines.[403] Within these two groups there exist various name brands — each with their slight differences and some with unique release mechanisms. Yet, all of these drugs are more alike than different. These substances are also marketed as safe and effective, but they are, in truth, categorized by the FDA as being some of the most dangerous and addictive legal drugs available.[404]

The Drugs' True Action

Although psychostimulants are prescribed by licensed medical doctors, approved by the FDA as medicines, and advertised as an effective treatment for ADHD, psychostimulants are actually chemical agents that attack the

---

[402] Pettus, "Psychiatry by Prescription: Do Psychotropic Drugs Blur the Boundaries between Illness and Health?" *Harvard Magazine Online*.

[403] Tranquilizers (which are better known as antipsychotics) are also sometimes prescribed to children (Megan Brooks, "Antipsychotics Frequently Part of a kid's ADHD Treatment," *Medscape Psychiatry Online*, January 20, 2017, http://www.medscape.com/viewarticle/874722?nlid= 112206_2051&src=WNL_mdplsnews_170127_mscpedit_psyc&uac=264124BV&spon=12&impID=1279804&faf=1; accessed 25 January 2017).

[404] Drug Enforcement Administration, http://www.justice.gov/ dea/druginfo/ds.shtml. See also Robert Whitaker, *Anatomy of an Epidemic*, 222-28.

nervous system and impair normal neurological functions.
Former NIMH full-time consultant and professor of psychiatry
at Harvard University, Peter Breggin, explains,

> All psychoactive drugs specifically impair the frontal lobes because
> they are among the most vulnerable areas in the brain and because
> the widespread disruption of neurotransmitters inevitably has a
> negative impact on them. As we examine the remaining categories of
> psychiatric drugs, keep in mind that all of them over time will
> impair frontal lobe function and produce a degree of apathy and
> indifference, with a related loss in quality of life.[405]

Ritalin, for example, has been a popular methylphenidate
prescription taken by millions of children, but Ritalin does not
treat an invisible disease; instead, the drug "binds to dopamine
transporters and *inhibits* dopamine reuptake [emphasis
added]."[406] Dopamine is the neurochemical that helps produce
the biological effects of pleasure,[407] and dopamine receptors are
impaired when psychostimulants enter the blood stream. Robert
Whitaker explains,

> Given that the biology of ADHD remains unknown [it does not
> exist], it is fair to say that Ritalin and other ADHD drugs "work" by
> perturbing neurotransmitter systems. Ritalin could best be described
> as a dopamine reuptake inhibitor. At a therapeutic dose, it blocks 70
> percent of the "transporters" that remove dopamine from the
> synaptic cleft and bring it back into the presynaptic neuron. Cocaine
> acts on the brain in the same way.[408]

---

[405] Peter Breggin, "Rational Principles of Psychopharmacology for
Therapists, Healthcare Providers and Clients," *Journal of Contemporary
Psychotherapy* 46 (2016): 3.

[406] Joseph Martin, Daniel Lowenstein, and Stephen Hauser, *Harrison's
Principles of Internal Medicine*, 16th ed. (New York: McGaw-Hill, 2005), 2340.

[407] Ibid., 2346. See also "Ritalin and Cocaine: The Connection and the
Controversy," University of Utah Health Sciences, http://learn.genetics.
utah.edu /content/addiction/ritalin/.

[408] Whitaker, *Anatomy of an Epidemic*, 221.

Psychostimulants are typically "dopamine agonists,"[409] which means that they work against the nervous system to produce down regulation or impairment. This perturbing of the nervous system is claimed to be the therapeutic effect. But the therapeutic effect does not heal the body; rather, it blocks normal healthy neurological function and "crushes behavior."[410] Psychiatrist Peter Breggin explains,

> All drugs that impact on the brain and mind "work" by partially disabling the brain and mind. No psychoactive substance corrects biochemical imbalances or any other real and presumed defects, deficits or disorders of the brain and mind, and none improve the function of the brain or mind. The so-called therapeutic effect is always a disability. The brain-disabling principle is key to understanding psychopharmacology and the unfortunate plight of so many patients. Because of the toxic effects of psychiatric drugs on the brain and body, they are vastly reducing the quality of life, health, and lifespan of millions of people.[411]

The true action of psychostimulants is not to change behavior, provide self-control, or increase attentiveness; it is, rather, to perturb the monoamine neurotransmitter dopamine (and others) which heightens pleasure and produces a state of euphoria or "transcendence." Transcendence is a mental/spiritual state which is in part defined as going beyond what is normal or the limits possible:

> Exceeding usual limits; extending or lying beyond the limits of ordinary experience; being beyond the limits of all possible experience and knowledge; being beyond comprehension; *transcending the universe or material existence* [emphasis added].[412]

---

409 "Altering Consciousness with Psychoactive Drugs," University of Minnesota, http://open.lib.umn.edu/intropsyc/chapter/5-2-altering-consciousness-with-psychoactive-drugs/.

410 Breggin, "Rational Principles of Psychopharmacology," 3.

411 Ibid., 2-3.

412 http://www.merriam-webster.com/dictionary/transcendent.

If normalcy is impairment, lack of self-control, misplaced attention, poor academic performance, and foolish behavior (as seen in the last chapter), then taking these stimulants in attempt to go beyond the normal depraved state (to transcend), explains why these drugs are so widely used. Stimulants are to the nervous system (the senses) what steroids are to the muscular system.

Although one might think that smaller dosages of psychoactive medications do not cause sensory highs or transcendence, in actuality, even small dosages of powerful psychostimulant increase the feeling of pleasure and mental alertness.[413] Dr. Breggin states,

> Many people do not develop a "high" from amphetamines, but their feeling of increased well-being may be a subtle high. Relatively small doses of any [psycho-] stimulant, including amphetamine or cocaine, may increase the sense of well-being without producing a gross high or euphoria.[414]

---

[413] It must be noted that caffeine is also a stimulant. However, caffeine belongs to a family of drugs called *methylxanthines* (which means that caffeine is a mild stimulant found in nature in contrast to synthetic or manufactured stimulants like amphetamines or methylphenidates), and it is not a powerful mind-altering substance. In other words, caffeine cannot cause transcendence or take control of the mind as cocaine, LSD, and many amphetamines and methylphenidates do. Instead, caffeine heightens mental awareness and affects the central nervous system: "Both caffeine and nicotine are classified as secondary stimulants because, unlike drugs such as amphetamines and cocaine, they affect the sympathetic nervous system more than the central nervous system. Also, unlike stimulants that are abused for recreational purposes, caffeine and nicotine produce only an increased energy level but not a feeling of intoxication" ("Stimulant Drugs - Caffeine and nicotine, Stimulants Used for Therapeutic Purposes, Abuse of Illegal Stimulants," *JRank Articles,* http://psychology.jrank.org/pages/615/Stimulant-Drugs.html#ixzz4OF8XIqXs).

[414] Breggin, *Toxic Psychiatry,* 432.

This effect also exposes why so many people abuse psychostimulants: these drugs do not just selectively block dopamine transmitters in children labeled as having ADHD; they affect every consumer in this way. One senior researcher on ADHD at the National Institutes of Health (NIH), Judith Rapoport, asserts,

> These drugs have the same effect in healthy and ADHD kids. Amphetamines seem to improve anyone's attention — whether they have a problem or not. Whatever the task is, you do it better. Football players and racehorses have known this for a long time.[415]

Pediatric psychiatrist Leon Eisenberg — often considered to be the "creator of ADHD" based upon his research into using drugs to treat children's behavior — is quoted in Harvard's medical journal as stating, "The trouble is that the drugs work across the board. Dexedrine makes not only hyperkinetic kids mellower and less distractable [sic], but normal kids as well."[416] Psychiatrist Joanna Moncrieff remarks about all psychoactive substances,

> Although there is variation in individuals' response to all drugs, psychoactive drugs produce their characteristic range of effects in anyone who takes them, regardless of whether or not they have a psychological problem. Most psychoactive drugs also have physical effects, and the physical and mental effects are often inextricably linked. Alcohol and benzodiazepines, for example, produce a state of both physical and mental relaxation, and *stimulant drugs, like amphetamines and cocaine, stimulate mental processes like attention and alertness, as well as physical processes like increasing heart rate and blood pressure* [emphasis added].[417]

---

[415] Judith Rapoport quoted in Ray Moynihan's interview with Judith Rapoport, "Dextro-amphetamine: Its Cognitive and Behavioral Affects in Normal Prepubertal Boys," *Science* 199 (1978): 560-63.

[416] Pettus, "Psychiatry by Prescription: Do Psychotropic Drugs Blur the Boundaries between Illness and Health?" *Harvard Magazine Online*.

[417] Moncrieff, *Bitterest Pills*, 11.

Other professionals, like psychologist John Rosemond and pediatrician Bose Ravenel, agree that psychostimulants have "the same effect on both the hyperactive child and the non-hyperactive individual."[418] This fact is why amphetamines and methylphenidates are regularly consumed as performance-enhancing drugs:

> Drugs like Adderall were once only prescribed to help highly distractible children with attention deficit disorders focus on their school work. Then college students found those drugs, amphetamine-like stimulants, could increase their ability to study. Now a growing number of workers use them to help compete, whether or not they have A.D.H.D.[419]

Students are not just receiving these pills from other students illegally; they are falsely claiming to have ADHD, being diagnosed, and then obtaining a psychostimulant prescription:

> Undergraduates, as well as high school SAT-takers, are increasingly turning to prescription stimulants like Ritalin and Adderall to boost concentration during long study sessions and all-nighters, according to drug abuse experts at the University of Florida, who cite a rise in the number of teen patients they see who openly admit to having conned unnecessary prescriptions from doctors.[420]

Psychostimulants provide the user with a performance enhancement or transcendence beyond their normal state or production. Dr. Breggin explains what is actually taking place when children consume psychostimulants:

> The addictive stimulant drugs given to children disrupt numerous neurotransmitter systems. Does this effect take place only if a child has ADHD? No, the same effect has been studied for many years in normal children, animals, and stimulant addicts (Grahame-Smith

---

[418] Rosemond and Ravenel, *Diseasing of America's Children*, 92.

[419] Elizabeth Herman, "Using Adderall to Get Ahead not to Fight A.D.H.D." *New York Times*, April 21, 2015, http://www.nytimes.com/ roomfordebate/2015 /04/21/using-adderall-to-get-ahead-not-to-fight-adhd; accessed 17 June 2015.

[420] "Risky Ritalin Abuse during College Exam Week," http://ihealthbulletin.com/archive/2007/05/14/risky-ritalin-abuse-during-college-exam-week/; accessed 4 November 2012.

and Aronson 1992, p. 141; Randrup and Munkva 1967; reviewed in Breggin 1999, 2008a, pp. 303–307). At clinical doses of stimulants in monkeys, all spontaneous behavior is reduced and sometimes crushed (Schiorring, 1977, 1979). The monkeys' repertoire of spontaneous behaviors diminishes or disappears including socializing, mutual grooming, playing, and exploring. At the same time, probably due to impact on the basal ganglia, the monkeys develop perseverative behaviors, defined as the repetition of meaningless activities. (In children on stimulants, perseverative behavior manifests as obsessive–compulsive behavior.) Instead of grooming, the monkeys will pick at their own skin; instead of socializing, they will stay by themselves; instead of playing, they will do boring things like chewing on the bars of their cage or fingering pebbles; and instead of exploring, they will pace a corner or stare out their cage. *Stimulants make seemingly good caged animals and they do the same thing to children, making them good caged children at school or at home. They stop their annoying socializing, lose their overall spontaneity, become more docile, and finally show willingness to perform behaviors that to them otherwise seem rote and meaningless* [emphasis added].[421]

Psychostimulants are not magic bullets, and they do not treat the invisible construct of ADHD. These powerful chemicals perturb the nervous system/brain, heighten the senses, and "crush" spontaneous behavior. The drug's true effect is precisely why the highly respected Dr. Allen Frances warns that "we shouldn't want to transform our kids into well behaved, well medicated little zombies."[422]

The Drug's True Nature

Amphetamines and methylphenidates were not created as medicines. Instead, they were synthesized in labs from existing and equally dangerous drugs. For example, the amphetamine Adderall has almost the exact identical chemical structure as methamphetamine, and is known by neuroscientists to produce the same behavioral effects.[423] Carl Hart, associate professor of neuroscience at Columbia University, affirms:

---

[421] Breggin, "Rational Principles of Psychopharmacology," 3-4.

[422] Frances, "Most Active Kids."

[423] Ronald Kuczenski, David S. Segal, Arthur K. Cho, and William Melega, "Hippocampus Norepinephrine, Caudate Dopamine and Serotonin, and'

It's the exact same drug. The only difference is that
methamphetamine has a methyl group attached to it. But we did a
study, along with other people, in which we tested a drug like
Adderall compared to methamphetamine, and they produce
identical effects. They are almost identical chemically in terms of
their chemical structure.[424]

He later notes that the biological and cognitive changes from
consuming these drugs are virtually identical.[425] It is no wonder,
then, that amphetamines like Adderall and Desoxyn (to name a
few) — claimed to treat ADHD — are classified as some of the
most addictive and dangerous drugs.[426] Cognitive neuroscientist
Martha Farah remarks on how addictive stimulant drugs truly
are:

A few years ago Adderall was touted as a "smart pill." But after
research showed little or no improvement in cognition under its
influence, *Adderall is now gaining a reputation as a "productivity pill."*. .
. *On the scales of risk and benefit, the risks of stimulant misuse
weigh more heavily against the benefits in most work contexts than
against survival in war. Second, frequency of use is a major determinant
of addiction risk. Regular use on the job is an invitation to dependence. And
drug dependence is a problem that makes ordinary workplace pressures look
delightful in comparison* [emphasis added].[427]

Behavioral Responses to the Stereoisomers of Amphetamine and
Methamphetamine," *Journal of Neuroscience* 75, no. 2 (February 1995): 1309-17.

[424] Carl Hart, https://www.youtube.com/watch?v=zhdqhIIm4cQ&
feature=youtu.be, min. 5:02-5:30; accessed 2 January 2017.

[425] Carl Hart, https://www.youtube.com/watch?v=VOCsIyIGNls; accessed
2 January 2017.

[426] Nikesh Patel and Robert Sade, "Ethical and Legal Aspects of Prescription
Stimulant Use by Medical Students," *Journal of South Carolina Medical Association*
110, no. 4 (January 2015): 131.

[427] Martha Farah, "The Risk Associated with 'Productivity Pills' Outweigh
the Benefits," *New York Times*, April 21, 2015, http://www.nytimes.com/
roomfordebate /2015/04/21/using-adderall-to-get-ahead-not-to-fight-
adhd/the-risks-associated-with-productivity-pills-outweigh-the-benefits.

Amphetamines are not unique medicines designed to treat alleged ADHD; they are simply mind-controlling drugs.

Take as another example, the methylphenidate Ritalin. The chemical properties and drug action of Ritalin and similar methylphenidates are virtually identical to cocaine.[428] They are so alike, that the prestigious *Journal of the American Medical Association (JAMA)* acknowledges that "Ritalin acts much like cocaine,"[429] and the drug is widely referred to as "kiddie cocaine."[430] Ritalin and many other psychostimulants can easily be considered synthetic cocaine — developed to mimic the 1950 results of cocaine's effect on people's minds and behavior.[431]

The major differences between Ritalin and cocaine lie both in the way they are perceived and classified and also in their method of consumption, which affects how they enter the bloodstream. The differences are not in their chemical structure or effects. The University of Utah's Health Science division notes the significant difference is how these drugs are consumed and thus how they enter the bloodstream. Cocaine is typically snorted or injected, while Ritalin is swallowed in a pill or liquid

---

[428] "Links between Methylphenidate (Ritalin) and Cocaine," http://www.drugrehab.us/news/links-between-ritalin-cocaine/.

[429] B. Vastag, "Pay Attention: Ritalin Acts Much Like Cocaine," *JAMA* 286, no. 8 (Aug 22-29, 2001): 905-6.

[430] "'Kiddie Cocaine': Behavior Drug Ritalin Abused by Children," http://www.cbsnews.com/news/kiddie-cocaine-behavior-drug-ritalin-abused-by-children/.

[431] Cocaine is widely known to be linked to early psychiatry practices and psychopharmacologic theory. For example, "From cocoa leaves came the ingredients to make cocaine, which connect to modern psychiatry" (Steven Moffic, "A Shaman and a Psychiatrist: A Supernatural Story?" *Psychiatric Times*, October 31, 2013, http://www.psychiatrictimes.com/ blogs/shaman-and-psychiatrist-supernatural-story); accessed 2 October 2016).

form.[432] This difference in means of ingestion determines the extent of the drug's effect on the nervous system. Cocaine is a dangerous class I illegal drug and public domain, while Ritalin is a just-as-dangerous class II legal, manufactured, and privately-owned drug. Despite these superficial differences, society in general views one of them as a medicine and the other as a public enemy.

Big Business

Though cocaine and methamphetamines are illegal drugs, their synthetic counterparts — amphetamines and methylphenidates — distributed by psychopharmacologists as legitimate medicines are legal. There is a great amount of money to be made in distributing any psychoactive substance, and many advocacy groups, government agencies, psychiatrists, and even some physicians are making large profits from drug sales. When drugs are claimed to be positively-life-altering medicines — indispensable tools — the stakes become even higher.

The overwhelming amount of money made each year from prescription psychoactive drugs has enabled research, dictated "scientific" conclusions, and funded over-the-top marketing. The APA and many of its psychiatrists, for example, receive large sums of money from often undisclosed partnerships with big pharmaceutical companies. [433] Many psychiatrists — who are considered "experts" or "authorities" in their field — receive large payments in both research and speaking on behalf of Big

---

[432] "Ritalin and Cocaine: The Connection and the Controversy," University of Utah Health Sciences, http://learn.genetics.utah.edu/content/addiction/ritalin/; accessed 2 January 2017.

[433] John Abramson, *Overdosed America: The Broken Promise of American Medicine* (New York: Harper Perennial, 2005), 89-90.

Pharma. Take for example, highly respected professor of psychiatry, chief of pediatric psychopharmacology at Massachusetts General Hospital, and former Harvard professor, Joseph Biederman, who has been instrumental in spreading the idea that psychostimulants are medicines that treat the alleged medical disorder of ADHD. Reporter Alan Schwarz comments,

> Dr. Conners called Dr. Biederman "unequivocally the most published psychopharmacology maven for A.D.H.D.," one who is well known for embracing stimulants and dismissing detractors. Findings from Dr. Biederman's dozens of studies on the disorder and specific brands of stimulants have filled the posters and pamphlets of pharmaceutical companies that financed the work. Those findings typically delivered three messages: The disorder was underdiagnosed; stimulants were effective and safe; and unmedicated A.D.H.D. led to significant risks for academic failure, drug dependence, car accidents and brushes with the law.[434]

But there is a problem with Biederman's research and published/marketed findings:

> Dr. Joseph Biederman, is currently under U.S. Congressional investigation for his undisclosed financial ties to the pharmaceutical industry. Dr.Biederman, whose studies are cited more than 70 times in the draft ADHD guidelines, has confessed to receiving up to US$1.6 million to research and promote specific drugs, clearly a conflict of interest.[435]

It is clear that Beiderman's and many other professionals' findings reflect, not empirical evidence or objective research, but their own financial gains. It is of no surprise, then, to learn that

---

[434] Alan Schwarz, "The Selling of Attention Deficit Disorder," *New York Times,* December 14, 2013, http://www.nytimes. com/2013/12/15/health/the-selling-of-attention-deficit-disorder.html? action=click&contentCollection= Health&module=RelatedCoverage&pgtype=article&region=Marginalia&utm_ca mpaign=Constant+Contact&utm_medium=email&utm_source=January+2015&_r=0; accessed 2 January 2017.

[435] "New Federal ADHD Guidelines Halted due to Undisclosed Drug Company Connections of US Psychiatrist," http://www.cchr.org.au/media-releases/189-new-federal-adhd-guidelines-halted-due-to-undisclosed-drug-company-connections-of-us-psychiatrist.

Biederman is the "most cited scientist on the subject of ADD and ADHD during the past decade."[436] It is largely his studies that have led many to falsely believe that ADHD is "a universal biological condition."[437]

Or take as another example, "internationally recognized authority on ADHD,"[438] author, and speaker Russell Barkley who also "receives or has received research support, acted as a consultant and/or served on a speaker's bureau for Eli Lilly and Company, Shire Pharmaceuticals Group plc, and McNeil Pediatrics."[439] The belief that psychostimulants are medications has come, in large part, from false information being spread by people who stand to make large financial gains to do so.

Many physicians and citizens alike have come to believe that if the FDA approves a drug, it must be safe—that there are no financial factors influencing such judgment. Often, however, drugs are granted approval without proper controls,[440] with fraudulent research,[441] and even with the FDA warnings on many of the psychiatric drugs labels that are approved and regularly prescribed attesting to the extreme dangers of

---

[436] Pettus, "Psychiatry by Prescription: Do Psychotropic Drugs Blur the Boundaries between Illness and Health?" *Harvard Magazine Online.*

[437] Joseph Biederman quoted by Ashley Pettus, Ibid.

[438] "Russell A. Barkley, Ph.D.," http://www.russellbarkley.org/.

[439] "Conflicts of Interest for Practice Parameters Not Listed in Parameter," http://www.aacap.org/AACAP/Resources_for_Primary_Care/Practice_Param eters_and_Resource_Centers/Conflicts_of_Interest_for_Practice_Parameters_Not _Listed_in_Parameter.aspx.

[440] For more on how medications are often granted approval without proper studies, see John Abramson, *Overdosed America.*

[441] See Marcia Angell, *The Truth about the Drug Companies: How They Deceive Us and What to do About It* (New York: Random House, 2005).

consuming these chemicals.[442] Dr. Breggin notes how Adderall was approved by the FDA as a long-term and safe solution for children after only three weeks of clinical trials.[443] It is no wonder, then, that most every professional who writes on the construct of ADHD is concerned with the unknown long-term effects of psychostimulants on children who consume them.[444]

Adverse Effects

Some "side-effects" or "adverse effects" are well known because all prescribed psychostimulants contain "side-effects" listed on the packaging that explain the drug's true action. However, there are also common side-effects that are not disclosed on the drug's label due to the limited research.

For example, because psychostimulants — which create euphoric highs or transcendent states — so perturb the nervous system, many children experience neurological crashes with long-term use. This effect regularly results in the child being diagnosed as having the construct of bipolar, depression, anxiety, and or oppositional defiant disorder. Dr. Robert Whitaker explains how these powerful drugs work against the healthy nervous system and regularly lead children to further diagnoses and subsequent prescriptions:

> Even before the prescribing of Ritalin took hold, it was well known that amphetamines could stir psychotic and manic episodes. . . . There is an even bigger problem with stimulants. They cause children to cycle through arousal and dysphoric states on a daily basis. When a child takes the drug, dopamine levels in the synapse increase, and this produces an aroused state. The child may show increased energy, an intensified focus, and hyperalertness. The child may become anxious, irritable, aggressive, hostile, and unable to

---

[442] Abramson, *Overdosed America*, preface viii.

[443] Breggin, "Rational Principles of Psychopharmacology," 6.

[444] Pliszka, *Treating ADHD and Comorbid Disorders*, 191

sleep. More extreme arousal symptoms include obsessive-compulsive and hypomanic behaviors. But when the drug exits the brain, dopamine levels in the synapse sharply drop, and this may lead to such dysphoric symptoms as fatigue, lethargy, apathy, social withdrawal, and depression. Parents regularly talk of this daily "crash."[445]

Whitaker later writes,

Yet there is an even bigger problem with stimulants. They cause children to cycle through arousal and dysphoric state on a daily basis. When a child takes the drug, dopamine levels in the synapse increase, and this produces an aroused state . . . . In short, every child on a stimulant turns a bit bipolar. [446]

The University of Minnesota published an article which also explains one of the clear long-term effects of a child's use of psychostimulants:

Used in moderation, some stimulants may increase alertness, but used in an irresponsible fashion they can quickly create dependency. A major problem is the "crash" that results when the drug loses its effectiveness and the activity of the neurotransmitters returns to normal. The withdrawal from stimulants can create profound depression and lead to an intense desire to repeat the high . . . . Amphetamines may produce a very high level of tolerance, leading users to increase their intake, often in "jolts" taken every half hour or so. Although the level of physical dependency is small, amphetamines may produce very strong psychological dependence, effectively amounting to addiction. Continued use of stimulants may result in severe psychological depression.[447]

Children whose nervous systems are perturbed long enough with powerful stimulants will inevitably crash; what goes up will eventually come down.

---

[445] Whitaker, *Anatomy of an Epidemic*, 235-37. Whitaker also asserts that "Ritalin and other ADHD medications cause a long list of physical, emotional, and psychiatric adverse effects" (Ibid., 228).

[446] Ibid., 237-38.

[447] "Altering Consciousness with Psychoactive Drugs," University of Minnesota, http://open.lib.umn.edu/intropsyc/chapter/5-2-altering-consciousness-with-psychoactive-drugs/.

The evidence is abundant[448] that psychostimulants (methylphenidates and amphetamines) are clearly not medicine designed to treat a valid illness, but rather, they are synthetic knockoffs of mind-altering and neurologically perturbing illicit drugs. In their 1994 edition of the *Textbook of Psychiatry*, the APA concluded from their studies on psychostimulants that,

> Stimulants do not produce lasting improvements in aggressivity, conduct disorder, criminality, education achievement, job functioning, marital relationships, or long-term adjustment. [449]

Though these substances are FDA approved and regulated, synthesized in a lab, and distributed by valid licensed physicians, these chemicals are not medicines that heal children in any way.[450]

The Scientific Tools

The claim that ADHD is scientifically proven to be a neurodevelopmental disorder is a popular belief. No one on any side of the ADHD construct argues that behavior cannot be observed and even measured, but does this fact make interpretations of behavior scientifically driven? Likewise, everyone understands that the brain is involved in behavior, but how does that prove or disprove that the spiritual mind does or

---

[448] For further study on psychoactive/psychotropic medications, see Berger, *Mental Illness: The Necessity for Dependence.*

[449] Quoted by Peter Breggin, "Psychostimulants in the Treatment of Children Diagnosed with ADHD," *International Journal of Risk and Safety in Medicine* 12 (1993): 3-35.

[450] The information offered in this chapter represents facts from various medical researchers and licensed physicians but is not intended in any way to be taken as medical advice. Going on or off any dangerous substance should be done only under the close supervision of a trained physician.

does not control the brain? In other words, proving scientifically that moral behavior is biologically caused is an impossible task.

Behavior can be studied through the scientific process, but only to a limited degree. There is not nor will there ever be scientific tools that can explain why someone behaves morally or immorally or study motives, desires, faith, fear, and intentions. This is one reason why the judicial system is necessary in every society — as some behavior must be discerned/interpreted within some type of moral system.

As we discussed in the first chapter, the ADHD construct was created by theorists who view humanity as being only biological in nature — denying the spiritual/moral nature. While these evolutionists deny the soul, they are still attempting to study, explain, and treat the soul/psyche within a disease model. At the same time, however, they admit that the concept of the human soul is not something that can be studied with scientific mechanisms. Psychiatrist Sally Satel and psychologist Scott Lilienfeld explain,

> As part of the supernatural realm, immaterial souls and a transcendent God are not amenable to the tools of science. So this strategy is a scientific dead end."[451]

Likewise, Dr. Frances remarks,

> The new biology of the brain would explain behaviors previously considered to be within the abstract provinces of the philosophers and the theologians. It might be impossible to plumb the depths of the human soul, but it should be possible to figure out the structural specifications and electrical connections of the human brain.[452]

Secularists are only able/willing to consider material matter that they can observe and study with scientific tools.

---

[451] Satel and Lilienfeld, *Brainwashed*, 130.

[452] Frances, *Saving Normal*, 125.

Alleged Science of the Mind

The problem with claiming ADHD as scientific is that no one can actually study the immaterial mind through the scientific process. Dr. Bruce Lipton explains,

> Spirit and other metaphysical concepts were devalued as "unscientific" because their truths could not be assessed by the analytic methods of science. The important "stuff" about life and the Universe became the domain of rational scientists.[453]

Children's moral behavior cannot fully be understood or explained through the scientific method.

Why a child's behavior is framed as a medical problem and why science claims to provide answers to children's behavioral problems has more to do with an underlying worldview than it does a physical reality. Evolutionary biologist and geneticist at Harvard University, Richard Lewontin, explains why materialists must attempt to fit every human mindset and experience into a medical/biological framework:

> Our willingness to accept scientific claims that are against common sense is the key to an understanding of the real struggle between science and the supernatural. We take the side of science is spite of the patent absurdity of some of its constructs, in spite of its failure to fulfill many of its extravagant promises of health and life, in spite of the tolerance of the scientific community of unsubstantiated just so stories, because we have a prior commitment, a commitment to materialism. It is not that the methods of and institutions of science somehow compel us to accept a material explanation of the phenomenal world, but on the contrary, that we are forced by our a priori adherence to material causes to create an apparatus of investigation and a set of concepts that produce material explanations, no matter how counterintuitive, no matter how mystifying to the uninitiated. *Moreover, that materialism is absolute, for we cannot allow a Divine Foot in the door* [emphasis added]."[454]

---

[453] Bruce H. Lipton, *The Biology of Belief: Unleashing the Power of Consciousness, Matter and Miracles* (New York: Hay House, 2005), 158.

[454] Richard C. Lewontin, "Billions and Billions of Demons," *New York Review of Books* (January 7, 1997): 31.

The construct of ADHD was created by materialists as an attempt to explain away God's authority and humanity's depravity. The construct of ADHD, therefore, does not explain or define children's true conditions nor is it scientifically sound; instead, the construct explains the theorists' worldview.

Those who claim to study the mind scientifically are either dishonest or they are attempting to reduce the spiritual mind to a biological function. Yet this is the common claim as to why a child's thoughts are biological. Dr. Eric Kandel, an outspoken reductionist, comments,

> Indeed, the underlying precept of the new science of mind is that *all* mental processes are biological. . . . Therefore, any disorder or alteration of those processes must also have a biological basis.[455]

But psychiatrist Niall McLaren offers his own perspective on reductionism,

> [Kandel and other psychiatrists] offer the view that "radical reductionism" will convert psychiatry and psychoanalysis into genuinely scientific fields. I argue instead that reductionism is a restricted model of science that can never account for the entirety of human behavior.[456]

Secular theorists argue that through science every facet of humanity can be explained, approached, and remedied. But nothing could be farther from the truth. Children are not just biological masses, and their spiritual minds and foolish nature can never be objectively studied with scientific tools. Atheist and professor of psychiatry Thomas Szasz acknowledges,

> For the past century or so, psychologists have considered themselves, and have been accepted by others, as empirical scientists whose methods and theories are ostensibly the same as those of the

---

[455] Kandel, *In Search of Memory,* 336.

[456] Niall McLaren, "Kandel's 'New Science of Mind' for Psychiatry and the Limits to Reductionism: A Critical Review." *Ethical Human Psychology and Psychiatry* 10, no. 2 (July 1, 2008).

biologists or physicist. Yet the fact remains that insofar as psychologists address themselves to the questions posed above, their work differs significantly from that of the natural scientist. *Psychologists and psychiatrists deal with moral problems which, I believe, they cannot solve by medical methods* [emphasis added].[457]

No one can search out/study the mind — only God can. Jeremiah 17:9-10 specifically states this point. Finite people can gain limited insight into the immaterial mind only by understanding both God's mind and by learning what He has shared in His Word about humanity's common mental condition.

Alleged Images of the Mind

One of the most prominent ways in which secular theorists have convinced many that ADHD is a medical problem — which science can explain and remedy — is through the use of neuroimaging/brain scans. Many children are now being diagnosed as allegedly having ADHD through fMRIs and EEGs. The common belief is that images of the brain offer a glimpse into the immaterial mind. But no picture of the brain — no matter how complex and detailed — can ever provide an objective explanation or valid glimpse of the mind. Drs. Satel and Liliendfeld assert,

> The illuminated brain cannot be trusted to offer an unfiltered view of the mind. Nor is it logical to regard behavior as beyond an individual's control simply because the associated neural mechanisms can be shown to be 'in the brain.'[458]

In fact, the *DSM* clearly states that neuroimaging is never diagnostic for ADHD:

> *No biological marker is diagnostic for ADHD.* As a group, compared with peers, children with ADHD display increased slow wave electroencephalograms [EEGs], reduced total brain volume on magnetic resonance imaging [MRIs], and possibly a delay in

---

[457] Szasz, *Myth of Psychotherapy*, 9.

[458] Satel and Lilienfeld, *Brainwashed*, 150.

posterior to anterior cortical maturation, *but these findings are not diagnostic* [emphasis added].[459]

Despite the fact that no brain scan can determine if a child can or cannot control moral behavior, a growing number of physicians are directly contradicting the *DSM* and choosing to convince parents that children have ADHD based on pictures of brain wave activity and brain size at a given moment in time. Psychiatrist Sally Satel and psychologist Scott Liliendfeld comment on one such case,

> In a worrisome recent development, a popular nationwide outfit called Amen Clinics promises patients that it can diagnose and treat depression, anxiety, and attention-deficit hyperactivity disorder using brain scans. Its founder, psychiatrist Daniel Amen, oversees an empire that includes book publishing, television shows, and a line of nutritional supplements. Single photon emission computed tomography, SPECT, a nuclear-imaging technique that measures blood flow, is the type of scan favored by Amen. His clinics charge over three thousand dollars for an assessment and, according to the *Washington Post*, grossed about $20 million in 2011. Despite near-universal agreement among psychiatrists and psychologists that scans cannot presently be used to diagnose mental illness, Amen insists that "it will soon be malpractice to not use imaging in complicated cases."[460]

Physical observations—which are key to the scientific process—are limited to only the physical nature in explaining facets of humanity. Dr. Abramson observes:

> Medical researchers observe with increasing sophistication the physical correlates of subjective experience, relying upon galvanic skin response (the lie detector test), electroencephalogram (EEG or brain wave) recordings, and functional MRIs of the brain. These objective observations can help us understand what kind of physical changes take place during different experiences, *but they get us not a bit closer to understanding what it feels like to be that person whose brain we are observing, nor to understanding the meaning of the experience for that person. This is why the extra scientific qualities that define personhood (and contribute so much to the personal decisions that are usually the most important determinants of our health) tend to get discounted or diminished in the world of biomedicine* [emphasis added].[461]

---

[459] APA, *DSM-5*, 61.

[460] Satel and Lilienfeld, *Brainwashed,* 23-24.

[461] Abramson, *Overdosed America,* 207.

By reducing human nature and specifically the mind to biological processes and explanations and producing images of the brain that are claimed to explain behavior, materialists have convinced many people to believe that ADHD is not a construct, but a valid medical/biological condition.[462]

---

[462] For further study on the limitations of neuroimaging and its false promises, see Berger, *Mental Illness: The Reality of the Physical Nature*, and Satel and Lilienfeld, *Brainwashed: The Seductive Appeal of Mindless Neuroscience*.

CHAPTER 5

ADHD HAS A REMEDY

"Your beliefs define your vision of the world; they dictate your
behavior; they determine your emotional responses to other human
beings. . . . They become part of the very apparatus of your mind,
determining your desires, fears, expectations and subsequent
behavior."[463] – Neuroscientist and Atheist, Sam Harris

"Learning how to harness your mind to promote growth is the secret
of life. . . . Of course the secret of life is not a secret at all. Teachers
like Buddha and Jesus have been telling us the same story for
millennia. Now science is pointing in the same direction. It is not our
genes but our beliefs that control our lives. . . . Oh ye of little
belief!"[464] – Former Stanford University researcher, Dr. Bruce Lipton

Despite the clear disagreement on how the *DSM* and
Scripture interpret, approach, and seek to remedy the behaviors
classified in the construct of ADHD, these two antithetical
worldviews at least agree that the identified behaviors in the
construct of ADHD are destructive and must be remedied.
Whereas the American Psychiatric Association (APA) focuses on
various forms of behaviorism and biological remedies, Scripture
focuses on changing the spiritual heart in order to change
behavior.

In addition to agreeing upon the destructive nature of
specific mindsets and behavior, these opposing perspectives of

---

[463] Sam Harris, *The End of Faith: Religion, Terror, and the Future of Reason*
(New York: Norton and Company, 2005), 12.

[464] Lipton, *Biology of Belief*, preface xxvi.

children's nature and bad behavior also agree that parents have an immense responsibility to actively engage their children and help the child to solve his/her attentional and behavioral problems. In most acclaimed secular books on ADHD, authors consistently assert that parents are not responsible for their child's maladaptive behavior. Scripture agrees, and declares that the foolishness bound in each child's heart causes foolish behavior and not something an authority has or has not done.

Both worldviews not only agree that the root problem rests in the child and that the behaviors are detrimental, they also concur that parents are responsible to address these behaviors. Clearly, however, within these two models, what is believed to be the child's true nature and the kind of advice and counsel that is given concerning parent's involvement are very different. So what can/should parents and educators do in order to help a child to change?

The Leading Secular Authorities

Leading secular experts insist that ADHD/ADD has nothing to do with parenting, yet they regularly teach and write about steps parents and educators must take to help children labeled as having ADHD. In other words, these theorists understand that the child's authority must do something to help the child pay attention and behave appropriately. For example, Julian Haber begins her book by stating,

> Parents can use many techniques to modify behavior of children with ADHD and to guide them. Some of these techniques are rule making, positive reinforcements, structured routines, information, color coding, limit setting, consequences, redirection, and posting reminders.[465]

---

[465] Haber, *ADHD*, 7.

Also consider entire books written by Russell Barkley which tell parents what they must specifically do: *Taking Charge of ADHD: The Complete Authoritative Guide for Parents*[466] and *Your Defiant Child: 8 Steps to Better Behavior.*[467] Likewise, Leon Eisenberg—one of the first psychiatrists to proclaim ADHD as a disease based upon his studies on Dexedrine—came to realize that his theory was wrong:

> Leon Eisenberg, Presley professor of social medicine emeritus, was among the first pediatric psychiatrists to conduct research into the biomedical treatment of ADHD in children. He recalls how the introduction, in the early 1960s, of Dexedrine to treat overactive and distracted kids brought a welcome sense of efficacy to doctors and great relief to parents, who could finally attribute their child's problem to an organic disorder, rather than to their own failings. Biological diagnosis also allowed for a more economical approach to treatment, he says: Give a pill and you're done. *But Eisenberg now believes that the short-term studies he conducted on Dexedrine were misleading.* We tracked kids for 12 weeks, and the results were clear and made sense: if you reduce distractibility, learning should improve. Yet subsequent long-term studies have shown that if you don't incorporate a psychosocial approach, *with a focus on family and learning environment, the gains don't hold* [emphasis added].[468]

While attentional struggles are part of every child's nature, it is clear that leading ADHD theorists understand that parents have a responsibility to do things (to discipline/educate) which will produce "better behavior" in their children.

The DSM

Secular authorities on ADHD are not alone in asserting that parents' involvement in their children's lives can minimize or

---

[466] Barkley, *TCoA*.

[467] Russell Barkley and Christine Benton, *Your Defiant Child: 8 Steps to Better Behavior* (New York: Guilford, 2013).

[468] Pettus, "Psychiatry by Prescription: Do Psychotropic Drugs Blur the Boundaries between Illness and Health?" *Harvard Magazine Online.*

eliminate bad behavior. The *DSM* — within the official construct of ADHD itself — recognizes that

> Signs [behaviors] of the disorder may be *minimal or absent* when the individual is *receiving frequent rewards* for appropriate behavior, is *under close supervision* [emphasis added].[469]

As observed in the clear statement of the APA committee who oversaw the construct of ADHD, parents' actions can positively affect children labeled as having alleged ADHD. Likewise, the *DSM-5* task force members rightfully recognize that these children can behave appropriately when they want, are made to do so, or when it is convenient for them. The APA's remark also undermines the spurious claim that children with the ADHD label cannot consider future reward (an alleged flaw in "executive functions" caused by evolution[470]). Clearly these children are able to behave appropriately if they find enough value in doing so or their parents are supervising their lives.

What the APA's statement reveals is not an exception to a speculated disease of ADHD. Rather, this clear statement points out that authority figures are by nature responsible to address the child's naturally foolish and immature heart by teaching the child how to pay attention, to pursue goals, and to behave appropriately. The APA's comments also expose the wrong presuppositional view that children will pay attention rightly and behave appropriately on their own without supervision or guidance. It is worth noting again, however, that the authority is not to blame for a child's misplaced attention or bad behavior; the natural depraved heart is the true cause in all children. A parent's involvement in the child's life, though, is a powerful

---

[469] APA, *DSM-5*, 61.

[470] Russell Barkley, *Executive Functions: What they Are, How They Work, and How They Evolved* (New York: Guilford, 2012).

influence in shaping attentional and behavioral patterns as well as desires and goals.[471]

The Book of Proverbs

Whereas secular theorists attempt to answer the question of how parents can take a child from behaving as the construct of ADHD describes to being normal — however they might define normal, Scripture explains how to take a child from behaving as naturally foolish to being wise (Christ-like). Although these two opposing worldviews/paradigms discuss the exact same mindsets and behavior, they present different interpretations and labels.

As with the APA's claim that the *DSM* is sufficient to accurately describe and explain the child's problems and lead to a remedy, Scripture also informs the believer that its description of human nature and the remedy are entirely profitable to provide wisdom and transform those who believe it from being foolish to being a wise citizen who does good. Second Timothy 3:16-17 states,

> All Scripture is breathed out by God and profitable for teaching, for reproof, for correction, and for training in righteousness, that the man of God may be complete, equipped for every good work.

Whether the child needs to be taught, confronted, corrected, or pointed in the way that he/she should go, the Bible is entirely profitable for changing the child's heart and improving behavior.

Though all of Scripture is profitable to positively transform lives, Proverbs is a unique book that focuses on a child's nature/tendencies, attention, behavior, and desires while

---

[471] See Berger, *Teaching a Child to Pay Attention: Proverbs 4:20-27.*

172

revealing God and His wisdom—the standard of normalcy to which every person needs to be restored. Proverbs states explicitly how parents can teach wisdom. Proverbs 13:1b declares, "A wise son accepts his father's discipline (NASB)." In Hebrew, the text literally says, "'A wise son [is] discipline of a father.'"[472] The commentator James Smith explains what this verse declares: "To make sense of this clause, NIV supplies the verb 'heeds,' NASB 'accepts.' The meaning is that on account of a father's discipline the son is wise."[473] The verse should be understood as a direct answer to the question of how parents and educators can lead children from being foolish to being wise. The way to achieve this important goal is through biblical discipline. The Jewish commentator, Abraham Cohen, explains,

> The Hebrew is literally "a wise son discipline of a father." A.AV. "a wise son heareth his father's instructions" supplies the verb from the second clause. Rashi offers two explanations: verbs like 'ask and loves' have to be understood; or, the meaning is that on account of the father's discipline the son is wise. The latter agrees better with the text: "a son is wise (as the effect of) a father's discipline."[474]

Therefore, parents and educators can make foolish children (labeled as ADHD) wise through biblical discipline.

Since discipline is clearly the vehicle to the biblical answer to the foolish behavior which secularists are content to frame as ADHD, understanding what biblical discipline looks like is vital to helping children. Proverbs not only insists that discipline is the answer, but it also offers specific practical ways to discipline

---

[472] James E. Smith, *The Wisdom Literature and Psalms*, Old Testament Survey Series (Joplin, MO: College Press Pub. Co., 1996), Prov 13:1.

[473] Ibid.

[474] Cohen, *Proverbs*, 80.

all children toward wisdom.[475] The biblical concept of discipline as the path to wisdom is a major theme in Proverbs; seventy percent of all usages of discipline (OT: *musar/yasar*) in Scripture are found in this single book.

A Biblical Definition

The biblical concept of discipline is far different from the secular ideas of behaviorism and punishment. The Bible emphasizes that right discipline takes a person from a current condition toward an established goal; it is the parents' effort to establish a clear path that their child can accept as the way in which he/she should go. More specifically, all children's natural condition/starting point is foolishness (point A; Proverbs 22:15), and all children need to be directed toward God's wisdom/holiness (point B; Proverbs 29:15; see illustration). Herein lies the two aspects of parenting: (1) exposing the child's true nature (reproving, correcting, warning, etc.) and (2) teaching/establishing the goal of change (teaching and instructing):

> The educator's task is both to tear down and to build up; he has to eradicate as well as to implant. There are elements of chaos in the mind of the youth and order has to be restored; his innate tendency is towards folly rather than wisdom, and only the *sebet musar* [discipline] will put a distance between him and folly.[476]

---

[475] The New Testament focuses less on practical aspects of discipline — those are established in Proverbs — and establishes more a theology of discipline (e.g., Ephesians 6:1-3; Hebrews 12:5-13; Titus 2:11-13).

[476] William McKane, *Proverbs: A New Approach* (Philadelphia: Westminster, 1970), 564-65.

Commentator William McKane later explains that both the parent and the child have specific duties in discipline:

> [Discipline] is the emphasis on the intellectual authority of the teacher and the duty of unbroken attentiveness and unquestioning acceptance which is laid upon the pupil.[477]

As will be discussed in this chapter, a parent's teaching and a child's attention are keys to biblical discipline. In fact, beginning to give attention to wisdom — finding it to be the highest value — is the starting point to "fearing the Lord."

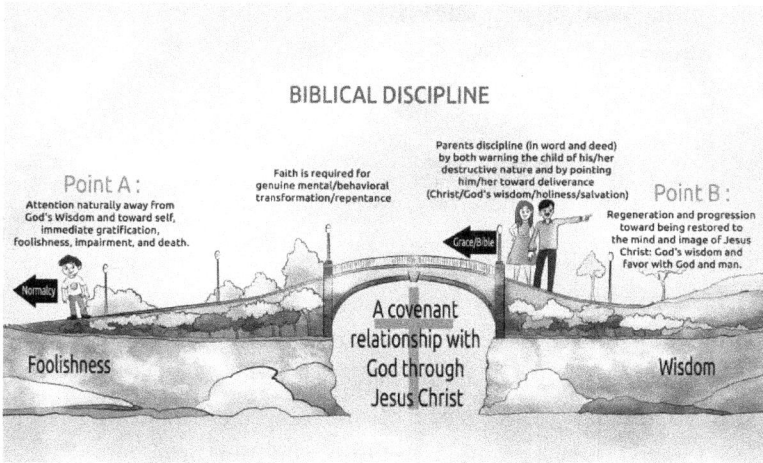

BIBLICAL DISCIPLINE

Point A :
Attention naturally away from God's wisdom and toward self, immediate gratification, foolishness, impairment, and death.

Faith is required for genuine mental/behavioral transformation/repentance

Parents discipline (in word and deed) by both warning the child of his/her destructive nature and by pointing him/her toward deliverance (Christ/God's wisdom/holiness/salvation)

Point B :
Regeneration and progression toward being restored to the mind and image of Jesus Christ: God's wisdom and favor with God and man.

Normalcy

Grace/Bible

A covenant relationship with God through Jesus Christ

Foolishness

Wisdom

A Goal Established

For discipline to occur, there must be a clearly established goal. If wrong values/desires/treasures are central to the child's struggles and right values/pursuits are central in teaching children to pay attention and disciplining them, then biblical discipline always requires that the wrong value be removed and the highest value be established and pursued. The necessity to establish and pursue a goal can also be observed in temporal

---

[477] Ibid.

disciplines (e.g., academics and sports). As observed in chapter three, Proverbs declares wisdom to be the highest value/priceless goal that humanity can pursue (more valuable than gold or silver). Thus, biblical discipline requires the goal of God's wisdom or holiness to be established and pursued. In other words, Christ must become the premier pursuit.

God the Father's goal for His children is to restore their minds to His holiness through a covenant father-son relationship. One commentator states, "Discipline in Proverbs is aimed at the shaping of godly character, character that reflects something of the wisdom and righteousness of God."[478] Bryan Chapell also notes,

> The writer of Hebrews makes it clear both that the goal of discipline is our holiness (Heb. 12:10), and that "without holiness no one will see the Lord" (v. 14). The connection is clear. Through the holiness that our discipline nurtures, we gain a clearer vision of God.[479]

Becoming Christ-like gives a child a new mindset (wisdom) from which to view life. Biblical discipline always aims at restoration to God's holy character. Without Christ's holiness/wisdom as the true goal, there can be no biblical discipline.

There are many aspects of biblical discipline — including reproof, rebuke, correction, instruction, and modeling, but all aspects are in accordance with the goal of the child's transformed character. Kidner explains,

> Instruction, or training (mûsār; 1:2a, 3a), a far from static term, is the first synonym, giving notice at once that *wisdom will be hard-won, a quality of character as much as of mind.* This word has usually (not invariably — see e.g. 4:1) a note of sternness, ranging from warning

---

[478] D.P. Kingdon, "Discipline," *New Dictionary of Biblical Theology*, ed. Desmond Alexander, Brian S. Rosner, D.A. Carson, and Graeme Goldsworthy (Downers Grove, IL: Intervarsity, 2000), 449.

[479] Bryan Chapell, *Holiness by Grace: Delighting in the Joy That Is Our Strength* (Wheaton, Ill: Crossway Books, 2001), 177.

(e.g. 24:32) to chastening (whether by the Lord, 3:11, or by the rod, 23:13; cf. the extreme instance: Isa. 53:5). Its frequent companion is correction, or reproof (tôkaḥat; 1:23; 3:11, etc.), a noun whose derivation emphasizes verbal rather than physical persuasion: an appeal to reason and conscience (cf. Isa. 1:18; cf. John 16:8 with the LXX's equivalent of tôkaḥat). The two terms together can be summed up as discipline; they give the reminder that wisdom is not to be had through extra-mural study: it is for disciples only. LXX The Septuagint (pre-Christian Greek version of the Old Testament).[480]

Biblical discipline is always in accordance with the established goal of wisdom/holiness.

The Rules Explained

Since discipline is moving the child from point A (his naturally foolish condition) toward point B (becoming wise), rules are necessary aids to help keep the child focused on the established goal—to help the child stay on the path. But the law (rules, standards, and regulations) is an assistant teacher and never the goal. Derek Kidner recognizes that the law "fundamentally means direction."[481] Rules and standards are never to be the focus or summary of discipline. The law simply helps with maintaining direction toward the worthy goal. In fact, rules, promises, warnings, and consequences are useless and often detrimental if they do not direct/point the child toward the established goal. Unfortunately, too many parents and educators lose sight of the goal of discipline and focus instead on the "discipline system." When outward conformity and maintaining a standard become the goal of discipline rather than the effect/result, children will tend to leave their home or school believing that discipline equals legalism—fulfilling the law on one's own merit—rather than understanding the biblical concept that leads the child into God's grace and holiness (Titus 2:11-13).

---

[480] Kidner, *Proverbs*, 34.

[481] Ibid., 51.

True Love Displayed

Correction and instruction are both vital aspects of discipline, but these activities differ greatly from punishment. Unlike biblical discipline, punishment does not need an established goal, a motive of love, or an intimate relationship to be carried out; evil dictators, for example, punish innocent people. Yet, one of the misconceptions of discipline is that it equals punishing the child. Scripture, however, makes it clear that at the cross everything changed when God bore His children's punishment: "But He was pierced because of our transgressions, crushed because of our iniquities; punishment for our peace was on Him, and we are healed by His wounds" (Isaiah 53:5). Punishment is retribution and not a loving act of turning a person back to a beneficial path — leading to a worthy goal. Bryan Chappell explains,

> Since God's justice has been fully satisfied, the remaining purposes of his discipline are to help those dear to him to know more of the riches of his grace, and to grow more like him. As indicated by the loving motives of the heart that administers it, divine discipline is intended to benefit the wayward rather than to exact retribution for wrong. Very simply put, understanding the difference between punishment and discipline enables us to consider God as a Father in heaven rather than an ogre in the sky.[482]

One of the key features of biblical discipline, then, is love (grace and mercy). Proverbs 3:12 says, "For the LORD disciplines [corrects; KJV] the one He loves, just as a father, the son he delights in."[483] The same truth applies to parents with their children. Proverbs 13:24 states, "He who withholds his rod hates his son, But he who loves him disciplines him diligently." What is taking place in biblical discipline is a loving parent doing

---

[482] Bryan Chapell, *Holiness by Grace: Delighting in the Joy That Is Our Strength* (Wheaton, Ill: Crossway Books, 2001), 177.

[483] *Holman Christian Standard Bible.*

his/her part to shape the child's heart into being a disciple. It does not mean that the father is constantly chasing his son around with a rod (see Appendix B), since the true meaning of discipline is

> Learning that molds character and enforces correct behavior; from a Latin word meaning "instruction" or "training." *To discipline a person or a group means to put them in a state of good order so that they function in the way intended.* Discipline, in spite of a popular misconception, is not inherently stern or harsh. Bible translators chose "disciple" as an appropriate term for one who learns by following.[484]

By disciplining their offspring as God disciplines His own children, earthly fathers reveal God's loving character and authority (Romans 13:1-5) and invite their children to receive God the Father and submit in the same way to His loving wisdom. The goal of the child becoming wise and holy could also be stated as making a disciple of Christ. As a parent knows and loves the heavenly father, he/she desires his/her child to have the same loving covenant relationship with God. Commentators Harris, Archer, and Waltke point out that it is God's covenant with the believer that forms the

> theological basis for an earthly father's discipline over his son... He [the father] bears the image of his covenant Lord, and as such stands in parallel relationship over his children – chastening, correcting, instructing, providing – which are expressions of an interpersonal relationship of love.[485]

Biblical discipline is not punishment; it is recognizing the child's naturally foolish nature and establishing the way and the goal that God intended the child to go (toward wisdom) through an

---

[484] Walter A. Elwell and Barry J. Beitzel, *Baker Encyclopedia of the Bible* (Grand Rapids: Baker Book House, 1988), 631.

[485] Robert Harris, Gleason Archer Jr., and Bruce Waltke, *Theological Wordbook of the Old Testament* (Chicago: Moody Press, 2003), 386-87.

"interpersonal relationship of love." Biblical parental discipline always intends to make disciples out of fools.

The administration of the rod of correction or spanking (not the rod of punishment or wrath) is an attempt to gain the attention of the child and reestablish him/her back onto the path toward the established goal.[486] The rod of correction is only one aspect of discipline, though. God disciplines all those whom He loves (Hebrews 12:5ff.) because we are living sacrifices who — like sheep — go astray and constantly wander off course. It is the grace of God — the same grace that brings salvation — that disciplines us to deny our ungodly tendencies and to stay focused on being restored to His holiness (Titus 2:11-15). True biblical discipline — patterned after God's discipline — always emphasizes staying on the path toward the priceless goal of Christ/wisdom (Hebrews 12:1-13 is one example) rather than focusing on retribution for wrong doing.

A Focus on Attention

Another foundational aspect of discipline is the child's giving attention. If the child will only naturally listen to his/her way of thinking and pursue his/her own desires, then God's wisdom can never be obtained. No wonder, then, that a child's attention and desires are key discussions throughout Proverbs. In fact, Proverbs 4:20-27 offers a pattern of giving attention that is vital to childrearing. One commentator understands this text as presenting the "anatomy of discipleship."[487] The passage is so important to a child's right attention that I wrote a separate book, *Teaching a Child To Pay Attention: Proverbs 4:20-27,* to

---

[486] For further discussion on Spanking, see Appendix B.

[487] D. A. Hubbard, *Proverbs* (Dallas: Word, 1989), 87.

provide practical steps from Scripture that parents and educators can use to teach their children to pay attention. It is also important to consider some thoughts from Proverbs 4 in regard to biblical discipline.

In Proverbs 4, the author shifts directions from explaining the two ways in which a child can choose to live in chapter 2-3 (wisely or foolishly) to discussing how the child is educated in chapter 4.[488] Kidner notes that the process/pattern offered in Proverbs 4 is much like a medical inspection "in which one's state of readiness in the various realms symbolized by [spiritual] heart, mouth, eyes, [ears], and feet, comes under review."[489] The elements of parental discipline that are presented, then, speak directly to or influence these receptive parts of the child. Whether it is through seeing his/her parents' lifestyle (the child's eyes engaged and the parent's feet in practice), or hearing his/her parents' instructions (the child's ears engaged and the parent's mouth in action), God designed the human body to receive and communicate information that will produce faith and will change — for better or worse — the spiritual heart and its outworking behavior. It is imperative, then, to diligently guard our hearts in order to walk in wisdom rather than according to naturally foolish inclinations.

Although numerous Scripture references offer parental wisdom which is directly applicable to the ADHD label, Proverbs 3 is one passage that provides both a framework of biblical parental discipline/discipleship and practical theology

---

[488] Waltke, *1-15*, 294.

[489] Kidner, *Proverbs*, 68.

within the parent/child relationship.[490] In fact, Kidner calls chapter 3 "the whole-hearted disciple,"[491] and in chapter 4, Solomon calls this wisdom "good teaching" that should be passed down through generations (Proverbs 4:2-4). This good teaching is just as necessary and sound today as it was in Solomon's lifetime. The first part of the passage (1-12) reads like a covenant between God and man. Waltke emphasizes that the odd verses list the obligations of the son or disciple (the human participant), and the even verses reveal God's detailed commitment to the covenant.[492]

The father's giving this wisdom, which he calls his own, indicates his desire to see his son enter into a covenant relationship with God and thus become a disciple of God. In other words, the beginning of a child's accepting wisdom occurs only through "the fear of the Lord." If all people are by nature foolish, then until a child enters into a covenant relationship with the Creator God by grace through faith, he/she cannot be expected to behave wisely or to please God. This point cannot be overstated: if a child is left to his/her foolish way and does not enter into a covenant relationship with the Creator God, then true life-changing wisdom cannot be received and the child's behaviors will only reflect this condition. Faith, then — that comes from hearing the Word of God, is essential to making wise disciples who give attention rightly and produce behavior that pleases God and benefits the community.

---

[490] One of the key counseling points that Ed Welch offers to parents is "become an expert in the book of Proverbs" (Edward T. , *A.D.D.: Wandering Minds and Wired Bodies* [Phillipsburg, NJ: Presbyterian and Reformed, 1999], 13).

[491] Kidner, *Proverbs*, 63.

[492] Bruce Waltke, "Does Proverbs Promise Too Much?" *Andrews University Seminary Studies* 34 (1996): 319-36.

Proverbs offers not only practical truths for the home but also desirable outcomes and hope to children who receive, retain, and live out God's wisdom. Children who embrace wise teaching can find hope in the promise of a good, long, and peaceable life (3:2) as well as in the prospect of finding favor with others (3:4).[493] However, the primary motive that must drive parents or children to pursue and keep God's wisdom is the desire for an intimate covenant relationship with God. Solomon expresses this underlying motive as the desire "to find favor and good success in the sight of God" (3:4).[494] Like Jesus in His youth (Luke 2:40, 52), the child who pursues wisdom will be growing in grace and be pleasing to God and those around him.[495]

Attention to the Parents

Throughout Scripture, the central component of godly discipline is the learner's observation of his parent's/teacher's genuine relationship with God. Though having godly models does not guarantee that a child will follow his parents' teaching, the parents' own lives are key aspects of biblical authoritative discipline. The father in Proverbs is one example of a parent who exhorts his son both to accept his spiritual teaching as well as to observe his ways (Proverbs 23:26). William McKane writes, "'Let your eyes observe my ways' means simply, 'Take my life as a

---

[493] Waltke sees Proverbs 3:1-12 revealing three key conditional blessings of receiving divine wisdom: (1) *social favor* (3:4), (2) *straight paths* (3:6b), and (3) *health* (3:8) (*1-15*, 238).

[494] *Favor* should be understood as the common word for *grace* (ibid., 242). See also Kidner, *Proverbs*, 63 and Longman, *Proverbs*, 132-33.

[495] Longman writes, "The reward, therefore, of obedience is that God and fellow human beings will respect such a person for having grace and good favor. They will be honored and sought after for their wisdom" (*Proverbs*, 133).

paradigm.'"[496] Proverbs 24:32 states the same idea but from the child's perspective: "Then I saw and considered it; I looked and received instruction." McKane comments,

> Here is a new way of accepting *musar* [discipline] — not by paying attention to the authoritative [verbal] instruction of a teacher and acting on his advice, but by direct observation, followed by reflection, then conviction.[497]

The New Testament reiterates the same principle of modeling: "A disciple is not above his teacher, but everyone when he is *fully trained*[498] will be like his teacher" (Luke 6:40).[499] Similarly, *Baker Encyclopedia of the Bible* defines a disciple as "someone who follows another person or another way of life and who submits himself to the discipline (teaching) of that leader or way."[500]

---

[496] McKane, *Proverbs*, 389-90.

[497] Ibid., 572; Waltke agrees: "The father probably emphasizes that 'I' did this to serve as a model to his son whom he instructed in his prologue to do the same (see 1:2-3; 22:17)" (*Proverbs 15-31*, 299-300).

[498] *Fully trained* (καταρτίζω) means to restore, to render fit, complete, or recreate (Morris, *Luke*, 153). When godly discipleship is complete, it brings about restoration or re-creation into the teacher's image. Therefore, the believing parent should increasingly resemble his Creator as the parent progresses in sanctification.

[499] "Tenderly and lovingly the Master now assures them that although they will never be able to outrank or surpass him, yet thorough training under his direction will, if they accept it, cause them to become like their Teacher; that is, like him not in degree of knowledge or wisdom but in truly reflecting his image to the world, so that people instructed by them will begin to say, 'We can notice that these men have been with Jesus' (see Acts 4:13b)" (William Hendriksen and Simon J. Kistemaker, *Exposition of the Gospel According to Luke*, vol. 11 of New Testament Commentary [Grand Rapids: Baker, 2012], 361).

[500] Walter A. Elwell, ed., *Baker Encyclopedia of the Bible* (Grand Rapids: Baker, 1997), 630-31.

Discipline, then, begins with modeling; thus the adage "do as I say, not as I do" is not good parental advice.

Children will by nature pursue their parents' desires and repeat their parents' behavior. Even secular advocates of the ADHD theory acknowledge that parents' mindsets and lifestyles are powerful influences in teaching children:

> Important to note but often unspecified in modern neuropsychological conceptualizations of working memory is that this ability [imitation] underlies the imitation of complex sequences of behavior by individuals. Imitation is a powerful tool by which humans learn new behaviors. The power to imitate another person's behavior requires the capacity to retain a mental representation of the behavior to be imitated. In many cases, that representation will be made through visual imagery or covert audition.[501]

Godly parents, however, are not to provide their children with merely good teaching or an outward display of right behavior, but are to manifest godly behavior from a heart that loves God (Deuteronomy 6:1-7). Thompson comments on Deuteronomy 6: *"You shall love Yahweh your God.* Israel's obedience was not to spring from a barren legalism based on necessity and duty. It was to arise from a relationship based on love."[502] In truth, becoming a good parent means growing more in love with God and knowing Him more intimately. A parent's own established goal/genuine path are prominent teachers in a child's life, and these desires and pursuits regularly become their children's desires, pursuits, and behavior.

One illustration that not only highlights a parent's influence in a child's life but also exposes that children labeled as having ADHD are in fact able to give attention and learn to behave as their parents do is the human ability to learn a primary language. ADHD theorists speculate that children cannot engage

---

[501] Barkley, *NoSC*, 164.

[502] Thompson, *Deuteronomy*, 138.

is certain behaviors because of genetic defects, but these spurious claims are disproven when children can learn their parent's same language (requiring their attention) and be able to speak it (a complex behavior). Dr. Peter Breggin comments, "Families share political outlooks, national feelings, cultural values and prejudices and languages; but nowadays scientists do not consider these traits to be genetic in origin."[503] Certainly, the influence of parents' lives is a predominant aspect of discipline that helps to shape the child's character.

Attention to the Unseen

Faith is essential for unseating the naturally foolish nature, allowing Christ to rule the child's heart, and providing self-control. Faith, however, comes from hearing, and saving faith comes from hearing the Word of God (Romans 10:17). In other words, attention must be given to spiritual things for the child to have faith.

Faith is the evidence of things not seen (Hebrews 11:1); it is a spiritual reality. But every physical reality that can be seen was first a spiritual idea. Proverbs 3:19 tells us that "the LORD by wisdom founded the earth; by understanding he established the heavens. " Hebrews 11:3 also states, "By faith we understand that the universe was created by the word of God, so that what is seen was not made out of things that are visible." In order to understand fundamental truths (such as origins) and correctly interpret that which can be seen, one must have proper faith. Humanity — created in God's image — follows the same pattern of creating by first conceptualizing an idea in the mind and then constructing its physical existence. This same truth applies to all moral human behavior; our immaterial thoughts determine our physical actions. If a child's behavior is to positively change to

---

[503] Breggin, *Toxic Psychiatry*, 95-96.

please God, then his/her thoughts and pursuits must first change. Faith in Christ/His wisdom is foundational to godly behavior, since without faith, it is impossible to please God (Hebrews 11:6). It is also by faith and hope in God that one can gain a good reputation (Hebrews 11:2).

Proverbs offers several ways in which a child's thoughts need to change and where understanding needs to occur through giving attention to that which cannot be seen. Through internalizing these passages and truths, the child's faith can be cultivated.

Metaphors

One way to reach children's spiritual hearts and help them to understand is by teaching with metaphors that expose spiritual truths. These illustrations highlight not only that God is the Creator of all—and thus the child's authority, but also that everything we see reflects a spiritual reality that must also be understood. Thought-provoking illustrations both gain the child's attention and provide him/her with understanding. Former dean of education at Bob Jones University, Dr. Walter Fremont, writes,

> A superior teacher knows how to illustrate and simplify each truth he presents. The purpose of the illustration is to capture the attention of the listener and to motivate him to accept the idea presented.[504]

God has designed all of creation to reveal His character and wisdom (Psalm 19:1-6); wise parents and educators will use both verbal and physical illustrations to encourage the acceptance of vital truth. John Calvin says of Psalm 19:1-6:

---

[504] Walter and Trudy Fremont, *Becoming an Effective Christian Counselor: A Practical Guide for Helping People* (Greenville, SC: Bob Jones University Press, 1996), 89.

> God is in himself invisible; but as his majesty shines forth in his
> works and in his creatures everywhere, men ought in these to
> acknowledge him, for they clearly set forth their Maker: and for this
> reason the Apostle in his Epistle to the Hebrews says that this world
> is a mirror, or the representation of invisible things.[505]

Children must learn that they are under authority and ultimately they will answer to their Creator God. The book of Proverbs not only emphasizes this truth, but also uses vivid imagery of animals, treasures, and common elements of life to reveal God's wisdom and authority. This imagery is intended to enable the fear of the Lord and begin wisdom. Solomon uses illustrations, metaphors, and comparisons to teach his son the importance of fearing God and receiving his wisdom:

> Proverbs . . . introduce[s] the reader to a style of teaching that
> provokes his thought, getting under his skin by thrusts of wit,
> paradox, common sense, and teasing symbolism, in preference to the
> preacher's tactic of frontal assault.[506]

In fact, the very Hebrew word *māšāl* (Proverbs 1:6) from which the book was named carries with it the idea of "illumination or comparison."[507] Proverbs and parables are important elements of biblical teaching and teaching the child to pay attention rightly, since all of God's creation points humanity toward faith in God.

Solomon's use of riddles and parables to teach his sons the importance of loving God was not original or exclusive to him

---

[505] John Calvin, *Romans*, electronic ed., Calvin's Commentaries (Albany, OR: Ages Software, 1998), Ro 1:20.

[506] Kidner, *Proverbs*, 58-59.

[507] Derek Kidner, *Psalms 73–150: An Introduction and Commentary*, vol. 16 of Tyndale Old Testament Commentaries, ed. Donald J. Wiseman (Downers Grove: InterVarsity, 1975), 311.

but was an important educational tool repeated throughout generations (Proverbs 4:4)[508] and described in Psalm 78:2-7:

> I will open my mouth in a parable; I will utter dark sayings from of old, things that we have heard and known, that our fathers have told us. We will not hide them from their children, but tell to the coming generation the glorious deeds of the Lord, and his might, and the wonders that he has done. He established a testimony in Jacob and appointed a law in Israel, which he commanded our fathers to teach to their children, that the next generation might know them, the children yet unborn, and arise and tell them to their children, *so that they should set their hope in God and not forget the works of God* [emphasis added], but keep his commandments.

This pattern of discipline is repeated throughout the Old Testament in passages such as Deuteronomy 6:1-8[509] and Proverbs 6:21, 7:3.[510]

Like the Old Testament, the New Testament also uses parables, proverbs and physical reminders of God's covenants, wisdom, works and character. One example is found in 2 Timothy 2:1-7, where Paul uses various metaphors to offer counsel and wisdom.

> You then, *my child*, be strengthened by the grace that is in Christ Jesus, and what you have heard from me in the presence of many witnesses entrust to faithful men who will be able to teach others also. Share in suffering as a *good soldier* of Christ. No soldier gets entangled in civilian pursuits, since his aim is to please the one who

---

[508] Proverbs 4:4 is often referred to as "the grandfather's lecture" since the father teaches his son what his father taught him. Many commentators see the father in these verses to be Solomon (Steveson, *Proverbs*, 58).

[509] Longman views Deuteronomy 6, Psalm 78:5-8, and Proverbs 4:4 as all showing how Jewish parents used illustrations/metaphors to pass down their religious traditions and teachings to the next generation (*Proverbs*, 148). For further reading on the *Shema* and Jewish parental customs, see Craig Hartman, *Through Jewish Eyes* (Greenville, SC: Bob Jones University Press, 2010), 20-29.

[510] In speaking of the use of metaphors in Proverbs 7:3, Longman writes, "By such an admonition, the father is instructing the son that the command must change him internally (in the heart) and externally in terms of his actions (via the fingers)" (*Proverbs*, 186). See also Waltke, *Proverbs 1-15*, 351.

enlisted him. *An athlete* is not crowned unless he competes according to the rules. It is the *hard-working farmer* who ought to have the first share of the crops. Think over what I say, for the Lord will give you understanding in everything (2 Tim 2:1-7, emphasis added).

Similarly, Christ is the perfect example of teaching with parables:

All these things Jesus said to the crowds in parables; indeed, he said nothing to them without a parable. This was to fulfill what was spoken by the prophet: 'I will open my mouth in parables; I will utter what has been hidden since the foundation of the world' (Matthew 13:34-35).

Christ used numerous parables in his teachings to give His disciples understanding of His special revelation (that which was physically unseen; Matthew 13:10-17).

Throughout the Old and New Testaments, physical object lessons remind God's people of His character, His covenants, and His works. In Joshua 24:24-27, Israel erected a stone to remind the people of their covenant with God, and to this day a rainbow is a reminder that God is just, longsuffering, merciful, and faithful to his promises. Likewise, the Lord's Supper uses symbolic physical elements to help believers remember Christ's suffering, sacrifice, and love for his people (1 Corinthians 11:20-34). God knew that the natural tendency of people would be to forget valuable teaching and to be drawn away by misplaced desires, so He provided humanity with visual aids to remind us of Christ's preeminence and the invisible realities of life.

Proverbs 22:19-21 provides three reasons for the "dark sayings of counsel and knowledge": that "man's trust may be in the Lord," that man might "make known what is right and true," and that man may "give a true answer to those who sent him." Proverbs, parables, and all physical realities when used to illuminate eternal truths increase faith in God's wisdom while also providing the hearer with discernment. This method of teaching becomes more important to parents whose child, in part because of his/her forgetfulness, has been given the ADHD label.[511] Seeing and accepting truth which is physically unseen (faith) is the beginning of wisdom and will positively change behavior.

Future Reward

All children—not just those labeled as having ADHD—struggle to look past immediate gratification and focus on future reward. This natural tendency directly relates to one's faith, established goals, and pursuits, and this tendency is identified by secular theorists as characteristic of children who allegedly have ADHD. But forgoing future reward and working toward a goal is difficult and unnatural for all children. Biblical parental discipline directly addresses the child's tendency to live for the now, to trust in one's own heart, and to lack vision for future reward.

Focusing on the future is foundational to having faith in Christ and genuine hope (Hebrews 11:1; Romans 15:13). Scripture, in large part, directs the reader's attention to focus on eternity and forsake living for this temporal world. Focusing on the future is not a normal mindset, and parents must utilize God's covenants and promises (Proverbs 3:16-18) to teach a child how to focus on value in the future.[512] Though the secular

---

[511] Rachel Ehmke, "Helping Kids Who Struggle with Executive Function: Learning Specialists Discuss How to Get Organized," http://www.childmind .org/en /posts/articles/2012-8-20-helping-kids-executive-functions-organization; accessed 26 March 2014. The therapist gives an example of using something familiar like a hamburger to teach a child something unfamiliar such as writing. She also points out that this method of teaching provides the student an object of familiarity to remember the associated lesson. The book of Proverbs utilizes similar methods using things like ants, ships, and treasure to help the reader understand and remember important truths.

[512] These promises in Proverbs 3 pertain to the blessings or results of acquiring divine wisdom (Kidner, *Proverbs*, 65). Cohen sees the promises of

191

concept of behavior modification must be rejected as manipulative and ultimately destructive, the practice of offering rewards and negative consequences is, in truth, a biblical concept that therapists have altered to fit their secular theories. However, without a perceived benefit—whether temporal or eternal—goals are pointless. Still, establishing any goal requires a view to the future.

In contrast to the secular idea of behavior modification— which focuses on outward changes,[513] God's promises encourage holiness (inward change that produces outward change) based on a loving and righteous relationship with God.[514] For example, Paul states, "Since we have these promises, beloved, let us cleanse ourselves from every defilement of body and spirit, bringing holiness to completion in the fear of God" (2 Corinthians 7:1). In other words, salvation is centered on a covenant promise from God the father. Our entire relationship with God is based on this reality by faith. In fact, it is God's promises that restore the mind and transform behavior. Second Peter 1:3 states that

> His divine power has granted to us all things that pertain to life and godliness, through the knowledge of him who called us to his own glory and excellence, by which he has granted to us his precious and very great promises, so that through them you may become partakers of the divine nature, having escaped from the corruption that is in the world because of sinful desire.

God's promises are mentally and behaviorally transformational; they restore the mind and transform behavior (Romans 12:1-3).

---

receiving God's wisdom to be material gain, luxury, a pleasant life, and happiness (*Proverbs*, 17).

[513] Wender, *ADHD*, 102-10.

[514] For further reading on the process of sanctification, see Bryan Chapell, *Holiness by Grace*.

Children, by nature, tend to focus on the now and lack faith in understanding future value.

In Proverbs 3, the father offers his son several desirable consequences (future rewards) for pursuing wisdom and entering a covenant relationship with God: length of days (2, 16), peace (2, 17), grace (4, 34), right relationships (4), security (6, 23, 26), physical health (8), provisions (10, 16), holiness (14, 24), honor (16, 22, 35), pleasant life (17), eternal life (18, 22), happiness (18), mental stability (24, 25), and a joyful home (33). On the other hand, Solomon also records negative consequences for those who continue in their own natural way: a cursed house (33), rejection and separation from God (34), and a dishonorable life (35). God's promises and warnings are intended to restore people both inwardly and, consequently, behaviorally to the image of God (2 Pet 1:3-11).

Attention to the Way

Proverbs uses the metaphor of a way, road, or path throughout the book to illustrate the importance of discipline (e.g., Proverbs 22:6). This metaphor denotes direction and ultimately destination.[515] Everyone chooses a way in life, and it is up to parents to decide the initial direction a child's life should go, though children will not always follow the same path that their parents have chosen. As noted previously, a child's naturally tendency is to want his or her own way — even sometimes when the child is outwardly conforming to the parents' wishes. What also regularly occurs is a child's tendency to wander off course or turn his/her attention to things outside of the way. When it comes to temporal goals, these things which grab attention away from the goal are called distractions, but when it comes to the goal of pleasing God, these deterrents are

---

[515] Kidner, *Proverbs*, 54-56

known as lusts/misplaced desires which can lead to a person's leaving the course (a sin or trespass) to pursue vanity (James 1:14-15).

Within the biblical concept of disciplining a child, God has lovingly provided several means of correcting misplaced attention, wrong pursuits, or wandering from the way. God supplies the same spiritual tools of correction for parents to discipline their children toward wisdom as He himself uses in correcting His spiritual children unto holiness (Hebrews 12:5-13).

Attention to the Holy Spirit

Scripture makes it abundantly clear that no parent can transform a child into a wise person. The Holy Spirit gives understanding — working through the Word of God — and enables the fear of the Lord — the beginning of wisdom. The parent's role is to share God's wisdom which enables transformational faith. Salvation and positive changes are the Lord's work, and not the responsibility of parents.

Though most parents understand that salvation is not their responsibility, too often they get frustrated when what they do does not seem to work. But no magic bullet exists to transform children from foolish youngsters into wise Christ-like and well-behaved citizens. Because of their foolish hearts, many children of Christian parents will choose to reject the wisdom of God, which they so desperately need (Proverbs 15:5; 32). It is not the parents' responsibility to ensure their child accepts their discipline. It is only the parents' responsibility to clearly establish the way that children should go and lead them down that right path.

Too many parents mentally beat themselves up and even give up when their child continues to not pay attention, forgets important things, disobeys, expresses anger, or lacks self-control and motivation. Too many parents have concluded that God's Word is not sufficient to provide lasting change in their child's heart because the changes are slow or not occurring according to expectations. We have come to believe in our fast-paced society that everything should be available for immediate enjoyment and utility. But character/heart changes do not typically occur in this way even after regeneration, and despite popular beliefs, no magic bullet exists to genuinely transform character.

God declares the process of moving from a fool to wise to be a life-long process that culminates when the disciple finally sees His Creator face to face. It is widely recognized among commentators that the son being educated in Proverbs was around twenty-one years old. Yet, ten times in the first nine chapters the son had to be reminded to give his father his attention.[516] Becoming wise is not an overnight occurrence and is often a difficult and long struggle for everyone involved.

In truth, one of the key features of discipline is that it is painful for a time (Hebrews 12:11). To untangle foolishness from the very fabric of a child's spiritual heart requires painful and often repeated spiritual operations. Parenting as God desires is not going to be easy, and the unseating of foolishness from the child's heart often continues into adulthood.

While wisdom is the remedy to foolishness, and discipline is the only means to apply wisdom, there is no guarantee — no matter how hard an authority tries or how much he or she loves God — that foolish children will receive wisdom and begin the process of restoration to Christ-likeness. Ultimately, the child must choose his/her pursuits and life's direction. When Proverbs 22:6 admonishes parents to train the child in the way

---

[516] See Berger, *Teaching a Child to Pay Attention: Proverbs 4:20-27* for further study.

that the child should go, the verse is not offering a guarantee that children will receive God's wisdom if parents do enough. Instead, the verse establishes that whatever direction and goal parents might have for their children, they are responsible to establish and lead their children in that way. If parents desire their children to remain faithful to a way of living even when they are old, they must establish that way from the earliest of years. Discipline—even if it is unbiblical and points children toward a destructive goal away from God's wisdom—is the parents' privilege/responsibility.

True heart changes, though, are the responsibility of the Holy Spirit as He works through the Word of God in a person's life. Galatians 5 is one illustration of how walking with the Spirit of God enables people to produce Christ-like/God-honoring behavior rather than living according to the naturally foolish or fleshly heart. It states,

> But if you are *led by the Spirit*, you are not under the law. Now the works of the flesh are evident: sexual immorality, impurity, sensuality, idolatry, sorcery, enmity, strife, jealousy, fits of anger, rivalries, dissensions, divisions, envy, drunkenness, orgies, and things like these. I warn you, as I warned you before, that those who do such things will not inherit the kingdom of God. But *the fruit of the Spirit* is love, joy, peace, patience, kindness, goodness, faithfulness, gentleness, self-control; against such things there is no law. And those who *belong to Christ Jesus have crucified the flesh* with its passions and desires. *If we live by the Spirit*, let us also keep in step with the Spirit. Let us not become conceited, provoking one another, envying one another [emphasis added].

The focus is on giving attention to the Spirit rather than on producing change. Behavioral changes are fruit or effects of spending time with God and not something about which to brag or to take blame. Behaviorism, psychostimulants, and physical restraints can, in fact, all control behavior, but these control mechanisms do not offer hope of genuine mental change. Furthermore, and most importantly, God desires a heart that values, desires, and pursues Him above all else and not merely outward conformity. When the child's heart changes to pursue

God and fellowship with the Spirit, his/her behaviors will also positively change.

Both secular theorists and the Bible agree that parents and educators are not passive bystanders in a child's life and his/her learning to pay attention and behave appropriately. While they disagree on what a child's authority should or should not do, they both agree that the child's attention and behavior must be addressed.

Scripture makes it clear that the child needs to have his/her natural desires confronted and replaced with God's way of thinking (wisdom). As the child listens to and receives God's wisdom, his/her life begins more and more to reflect the life of Christ. Because parents have the unique responsibility to choose which direction their children's lives will initially go, their discipline must be theocentric if it is to meet the child's greatest needs and remedy the child's greatest problem: foolishness that leads to destruction.

Though it may seem that the child labeled as ADHD has as his/her most pressing need to change behavior or improve performance, his or her greatest need is to be regenerated (made new) and restored to God's original intent. All children either need to be saved or to grow in sanctification. The real change agent that alone can make these necessary changes is the Holy Spirit working through the Word of God to produce faith and good behavior. Parents must do their part by administering biblical discipline, which leads the child toward wisdom.

CONCLUSION

"Whatever was written in former days was written for our
instruction [now], that through endurance and through the
encouragement of the Scriptures we might have hope."
– Romans 15:4

Millions of children have been diagnosed with ADHD, yet
these children do not have a biological disease. What they have
is a tendency to behave in a naturally detrimental way. More
specifically, the ADHD construct is the APA's attempt to
describe and categorize children who do not listen, obey, or
behave according to expectations. But these children are not
abnormal as the construct of ADHD suggests; they simply
express their naturally depraved hearts in clear behavioral
patterns.

To deny the construct of ADHD as defining children and
explaining their behavior is not dismissing or rejecting that these
children have genuine and destructive problems. Denying the
secular construct of ADHD enables a person to consider a
proved and effective alternative approach — an approach that has
existed for thousands of years and found in the Word of God.
This right perspective clearly and perfectly defines every child
and contains the remedy to children's poor attentional and
moral behavioral problems.

Despite Scripture's reliable vantage point, many people have
chosen to ignore or reject God's wisdom and insist the Bible does
not speak on these matters. In setting aside Scripture's view of
the child, however, parents also set aside the very wisdom

necessary to lead the child out of his/her foolish condition and into God's wisdom. Instead of establishing the child's desperate need to enter into a covenant relationship with God and producing a wise son/daughter, many parents have decided that enhancing academic performance and stifling bad behavior are the true priorities. But behaviorism cannot reach the heart — the center of attention, and psychostimulants are not medications that correct or attack an invisible disease. These powerful drugs are only chemical agents that work against or perturb a child's healthy nervous system to crush behavior, enhance academic performance, and heighten the senses

Not only are psychostimulants not medications, ADHD is not a medical condition; it is a construct without biological markers, a biological etiology, or a biological remedy. Unlike valid impairments or syndromes — which hinder a child's paying attention across all areas of life — the child who is considered to have ADHD struggles morally with the natural tendency to pursue wrong interests, ignore authority, lack self-control, and esteem self too highly. Children (without biological impairment) who have been diagnosed as allegedly having ADHD are normal, depraved people; they act foolishly because their spiritual hearts are foolish.

Though these children are normal, they have genuine problems with attention and behavior that must be addressed and remedied. Unless God's vantage point is accepted by parents and the child, though, no ultimate remedy exists. Children — whether fit into one of the APA's diagnostic categories or not — must begin to see themselves as God sees them. Instead of accepting the stigmatizing and misleading label of ADHD, children must learn who they are in comparison with the perfect standard of normalcy: Jesus Christ. It is His wisdom/ grace alone that can move a child from his/her normal/

impairing/depraved condition to a place of wisdom and approval.

Parents have the privilege and responsibility to point their children in the way that they should go, but ultimately the decision to give attention to their own way or to God's directives is between the child and the Holy Spirit. Parents who simply assume that a child will pay attention rightly and will pursue worthy goals lack understanding of the child's true condition. Every child left to his/her natural way — left unsupervised and undisciplined — will remain a fool who may digress to become a rebellious scoffer. However, because of God's grace through faith, there is hope for all children. Faith is the very substance of hope, and transformational faith comes from giving attention to the Word of God.

The truth about ADHD is that it is a false humanistic gospel which defines and explains a child's natural condition through an evolutionary/materialistic/deterministic lens. The ADHD construct is not a gimmick, nor is it a medical condition; it is, however, a key component of humanistic anthropology necessary to deny human morality, responsibility, and God as humanity's gracious but just Creator.

APPENDIX A

THE BIBLICAL FOOL

Since one of the most important discussions surrounding ADHD is anthropology, it is necessary to carefully examine some of the key biblical terms in Proverbs that directly relate to the child's heart and behaviors. Specifically, one needs to understand humanity's natural position before God in relation to divine wisdom. By extension, such a definition should include discussion on who can receive God's wisdom. While the term *biblical fool* can refer to one who has a hardened heart, which is set against God, the term is also used to describe the natural hearts of all unregenerate people without understanding of divine wisdom.[517]

General Description

Scripture states that a fool is anyone who trusts in his own mind over God's wisdom. For example, Proverbs 28:26 states this important definition: "Whoever trusts in his own mind is a fool, but he who walks in wisdom will be delivered."[518] Waltke points

---

[517] Bruce Waltke, *The Book of Proverbs: Chapters 1-15*, 93-94; Kidner, *Proverbs*, 39-42.

[518] Cohen writes that the fool is one who "neglects the principles of wisdom and follows his own judgment" (*Proverbs*, 192). Likewise, Longman comments: "To trust in one's own heart (note the linkage by contrast to the second colon of the previous proverb) is the epitome of folly because the heart is limited in its

out that the word *fool* is often used in Proverbs "as a standard of comparison for one who is wise in his own eyes."[519] He also notes that this verse implies the depravity of the human heart and its need for divine wisdom.[520] Based on this understanding, everyone without God's wisdom is naturally a fool.[521] It is no wonder that Proverbs 22:15 declares that foolishness is bound in the heart of every child, since the natural bent of every child is to trust in his own mind.[522] Proverbs 22:15 has even been called "the

---

knowledge and also, apart from relationship with God, wicked" (Longman, *Proverbs*, 496-97). Wiersbe sees the comparison between the fool's pride and Satan's lie to mankind in the Garden of Eden: "You will be like God (Gen 3:5; NKJV)" (Warren W. Wiersbe, *Be Skillful: Tapping God's Guidebook to Fulfillment* (Wheaton: Victor Books, 1995), 77).

[519] Waltke, *Proverbs 1-15*, 50.

[520] Waltke, *Proverbs 15-31*, 427.

[521] Kidner writes, "The fact the fool, by whatever name he goes, is by definition one whose mind is closed, for the present, at least, to God (like the *nabal* of Psa 14:1) and to reason (like the *Nabal* of whom of whom his wife said, 'One cannot speak to him', 1 Sam 25:17), since he has rejected the first principle of wisdom, the fear of the Lord" (*Proverbs*, 41).

[522] Longman comments on Proverbs 22:15 that "the first colon states the sorry condition of youth, and the second gives the prescription for rectifying the problem. . . . The 'heart,' roughly equivalent to what we would call character, of the young is bad. The term 'stupidity' is closely associated with folly. It takes the application of discipline to remove their stupidity, which is so integrally and naturally a part of a person" (*Proverbs*, 408). Whereas Proverbs 22:15 focuses on the foolishness of the natural heart of every child and the necessary remedy being the rod of discipline, Proverbs 29:15 states that wisdom, the antithesis of foolishness, is the benefit of discipline. Whybray writes that when a child is "freed from proper discipline," he will shame his mother (R. N. Whybray, *Proverbs*, 402). Motivating a foolish child to receive wisdom requires verbal teaching but also physical instruction (McKane, *Proverbs*, 565). See also Cohen, *Proverbs*, 148.

doctrine of 'original folly.'"[523] Though born foolish, the one who
walks in God's wisdom will be delivered (Proverbs 28:26).[524]
Although the context of Proverbs would indicate that
deliverance in verse 26 is general in nature (from danger, social
problems, and even death), Longman has the New Testament
perspective in mind and sees this passage as also explaining
future salvation that Christ would accomplish.[525] Both in
temporal and eternal applications, God's wisdom is the
antithesis of the fool/self-reliance.[526] Proverbs 3:5-6 also states a
similar idea, contrasting self-trust with whole-hearted trust in
the Lord through intimate relationship with him.[527] The common
characteristics of all three types of biblical fools are that they live
in pursuit of their desires,[528] they lack divine wisdom,[529] they are

---

[523] Whybray, *Proverbs,* 125.

[524] Longman notes that the walking of the wise is in keeping with the
proverbial metaphor of *the way.* In light of New Testament truths, one can see the
idea of progressive sanctification as the disciple, who has received wisdom,
walks with Christ, who is wisdom (*Proverbs,* 497).

[525] Longman, *Proverbs* 497; Waltke sees the deliverance of the wise referring
to the Lord's punishment of fools (1:32-33; 2:20-22) (*Proverbs 15-31,* 427-28).

[526] "Wisdom entails fear of Yahweh (1:7) and an aversion to self-reliance
(3:5, 7; 26:12; 27:1; 28:11)" (Longman, *Proverbs,* 497).

[527] The prepositional phrases "unto Yahweh" and "unto your own
discernment" are antithetical, or as Phillips points out, "They are two rival ways
of thinking, two antagonists. The one leaves me locked into my own inborn
foolishness and waywardness (Prov 12:15; 22:15; cf. Ps. 51:5). The other puts me
in the way of God" (*God's Wisdom in Proverbs: Hearing God's Voice in Scripture*
[The Woodlands, TX: Kress Biblical Resources, 2011], 136).

[528] Tedd Tripp, *Shepherding a Child's Heart* (Wapwallopen, PA.: Shepherd
Press, 1995), 106; Cohen, *Proverbs,* 6; Waltke, *Proverbs 1-15,* 202-4.

headed toward destruction,[530] "they lack self-control" (Proverbs 12:16),[531] and they behave foolishly (by doing so they reflect the absence of God's wisdom in their lives; Proverbs 13:16).[532]

While Scripture considers all unsaved who are capable of understanding divine wisdom to be fools,[533] believers can also play the fool by trusting in their own minds and behaving accordingly. In Ephesians 5:17 Paul reveals this truth by giving the believer an imperative: "Therefore do not be foolish, but understand what the will of the Lord is [wisdom]."[534] Even those

---

[529] See Kidner's discussion on *nabal* (*Proverbs*, 41); Waltke, *Proverbs 1-15*, 111-12; Paul points out in Titus 3:3 that prior to receiving Christ, all Christians were foolish (*anoetos*) or without understanding (Guthrie, *Pastoral Epistles*, 224); Cohen, *Proverbs*, 6.

[530] Longman, *Proverbs*, 497; Waltke, *15-31*, 428.

[531] Bruce Waltke, *The Book of Proverbs: Chapters 15-30*, New International Commentary on the Old Testament, ed. R. K. Harrison and Robert L. Hubbard Jr. (Grand Rapids: Eerdmans, 2005), 344; Kidner, *Proverbs*, 97; Cohen, *Proverbs*, 76.

[532] "*Paras*, glossed *spreads out* (*yipros*), takes as its objects a garment, fishing net, snare, and so on. Here it is used metaphorically with the particular sense of 'to display,' 'like a peddler who openly spreads his wares before the gaze of all men.' Its parallels are 'proclaims' (12:13) and 'gushes' (15:3). By its antithesis to 'take cover' ('to protect himself'), 'to spread out folly' entails that he ruins himself thereby. Among other things, the fool shows his annoyance at once (12:16)" (Waltke, *1-15*, 298, 566-67); Longman, *Proverbs*, 288-89.

[533] Waltke writes that "Proverbs divides humanity into two classes: the wise and righteous over against fools and the wicked. These wisdom and ethical terms are correlative, for though they do not mean the same thing, they have the same referent" (*Proverbs 1-15*, 93).

[534] Lincoln comments on Ephesians 5:17: "Those who have already been exhorted not to live as unwise people in v 15 are now again warned not to succumb to folly. . . . The contrast between wise and unwise is now replaced by that between being foolish and having understanding. Just as the children of light will learn what is pleasing to the Lord (5:10), so those who are wise will

who possess God's wisdom can behave foolishly when they lack a right desire to please the Lord and demonstrate in their behaviors that they are walking in the flesh.

Specific Types

Although Proverbs uses the word *fool* in a general sense to describe all people who are able to understand and accept divine wisdom yet they have not received God's wisdom,[535] Proverbs also describes three specific types of fools:[536] (1) the simple, naïve, or "inexperienced" fool (Proverbs 14:15),[537] (2) the dull, stupid, or "ordinary fool"[538] (Proverbs 1:32; 26:11; 27:22),[539] and (3) the scornful, mocker, or "hardened" fool (Proverbs 1:22, 29;

---

understand what the will of the Lord is. Indeed, understanding the will of the Lord is the heart of wisdom (cf. also Col 1:9, 'filled with the knowledge of his will in all spiritual wisdom and understanding'). For believers, wise living involves a practical perception dependent on the direction of their Lord" (Andrew T. Lincoln, *Ephesians*, vol. 42 of Word Biblical Commentary [Dallas: Word, 1990], 342-43).

[535] The book of Proverbs contains three different Hebrew words along with three different names to describe fools. Some commentators include a sluggard as potentially a fourth type of fool. For more reading on the three types of proverbial fools, see Waltke, *Proverbs 1-15*, 109-15 and Kidner, *Proverbs*, 39-42.

[536] Kidner, *Proverbs*, 39-41; Waltke, *Proverbs 1-15*, 93-94.

[537] Waltke, *Proverbs 15-31*, 252; Kidner, *Proverbs*, 39.

[538] Kidner, *Proverbs*, 42.

[539] Many theologians see the three Hebrew words *kesil*, *'ewil*, and *nabal* as best describing the ordinary fool, though they note that these "terms are virtually interchangeable" with the other names of the simple fool and the scorner (ibid., 39-41); Waltke, *Proverbs 1-15*, 93-94.

3:34-35; 14:6-7; 19:29).[540] Waltke explains Proverbs' use of these names:

> These ethical terms imply the fool's moral culpability, not his lack of intelligence. The wisdom terms for the unwise, however, are not correlatives but distinguish three of four classes of fools according to their educative capacities: the gullible, the fool, and the mocker.[541]

As Waltke emphasizes, the determining factor for a fool is not his intellectual capabilities, but rather his lack of God's wisdom and trust in the fool's own understanding.[542]

General Applications

All children (and adults) who should understand and receive divine wisdom, yet are without it, are biblical fools (simple, ordinary, or hardened [scorner] fools). Biblical understanding of the fool is important in order for biblical parental discipline to occur. Specifically, having this understanding helps parents discern the current direction of the child diagnosed with ADHD through both his reactions to God's wisdom as well his behaviors, which can reveal the position of his foolish heart.

Conclusion

When Scripture refers to someone as a fool, it does not imply that he lacks intelligence, but that he lacks divine wisdom. Though it is likely best to not call a child a *fool*, the biblical concepts are nonetheless key to right anthropology and to both

---

[540] Kidner, *Proverbs*, 41-42, Waltke, *Proverbs 1-15*, 114.

[541] Waltke, *Proverbs 1-15*, 111.

[542] Cohen states of fools: "They are morally, rather than intellectually, defective, and despise a father's correction" (*Proverbs*, 3).

understanding and helping the child whom secularists have diagnosed as having ADHD.

If you wish to read the full article, "The Biblical Fool," please visit https://www.drdanielberger.com/samples

APPENDIX B

A BIBLICAL VIEW OF SPANKING

Scripture advocates spanking ("the rod of correction") as one aspect of discipline that purposely returns a child to the way.[543] However controversial it may be,[544] Scripture states that the "rod of correction"[545] is essential to both teaching and correcting children in God's wisdom (Proverbs 22:15; 23:13-14). Concerning Proverbs 22:15, Waltke writes:

> *Folly*, not purity, *is bound up* [see 3:3; Gen 44:30] *in the heart* [see 2:11] *of youth* (see 1:4; 22:6). *The rod* [see 22:8] *of discipline* (*musar*; see 1:2) *will remove it far* [see 19:7] *from him* (see 22:5, 6). Youth's intractable insolence and his immoral propensity for laziness (13), lust (14), and greed (16) are tightly bound within his very constitution (15a; cf. Gen 8:21; Job 14:4; 25:4; Ps 51:5[7]; Isa 48:8), but the father's disciplining rod breaks folly's hold and frees him (v 15b).[546]

---

543 For further study on the rod of correction, see Lou Priolo, *Teach Them Diligently: How to Use the Scriptures in Child Training* (Woodruff, SC: Timeless Texts, 2000) 95-100.

544 Hallowell and Ratey, *Driven to Distraction,* 272.

545 The physical act of spanking is set forth in the book of Proverbs as characteristic of wise parental discipline since it illuminates various spiritual realities. The New Testament does not mention this topic specifically as it relates to the father/child relationship and assumes that this wise parental practice should continue.

546 Waltke, *15-31,* 215-16.

Correction is important to lead a child to wisdom because children (and adults) are by nature off course and prone to wander; foolishness is bound in everyone's heart. The rod of correction, paired with verbal correction (Proverbs 29:15), is an important part of God's plan for parental discipleship.[547]

It is also worth noting that there exist two ways of looking at the rod of correction: literally and metaphorically. As discussed, God uses metaphor throughout Proverbs to illuminate important truths. Many people view spanking as one such metaphor; it exposes how important correcting a child's depraved nature truly is. Others, however, see a physical or literal spanking as instructive, necessary for correction, and as a means to gain the child's attention when they are not giving it otherwise. It certainly is a historical practice that dates back to antiquity. Either viewpoint one chooses, though, it is important that spanking be taken in the context of Scripture as always being identified as a tool of correction and way to get attention; it is never a means of retribution, abuse, or expression of anger within a parent/child relationship.

When a child is confronted and disciplined for veering off the path of wisdom, correction/redirection toward the established goal and not punishment must be the parental action taking place. If parents are punishing their children for wrong doing, rather than correcting or turning the natural heart back toward wisdom, then a wrong view of God and His purpose for the rod are being taught to the children. God the Father disciplines those he loves, but He took our punishment upon Himself (Isaiah 53:5). In fact, it was by his being crushed and receiving stripes that He healed us. The rod of correction is not

---

[547] Ibid., 442-43. Jewish commentator Cohen writes about Proverbs 29:15: "*Foolishness.* The Hebrew refers to delinquency which is here said to be *bound up* in a child, i.e., a natural state in the early period of life" (*Proverbs,* 148).

violent or abusive, it is not primarily to be used as retribution for wrong doing, and it is not intended to be corporal punishment; it is a loving way to get a child's attention when they refuse to give it through their eyes and ears and to help the child to redirect his steps toward wisdom. Punishment requires no verbal instruction, whereas correction aims to refocus the disciple toward the established goal.

One way to understand the value of applying the rod and distinguish its use from violence is by comparing it to the vaccination process. This process is a clear illustration that a temporary sting can prevent death.[548] This comparison conveys God's intent for the parents' application of the rod to be for the loving purpose of protection and prevention. Loving parents would not think of holding their child down while another stabs the child in the leg with fine metal tubes that inject him with chemicals, yet most parents realize that a little pain applied by a physician can potentially prevent diseases and save a child from more severe pain and suffering, and even from death.

Much like the theory of vaccines, the application of the rod, as described by Scripture, inflicts a physical sting in order to produce spiritual life and health that can lead the child from the pain and destruction of spiritual death (Proverbs 23:13-14). Parents who love their children (Proverbs 13:24) use this aspect of biblical discipline to teach their children vital truths that guide them to the Savior. Spanking is not intended to be violent, abusive, or destructive,[549] but to gently and lovingly teach wisdom that will lead the child to the Savior (Proverbs 22:15; 29:15). This application of discipline — as with all teaching —

---

[548] Vaccinations are used as an illustration and not as advice.

[549] John MacArthur, "Parenting in an Anti-Spanking Culture," http://www.gty.org/Resources/articles/3127; accessed 7 December 2012.

speaks directly to the senses of the child and demands he or she pay attention.

APPENDIX C

"TALKS EXCESSIVELY" WORKSHEET

INSTRUCTIONS: Name: _____

-   *This week: Memorize Proverbs 18:7 and 29:20*
-   *Please read the following passages of Scripture together and then answer the questions below:*

STUDY VERSES:

Proverbs 10:19-20; 13:3   Proverbs 14:3; 15:2
Proverbs 16:23; 17:27-28   Proverbs 18:7; 29:20
James 1:26

STUDY QUESTIONS:

1. Where do the words of one's mouth come from?

2. What do one's words reveal about the heart?

3. What are the characteristics of a wicked man's mouth?

4. What does Scripture say about someone unable to control his/her mouth?

5. What does Scripture say about people who say they love God, yet they do not control their tongue?

6. Are one's words important to God? If they are, why or why not?

7. Why does it displease God when you say everything that you think?

APPENDIX D

IMPULSIVITY WORKSHEET

INSTRUCTIONS: Name: _____

- *This week: Memorize Philippians 2:2-5*
- *Please read the following passages of Scripture together and answer the questions below:*

STUDY VERSES:

1. Blurts out answers before the question is finished. (Proverbs 18:13; 29:20)
2. Struggles to wait his/her turn. (Proverbs 16:32; 1 Corinthians 13:4a; Galatians 5:16-24)
3. Interrupts others. (Proverbs 17:27; Philippians 2:2-5; James 1:26)

STUDY QUESTIONS:

1. How does God view your lack of control and behavior?

2. What are some common words that you noticed in the above verses that describe the heart of these behaviors?

3. According to the above verses, how can you overcome your naturally selfish heart?

4. According to the above verses, when you interrupt others or are not willing to wait your turn, whose needs are you looking out for?

5. Write at least two things that need to change in your life.

APPENDIX E

DISOBEDIENCE WORKSHEET

INSTRUCTIONS: Name: _____

- *This week: Memorize Ephesians 6:1-3*
- *Please read the Following verses then answer the question below on a separate sheet of paper.*

STUDY VERSES:

1. Does not follow through with instruction and fails to finish tasks. (Proverbs 4:1-2; 6:6-11; 10:4-5, 26; 15:19; 20:4)

2. Gets out of his/her seat when told to stay seated. (Ephesians 6:1-3)

3. Runs around out of control and climbs things he/she is not supposed to. (Proverbs 25:28; Colossians 3:20)

STUDY QUESTIONS:

1. How does God view not listening to your authority (theology)?

2. When you disobey your authority, what do you reveal about your heart (anthropology)?

3. What are three steps you can take to help overcome your disobedience (application)?

4. According to the above verses, what attitude or motive should you have when you obey your authority? Why?

APPENDIX F

ANGER WORKSHEET

INSTRUCTIONS: Name: _____

- *This week: Memorize James 1:19-20 and Proverbs 14:29*
- *Please read the following verses, and then answer the questions below on separate paper.*

STUDY VERSES:

Proverbs 15:1; 29:22   Proverbs 14:29; 19:11
Galatians 5:16-24   Ephesians 4:26, 31-32
James 1:19-20; 4:1-6

QUESTIONS:

1. How does God view anger and violence (theology)?

2. When you act out in anger or violence, what do you reveal about your heart (anthropology)?

3. What steps can you take in your life to overcome your natural tendency to be angry (application)?

4. According to the above verses, why do you get angry (motives)?

BIBLIOGRAPHY

Abramson, John. *Overdosed America: The Broken Promise of American Medicine*. New York: Harper, 2005.

Alden, Robert L. *Proverbs: A Commentary on an Ancient Book of Timeless Advice*. Grand Rapids: Baker, 1983.

American Academy of Pediatrics. "Clinical Practice Guideline for the Diagnosis, Evaluation, and Treatment of Attention-Deficit/Hyperactivity Disorder in Children and Adolescents.": http://pediatrics.aappublications .org/content/early/2011/10/14/peds.2011-2654. accessed 23 April 2012.

American Psychiatric Association. *Diagnostic and Statistical Manual of Mental Disorders*. 5th ed. Washington, DC: American Psychiatric Publishing, 2013.

_____ . *Diagnostic Criteria from the DSM-IV-TR*. Washington, D.C.: American Psychiatric Association, 2000.

Arnsten, Amy F. T., Mary V. Solanto, and F. Xavier Castellanos, eds. *Stimulant Drugs and ADHD: Basic and Clinical Neuroscience*. New York: Oxford University Press, 2001.

216

Atkison, David. *The Message of Proverbs*. Downers Grove: InterVarsity, 1996.

Baldwin, Joyce G. *1 and 2 Samuel: An Introduction and Commentary*. Vol. 8 of Tyndale Old Testament Commentaries. Edited by Donald J. Wiseman. Downers Grove: InterVarsity, 1988.

Barkley, Russell. "ADD, ODD, Emotional Impulsiveness, and Relationships.": http://www.youtube.com/watch?v=rcwp9T3zNcM&feature=related. accessed 4 March 2012.

_____ . *ADHD and the Nature of Self-Control*. New York: Guilford, 2005.

_____ . "ADHD Intention Deficit Disorder." Available from http://www.youtube.com/watch?v=wF1YRE8ff1g. accessed 28 February 2012.

_____ . "ADHD — To Medicate or Not?": http://www.youtube.com/watch?v=V724jfgabKE&feature=related. accessed 27 February 2012.

_____ . *Defiant Children: A Clinician's Manual for Assessment and Parent Training*. 2nd ed. New York: Guilford, 1997.

_____ . *Taking Charge of ADHD: A Complete, Authoritative Guide for Parents*. Rev. ed. New York: Guilford, 2000.

Barkley, Russell A., Kevin R. Murphy, and Mariellen Fischer. *ADHD in Adults: What the Science Says*. New York: Guilford, 2008.

BBC News. "Bad Behaviour 'Linked to Smoking.'":
http://news.bbc.co.uk/2/hi/health/4727197.stm. accessed 10
August 2010.

Beale, G. K., and D. A. Carson, eds. *Commentary on the New Testament
Use of the Old Testament.* Grand Rapids: Baker, 2007.

Benedek, Elissa P. Review of *ADHD in Adults: What the Science Says,* by
Russell A. Barkley, Kevin Murphy, and Mariellen Fischer.
Bulletin of the Menninger Clinic 73, no. 1 (Winter 2009).

Benner, David, ed. *Baker Encyclopedia of Psychology.* Grand Rapids:
Baker, 1985.

Benner, David and Peter Hill, eds. *Baker Encyclopedia of Psychology and
Counseling.* 2nd ed. Grand Rapids: Baker, 1999.

Bentall, Richard. *Madness Explained: Psychosis and Human Nature.* New
York: Penguin, 2003.

Berger II, Daniel. *Mental Illness: The Influence of Nurture.* Taylors, SC:
Alethia International Publications, 2016.

_____ . *Mental Illness: The Necessity for Faith and Authority.* Taylors, SC:
Alethia International Publications, 2016.

_____ . *Mental Illness: The Reality of the Spiritual Nature.* Taylors, SC:
Alethia International Publications, 2016.

_____ . *Mental Illness: The Reality of the Physical Nature.* Taylors, SC:
Alethia International Publications, 2016.

_____. *Teaching a Child to Pay Attention*. Taylors, SC: Alethia
        International Publications, 2015.

Boice, James Montgomery. *Psalms 107-150*. Vol. 3 of *Psalms*. Expositional
        Commentary. Grand Rapids: Baker, 1998.

Boyd, Carrie Anne. "The Role of Music in Counseling and
        Discipleship." Master's thesis, Master's College, 2002.

Boyles, Salynn. "Immaturity Mistaken for ADHD? Youngest Kids in
        Classroom More Likely to Be Diagnosed." *WebMD Health
        News:* http://children.webmd.com /news/20120305/is-
        immaturity-being-mistaken-adhd?ecd=wnl_prg_031112.
        accessed 9 March 2012.

Braune, Karl. *The Epistle of Paul to the Ephesians*. Translated by M.B.
        Riddle. Vol. 7 of *Lange's Commentary on the Holy Scriptures*.
        Edited by Philip Schaff. 1874; reprint, Grand Rapids:
        Zondervan, n.d.

Breggin, Peter. *Medication Madness: The Role of Psychiatric Drugs in Cases
        of Violence, Suicide and Murder*. New York: St. Martin's Press,
        2008.

_____. "Medication Madness: The Role of Psychiatric Drugs in Cases of
        Violence, Suicide and Murder.":
        http://www.breggin.com/index.php?
        option=com_content&task=view&id=55&Itemid=79. accessed
        12 July 2012.

_____. *Toxic Psychiatry*. New York: St. Martin's Press, 1991.

_____ . "Rational Principles of Psychopharmacology for Therapists, Healthcare Providers and Clients," *Journal of Contemporary Psychotherapy* 46, 2016.

Breggin, Peter, and Ginger Breggin. "The Hazards of Treating 'Attention-Deficit/Hyperactivity Disorder' with Methylphenidate (Ritalin)." *Journal of College Students Psychotherapy* 10, no. 2 (1995): 55-72.

Cherry, Kendra. "What is Humanistic Psychology?" http://psychology.about.com

Chisholm, G. Brock. *Psychiatry: Journal of Biology and Pathology of Interpersonal Relations* 9, no. 1, (February 1946).

Brown, Raymond Edward, Joseph A. Fitzmyer and Roland Edmund Murphy. *The Jerome Biblical Commentary.* Vol. 1. Englewood Cliffs, N.J.: Prentice-Hall, 1996.

Bruce, F. F. *Romans: An Introduction and Commentary.* Vol. 6 of Tyndale New Testament Commentaries. Downers Grove: InterVarsity, 1985.

Calvin, John. *Acts.* Vol. 10 of Crossway Classic Commentaries. Edited by Alister McGrath and J. I. Packer. Wheaton: Crossway, 1995.

_____ . *Commentaries on the Book of the Prophet Jeremiah and the Lamentations.* vol. 2. Translated and edited by John Owen. Edinburgh: Calvin Translation Society, 1851.

_____ . *Commentaries on the Catholic Epistles.* Translated and edited by John Owen. Edinburgh: Calvin Translation Society, 1855.

_____ . *Commentaries on the Epistle of Paul the Apostle to the Romans.*
Translated and edited by John Owen. Edinburgh: Calvin
Translation Society, 1849.

_____ . *Genesis.* Vol. 25 of Crossway Classic Commentaries. Edited by
Alister McGrath and J.I. Packer, Wheaton: Crossway, 2001.

Carey, William B. "What to Do about the ADHD Epidemic." *American
Academy of Pediatrics: Developmental and Behavioral Pediatrics
Newsletter* (Autumn 2003): 6-7.
http://www.ahrp.org/children/CareyADHD0603.php.
accessed 3 May 2012.

Carter, James E., and Joe E. Trull. *Ministerial Ethics: Moral Formation for
Church Leaders.* Grand Rapids: Baker, 2004.

Chapell, Bryan. *Holiness by Grace: Delighting in the Joy That Is Our
Strength.* Wheaton: Crossway, 2001.

Cherry, Kendra. "Social Learning Theory: An Overview of Bandura's
Social Learning Theory.": http://psychology.
about.com/od/developmentalpsychology
/a/sociallearning.htm. accessed 2 September 2012.

Chriss, James J. *Social Control: An Introduction.* Cambridge: Polity, 2007.

Christensen, Duane L. *Deuteronomy 1–21:9.* Vol. 6A of Word Biblical
Commentary. Dallas: Word, 2001.

Cohen, Abraham. *Proverbs.* London: Soncino Press, 1973.

Collingwood, Jane. "The Genetics of ADHD." http://psych
central.com/lib/2010/the-genetics-of-adhd. accessed 16
September 2010.

Cousins, Leigh Pretnar. "Might Schools Be Teaching ADHD?":
http://psychcentral.com/lib/ 2010/might-schools-be-
teaching-adhd/. accessed 16 September 2010.

Denoon, Daniel. "Kids' Poor Bedtime Habits May Bring ADHD
Misdiagnosis." http://www.webmd.com/add-
adhd/news/20110919/kids-poor-bedtime-habits-may-bring-
adhd-misdiagnosis. accessed 23 September 2011.

Dunn, James D. G. *The Epistle to the Colossians and to Philemon*. New
International Greek Testament Commentary. Grand Rapids:
Eerdmans, 1996.

_____ . *Romans 1–8*. Vol. 38A of Word Biblical Commentary. Dallas:
Word, 1998.

_____ . *Romans 9–16*. Vol. 38B of Word Biblical Commentary. Dallas:
Word, 1998.

Eagleman, David. *The Brain: The Story of You*. New York: Pantheon
Books, 2015.

Easton, M. G. *Easton's Bible Dictionary*. New York: Harper and Brothers,
1893.

Ellingworth, Paul. *The Epistle to the Hebrews*. New International Greek
Testament Commentary. Grand Rapids: Eerdmans, 1993.

Ellison, Katherine. "Brain Scans Link ADHD to Biological Flaw Tied to Motivation." http://www.washingtonpost.com /wpdyn/content/article/2009/09/21/AR2009092103100.html. accessed 22 September 2010.

Elwell, Walter A., ed. *Baker Encyclopedia of the Bible*. 4 vols. Grand Rapids: Baker, 1997.

English Standard Version. Wheaton: Good News, 2001.

Erickson, Millard J. *Christian Theology*. 2nd ed. Grand Rapids: Baker, 1999.

Fletcher-Janzen, Elaine, and Cecil Reynolds, eds. *Disorders Diagnostic Desk Reference*. Hoboken, N.J.: John Wiley and Sons, Inc., 2003.

Flora, Stephen. *Taking America off Drugs: Why Behavioral Therapy is More Effective for Treating ADHD, OCD, Depression, and Other Psychological Problems*. Alba, N.Y.: State University of New York Press, 2007.

Foulkes, Francis. *Ephesians*. Rev. ed. Vol. 10 of Tyndale New Testament Commentaries. Grand Rapids: Eerdmans, 1989.

Frances, Allen. *Saving Normal: An Insider's Revolt against Out-of-Control Psychiatric Diagnosis, DSM-5, Big Pharma, and the Medicalization of Ordinary Life*. New York: HarperCollins, 2013.

Fronmüller, G.F.C. and J. Isidor Mombert. *The First Epistle General of Peter*. Vol. 9 of *Lange's Commentary on the Holy Scriptures*. Translated and edited by Philip Schaff. 1871; reprint, Grand Rapids: Zondervan, n.d.

_____ . *The Second Epistle General of Peter*. Vol. 9 of *Lange's Commentary on the Holy Scriptures*. Translated and edited by Philip Schaff. 1871; reprint, Grand Rapids: Zondervan, n.d.

Garcia, Ricky. "The Truth about ADHD from their Mouth!" http://www.youtube.com/watch?v=MKZXH7MOwjI&feature=related. accessed 28 February 2012.

Generation RX. DVD. Directed by Kevin Miller. Vancouver: Common Radius Films, 2008.

Goldstein, Sam, and Barbara Ingersoll. *Attention Deficit Disorder and Learning Disabilities: Realities, Myths and Controversial Treatments*. New York: Double Day Publications, 1993.

Gray, Peter. "The 'ADHD Personality': Its Cognitive, Biological, and Evolutionary Foundations." http://www. psychologytoday.com/blog/freedom-learn/201008/the-adhd-personality-its-cognitive-biological-and-evolutionary-foundations. accessed 15 September 2010.

Grudem, Wayne A. *1 Peter: An Introduction and Commentary*. Vol. 17 of Tyndale New Testament Commentaries. Downers Grove: InterVarsity, 1988.

Guelich, Robert A. *Mark 1–8:26*. Vol. 34A of Word Biblical Commentary. Dallas: Word, 1998.

Guthrie, Donald. *Hebrews: An Introduction and Commentary*. Vol. 15 of Tyndale New Testament Commentaries. Downers Grove: InterVarsity, 1983.

Guthrie, Donald. *Pastoral Epistles: An Introduction and Commentary*. Vol. 14 of Tyndale New Testament Commentaries. Downers Grove: InterVarsity, 1990.

Haber, Julian. *ADHD: The Great Misdiagnosis*. New York: Taylor Trade, 2003.

Hagner, Donald A. *Matthew 14–28*. Vol. 33B of Word Biblical Commentary. Dallas: Word, 1998.

Hallowell, Edward M. "Dr. Hallowell's Response to NY Times Piece 'Ritalin Gone Wrong.'": http://www.drhallowell .com/blog/dr-hallowells-response-to-ny-times-piece-ritalin-gone-wrong/. accessed 10 August 2012.

Hallowell, Edward M., and John J. Ratey. *Delivered from Distraction: Getting the Most out of Life with Attention Deficit Disorder*. New York: Ballantine Books, 2005.

_____ . *Driven to Distraction: Recognizing and Coping with Attention Deficit Disorder from Childhood through Adulthood*. New York: Pantheon Books, 1994.

Harris, R. Laird, Gleason Archer Jr., and Bruce Waltke. *Theological Wordbook of the Old Testament*. Chicago: Moody, 2003.

Harrison, R. K. *Jeremiah and Lamentations: An Introduction and Commentary*. Vol. 21 of Tyndale Old Testament Commentaries. Edited by Donald J. Wiseman. Downers Grove: InterVarsity, 1973.

Hartwell-Walker, Marie. "It May Not Be ADHD.":
http://psychcentral.com/lib/2010/it-may-not-be-adhd.
accessed 16 September 2010.

Healy, David. *Let Them Eat Prozac: The Unhealthy Relationship between the Pharmaceutical Industry and Depression*. New York: New York University Press, 2004.

Hendriksen, William, and Simon J. Kistemaker. *Exposition of the Gospel According to Luke*. Vol. 11 of New Testament Commentary. Grand Rapids: Baker, 2012.

Henry, Matthew. *Matthew Henry's Commentary on the Whole Bible*. Peabody, Mass.: Hendrickson, 1991.

Hodge, Charles. *1 Corinthians*. Vol. 11 of Crossway Classic Commentaries. Edited by Alister McGrath and J. I. Packer. Wheaton: Crossway, 1995.

_____ . *2 Corinthians*. Vol. 12 of Crossway Classic Commentaries. Edited by Alister McGrath and J. I. Packer. Wheaton: Crossway, 1995.

_____ . *Ephesians*. Vol. 7 of Crossway Classic Commentaries. Edited by Alister McGrath and J.I. Packer. Wheaton: Crossway, 1994.

_____ . *Romans*. Crossway Classic Commentaries. Edited by Alister McGrath and J.I. Packer. Wheaton: Crossway, 1993.

Hosenbocus, Sheik, and Raj Chahal. "A Review of Executive Function Deficits and Pharmacological Management in Children and Adolescents." *Journal of the Canadian Academy of Child and Adolescent Psychiatry* 21, no. 3 (2012): 223–29.

Hubbard, D. A. *Proverbs*. Dallas: Word, 1989.

Hubble, Mark, Barry Duncan, and Scott Miller. *The Heart and Soul of Change: What Works in Therapy*. Washington, D.C.: American Psychological Association, 1999.

Hughes, P. E. "The Priesthood of Believers." *Evangelical Dictionary of Theology*. Edited by Walter A. Elwell. Grand Rapids: Baker, 1996.

iHealthBulletin News Archive. "Risky Ritalin Abuse during College Exam Week." http://ihealthbulletin.com/archive/2007/05/14/risky-ritalin-abuse-during-college-exam-week/. accessed 17 September 2010.

Insel, Thomas. "Brain Scans: Not Quite Ready for Prime Time." http://www.nimh.nih.gov/about/director/index-adhd.shtml. accessed 4 May 2013.

_____ . "Transforming Diagnosis." http://www.nimh.nih.gov /about/director/2013/transforming-diagnosis.shtml. accessed 4 May 2013.

Jamieson, Robert, A. R. Fausset, and David Brown. *Commentary Critical and Explanatory on the Whole Bible*. Peabody: Hendrickson Publishers Marketing, 1996.

Jenni, Ernst, and Claus Westermann. *Theological Lexicon of the Old Testament*. Peabody, Mass.: Hendrickson, 1997.

Johnston C., and E. J. Mash. "Families of Children with Attention Deficit/Hyperactivity Disorder: Review and

Recommendations for Future Research." *Clinical Child Family Psychology* 4:3 (2001): 183-207.

Kandel, Eric. *In Search of Memory: The Emergence of a New Science of Mind.* New York: Norton Publishing Company, 2006.

Kidner, Derek. *Proverbs: An Introduction and Commentary.* Tyndale Old Testament Commentaries. Edited by Donald J. Wiseman. Downers Grove: InterVarsity, 1975.

_____ . *Psalms 73–150: An Introduction and Commentary.* Vol. 16 of Tyndale Old Testament Commentaries. Edited by Donald J. Wiseman. Downers Grove: InterVarsity, 1975.

_____ . *John: An Introduction and Commentary.* Vol. 4 of Tyndale New Testament Commentaries. Downers Grove: InterVarsity, 2003.

Kutchins, Herb, and Stuart A. Kirk. *Making Us Crazy: DSM: The Psychiatric Bible and the Creation of Mental Disorders.* New York: Free Press, 1997.

Lane, Christopher. "The NIMH Withdraws Support for the *DSM*-5." http://www.psychologytoday.com /blog/side-effects/201305/the-nimh-withdraws-support-dsm-5. accessed 4 May 2013.

Lane, William L. *Hebrews 9–13.* Vol. 47B of Word Biblical Commentary. Dallas: Word, 1998.

Langston, Evelyn. *Lord, Help Me Love This Hyperactive Child.* Nashville: Broadman, 1992.

228

Larimore, Walt. "Facts about ADHD." http://www.focusonthe
family.com/parenting/parenting_challenges/
adhd/facts_about_adhd .aspx. accessed 20 February 2012.

Leaf, Caroline. *Switch on Your Brain: The Key to Peak Happiness, Thinking,
and Health*. Grand Rapids: Baker, 2013.

Lieberman, Jeffrey A. *Shrinks: The Untold Story of Psychiatry*. New York:
Little, Brown and Company, 2015.

Lifton, Robert Jay. *The Nazi Doctors: Medical Killing and the Psychology of
Genocide*. New York: Basic Books, 1986.

Lightfoot, Joseph Barber. *Colossians and Philemon*. Vol. 13 of Crossway
Classic Commentaries. Edited by Alister McGrath and J. I.
Packer. Wheaton: Crossway Books, 1997.

_____ . *Philippians*. Vol. 8 of Crossway Classic Commentaries. Edited by
Alister McGrath and J. I. Packer. Wheaton: Crossway, 1994.

Lipton, Bruce H. *The Biology of Belief: Unleashing the Power of
Consciousness, Matter and Miracles*. New York: Hay House,
2005.

Lloyd, John Wills, Edward J. Kameenui, and David Chard, eds. *Issues in
Educating Students with Disabilities*. Mahwah, N.J.: Routledge,
1997.

Longman III, Tremper. *Proverbs*. Baker Commentary on the Old
Testament Wisdom and Psalms. Grand Rapids: Baker, 2006.

MacArthur, John F., Jr. *2 Timothy*. MacArthur New Testament Commentary. Chicago: Moody Press, 1995.

_____ . *Ephesians*. MacArthur New Testament Commentary. Chicago: Moody, 1986.

_____ . "Parenting in an Anti-Spanking Culture." Available from http://www.gty.org/Resources/articles/3127. accessed 7 December 2012.

_____ . *What the Bible Says about Parenting: God's Plan for Rearing Your Child*. Nashville: Word, 2000.

McCabe, Robert V. *Old Testament Studies: Interpreting Proverbs*. http://www.oldtestamentstudies.org/ my-papers/other-papers/wisdom-literature/ interpreting-proverbs. accessed 20 April, 2013.

McKane, William. *Proverbs: A New Approach*. Philadelphia: Westminster, 1970.

McLaren, Niall. *Humanizing Psychiatry*. Ann Arbor, MI: Future Psychiatry Press, 2010.

_____ . "Kandel's 'New Science of Mind' for Psychiatry and the Limits to Reductionism: A Critical Review." *Ethical Human Psychology and Psychiatry* 10, no. 2 (July 1, 2008).

Meek, Will. "TV & ADHD." http://psychcentral.com/blog/ archives/ 2007/09/08/tv-adhd/. accessed 16 September 2010.

Menhard, Francha Roffé. *Drugs: The Facts about Ritalin*. New York: Marshall Cavendish Benchmark, 2007.

Micale, Mark, and Roy Porter, eds. *Discovering the History of Psychiatry*. New York: Oxford University Press, 1994.

Michaels, J. Ramsey. *1 Peter*. Vol. 49 of Word Biblical Commentary. Dallas: Word, 1998.

Monastra, Vincent J. *Parenting Children with ADHD: 10 Lessons that Medicine Cannot Teach*. Washington, D.C.: American Psychological Association, 2005.

Moo, Douglas J. *James: An Introduction and Commentary*. Vol. 16 of Tyndale New Testament Commentaries. Downers Grove: InterVarsity, 1985.

Morganthaler, Timothy. "How Many Hours of Sleep Are Enough for Good Health?" http://www.mayoclinic. org/healthy-living/adult-health/expert-answers/how-many-hours-of-sleep-are-enough/faq-20057898. accessed 21 May 2014.

Morris, Leon. *The First Epistle of Paul to the Corinthians*. Rev. ed. Vol. 7 of Tyndale New Testament Commentaries. Downers Grove: InterVarsity, 1985.

_____ . *The Gospel According to Luke*. Vol. 3 of Tyndale New Testament Commentaries. Downers Grove: InterVarsity, 1988.

Moss, Robert. *Why Johnny Can't Concentrate: Coping with Attention Deficit Problems*. New York: Bantam, 1990.

Murphy, Roland. *Ecclesiastes*. Vol. 23A of Word Biblical Commentary. Dallas: Word, 1998.

_____ . *Proverbs*. Vol. 22 of Word Biblical Commentary. Dallas: Word, 1998.

Myers, Allen C. *Eerdmans Bible Dictionary*. Grand Rapids: Eerdmans, 1987.

National Institute of Neurological Disorders and Strokes. "Brain Basics: Understanding Sleep." http://www.ninds .nih.gov/disorders/brain_basics/ understanding_ sleep.htm. accessed 14 August 2012.

Neven, Ruth S., Vicki Anderson, and Tim Godber. *Rethinking ADHD: An Illness of Our Time*. Sydney, Australia: Allen and Unwin, 2002.

Newheiser, Jim. *Opening Up Proverbs*. Leominster, England: Day One Publications, 2008.

Nigg, Joel. *What Causes ADHD? Understanding What Goes Wrong and Why*. New York: Guilford, 2006.

Nolland, John. *Luke 1:1–9:20*. Vol. 35A of Word Biblical Commentary. Dallas: Word, 2002.

Norcross, John, ed. *Psychotherapy, Relationships That Work: Therapist Contributions and Responsiveness to Patients*. New York: Oxford University, 2002.

Nordqvist, Christian. "Premature Babies Much More Likely to Have ADHD." http://www.medicalnewstoday.com /articles/44574.php. accessed 18 September 2010.

O'Brien, Peter T. *Colossians, Philemon*. Vol. 44 of Word Biblical Commentary. Dallas: Word, 1998.

O'Dell, Nancy, and Patricia Cook. *Stopping ADHD: A Unique and Proven Drug-Free Program for Treating ADHD Children and Adults*. New York: Avery, 2004.

Ohene, S. A., M. Ireland, C. McNeely, and I.W. Borowsky. "Parental Expectations, Physical Punishment, and Violence among Adolescents Who Score Positive on a Psychosocial Screening Test in Primary Care." *Pediatrics* 117, no. 6 (2006): 441-47.

Olasky, Marvin. "Psychology Today: What Should Christians Make of Neuroscience?" *World Magazine*, September 8, 2012.

Oz, Cengiz. "Could You Have ADHD?" http://www.doctoroz. com/quiz/could-you-have-adhd. accessed 16 September 2010.

Panksepp, Jaak, ed. *Textbook of Biological Psychiatry*. New York: John Wiley and Sons, 2004.

Pantley, Elizabeth. "Should Babies and Toddlers Watch Television?" http://pregnancy.about.com/od /yourbaby/a/babiesandtv.htm. accessed 20 May 2008.

Parvaresh, Nooshin, Ziaaddini Hassan, Kheradmand Ali, and Bayati Hamidreza. "Attention Deficit Hyperactivity Disorder (ADHD) and Conduct Disorder in Children of Drug

Dependent Parents." *Addiction and Health* 2, no. 3-4 (Summer and Autumn 2010): 89-94.

Patel, Vikram, Alistair Woodward, Valery L. Feigin, Kristian Heggenhougen, and Stella R. Quah, eds. *Mental and Neurological Public Health: A Global Perspective*. San Diego: Academic Press, 2010.

Pennington, Bruce. *Diagnosing Learning Disorders: A Neuropsychological Framework*. 2nd ed. New York: Guilford, 2009.

Pert, Candace B. *Molecules of Emotion: The Science behind Mind-Body Medicine*. New York: Scribner, 1997.

Petersen, Melody. *Our Daily Meds*. New York: Sarah Crichton Books, 2008.

Phillips, Dan. *God's Wisdom In Proverbs: Hearing God's Voice in Scripture*. The Woodlands, Tex.: Kress Biblical Resources, 2011.

Pliszka, Steven R. *Treating ADHD and Comorbid Disorders: Psychosocial and Psychopharmacological Interventions*. New York: Guilford, 2009.

Porter, Roy. *Madness: A Brief History*. New York: Oxford University Press, 2002.

Porter, Stanley E., and Craig A. Evans. *Dictionary of New Testament Background: A Compendium of Contemporary Biblical Scholarship*. Downers Grove: InterVarsity, 2000.

234

Powlison, David. *Anger: Escaping the Maze*. Phillipsburg, N.J.:
Presbyterian and Reformed, 2000.

_____ . "Is the Adonis Complex in Your Bible?" *Journal of Biblical Counseling* 22, no. 2 (2004).

Pressman, Robert, and Steve Imber. "Relationship of Children's Daytime

Behavior Problems with Bedtime Routines/Practices: A Family Context and the Consideration of Faux-ADHD." http://www.pedipsyc.com/ abstract_FauxADHD.php. accessed 21 September 2011.

Priolo, Lou. *The Heart of Anger: Practical Help for the Prevention and Cure of Anger in Children*. Amityville, N.Y.: Calvary, 1997.

_____ . *Selfishness: From Loving Yourself to Loving Your Neighbor*. Phillipsburg, N.J.: Presbyterian and Reformed, 2010.

Ramachandran, V.S., and Sandra Blakeslee. *Phantoms in the Brain: Probing the Mysteries of the Human Mind*. New York: William Morrow and Company, 1998.

Rankin, Lissa. *Mind over Medicine: Scientific Proof that You Can Heal Yourself*. New York: Hay House Inc., 2013.

Restak, Richard. *The Brain has a Mind of Its Own: Insights from a Practicing Neurologist*. New York: Crown Publishers, 1991.

_____ . *Peddling Mental Disorder: The Crisis in Modern Psychiatry*. Jefferson, NC: McFarland, 2016.

Reznek, Lawrie. *Evil or Ill?: Justifying the Insanity Defense*. New York: Routledge, 1997.

Rice, David. "Psychotherapy for Oppositional-Defiant Kids with Low Frustration Tolerance.": http://www.psycho therapy.net/article/oppositional-defiants-kids: accessed 15 September 2010.

Rief, Sandra F. *How to Reach and Teach ADD/ADHD Children: Practical Techniques, Strategies, and Interventions for Helping Children with Attention Problems and Hyperactivity*. West Nyack, N.Y.: Center for Applied Research in Education, 1993.

Ritalin Death. "Conditions that Mimic ADD or ADHD." http://www.ritalindeath.com /Conditions-that-Mimic-ADHD.htm. accessed 17 September 2010.

Rosemond, John, and Bose Ravenel. *The Diseasing of America's Children: Exposing the ADHD Fiasco and Empowering Parents to Take Back Control*. Dallas: Thomas Nelson, 2008.

Ryle, John Charles. *Matthew*. Crossway Classic Commentaries. Edited by Alister McGrath and J. I. Packer. Wheaton: Crossway, 1993.

Satel, Sally, and Scott Lilienfeld. *Brainwashed: The Seductive Appeal of Mindless Neuroscience*. New York: Basic Books, 2013.

Saul, Richard Saul. *ADHD Does Not Exist: The Truth about Attention Deficit and Hyperactivity Disorder*. New York: HarperCollins, 2014.

Schwarz, Allen. "Idea of New Attention Disorder Spurs Research, and Debate." *New York Times*, April 11, 2014.

_____ . "Still in a Crib, Yet Being Given Antipsychotics." *New York Times*, December 10, 2015.

Scott, Stuart, and Heath Lambert, eds. *Counseling the Hard Cases: True Stories Illustrating the Sufficiency of God's Resources in Scripture*. Nashville: B&H, 2012.

Scull, Andrew. *Madness in Civilization: A Cultural History of Insanity from the Bible to Freud, from the Madhouse to Modern Medicine*. Princeton, NJ: Princeton University Press, 2015.

Seife, Charles. "How Drug Company Money Is Undermining Science." *Scientific American* 307, no. 6 (December 1, 2012).

Shorter, Edward. *A History of Psychiatry: From the Era of the Asylum to the Age of the Prozac*. New York: John Wiley and Sons, 1997.

Silver, Larry. *Dr. Larry Silver's Advice to Parents on Attention-Deficit Hyperactivity Disorder*. Washington, D.C.: American Psychiatric Press Inc., 1993.

Southall, Angela. *The Other Side of ADHD: Attention Deficit Hyperactivity Disorder Exposed and Explained*. Abingdon, England: Radcliffe, 2007.

_____ . *The Treasury of David*. Vol 2. New York: Funk and Wagnalls, 1885.

Stein, David. *Ritalin Is Not the Answer*. San Francisco: Jossey-Bass Publishers, 1999.

Stein, Martin T. "When Preschool Children Have ADHD." http://pediatrics.jwatch.org/cgi/content/full/2007/110/1. accessed 17 September 2010.

Still, George. "Some Abnormal Physical Conditions in Children." *Lancet Medical Journal* 1 (1902): 1008-12.

Szasz, Thomas S. *Pharmacracy: Medicine and Politics in America*. New York: Praeger, 2001.

Taylor, John. *Helping Your ADD Child: Hundreds of Practical Solutions for Parents and Teachers of ADD Children and Teens - with or without Hyperactivity*. Roseville, Calif.: Prima Publishing, 2001.

Taylor, Robert L. *Finding the Right Psychiatrist: A Guide for Discerning Consumers*. New Brunswick, NJ: Rutgers University Press, 2014.

Thompson, J. A. *Deuteronomy: An Introduction and Commentary*. Vol. 5 of Tyndale Old Testament Commentaries. Edited by Donald J. Wiseman. Downers Grove: InterVarsity, 1974.

Thorlakson, Catherine. "The Experience of Learning for Youth Diagnosed with Attention Deficit Hyperactivity Disorder." PhD diss., Capella University, 2010.

Thornton, Stephen P. "Sigmund Freud (1856-1939)." http://www.iep.utm.edu/freud/#H2. accessed 21 April 2014

Tripp, Tedd. *Shepherding a Child's Heart*. Wapwallopen, Pa.: Shepherd
    Press, 1995.

Turner, Barry. "ADHD and the Meaning of Evidence."
    http://www.ritalindeath.com/ADHD-Evidence.htm. accessed
    17 September 2010.

Waltke, Bruce. *The Book of Proverbs: Chapters 1-15*. New International
    Commentary on the Old Testament. Edited by R. K. Harrison
    and Robert L. Hubbard Jr. Grand Rapids: Eerdmans, 2004.

_____ . *The Book of Proverbs: Chapters 15-30*. New International
    Commentary on the Old Testament. Edited by R. K. Harrison
    and Robert L. Hubbard Jr. Grand Rapids: Eerdmans, 2004.

_____ . "Does Proverbs Promise Too Much?" *Andrews University
    Seminary Studies* 34 (1996): 319-36.

WebMD. "ADHD and Sleep Disorders."
    http://www.webmd.com/add-adhd/guide/adhd-sleep-
    disorders. accessed 14 August 2012.

_____ . "ADHD Diets." http://www.webmd.com/add-
    adhd/guide/adhd-diets?page=2. accessed 14 August 2012.

_____ . "Stimulant Drugs for ADHD." http://www.webmd.com/add-
    adhd/guide/adhd-stimulant-therapy. accessed 10 July 2011.

Weiss, Gabrielle, and Lily Trokenberg Hectman. *Hyperactive Children
    Grown Up: ADHD in Children, Adolescents, and Adults*. 2nd ed.
    New York: Guilford, 1993.

Weiss, Robin. "Babies and TV." http://pregnancy.about.com/od
/yourbaby/a/babiesandtv.htm. accessed 11 August 2010.

Welch, Edward. *A.D.D. Wandering Minds and Wired Bodies*. Phillipsburg,
N.J.: Presbyterian and Reformed, 1999.

_____ . *Blame it on the Brain? Distinguishing Chemical Imbalances, Brain
Disorders, and Disobedience*. Phillipsburg, N.J.: Presbyterian and
Reformed, 1998.

Wender, Paul. *ADHD: Attention-Deficit Hyperactivity Disorder in Children,
Adolescents, and Adults*. New York: Oxford University Press,
2000.

_____ . *The Hyperactive Child, Adolescent, and Adult: Attention Deficit
Disorder through the Lifespan*. New York: Oxford University
Press, 1987.

Wiersbe, Warren W. *Be Skillful: Tapping God's Guidebook to Fulfillment*.
Wheaton: Victor Books, 1996.

Whybray, R. N. *Proverbs*. New Century Bible Commentary. Grand
Rapids: Eerdmans, 1994.

Wood, D. R. W., and I. Howard Marshall. *New Bible Dictionary*. Downers
Grove: InterVarsity, 1996.

Yager, Joel. "New Findings in the Pathogenesis, Genetics, and
Comorbidity of ADHD." *Journal Watch Psychiatry*, December
30, 2005. http://pediatrics.jwatch.org
/cgi/content/full/2005/1230/9. accessed 17 September 2010.

Valenstein, Elliot. *Blaming the Brain: The Truth about Drugs and Mental Health*. New York: Basic Books, 1998.

Van der Kolk, Bessel. *The Body Keeps the Score: Brain, Mind, and Body in the Healing of Trauma*. New York: Penguin, 2014.

Watkins, Alan, ed. *Mind-Body Medicine: A Clinician's Guide to Psychoneuroimmunology*. New York: Churchill Livingstone, 1997.

Whitaker, Robert. *Anatomy of an Epidemic: Magic Bullets, Psychiatric Drugs, and the Astonishing Rise of Mental Illness in America*. New York: Broadway Books, 2015.

Whitfield, Charles L. *The Truth about Mental Illness: Choices for Healing*. Deerfield Beach, FL: Health Communications, 2004.

241

www.ingramcontent.com/pod-product-compliance
Lightning Source LLC
Chambersburg PA
CBHW070247290326
41930CB00042B/2755